The Study
of Government

The Study of Government

POLITICAL SCIENCE
AND PUBLIC ADMINISTRATION

BY

F. F. RIDLEY

Professor of Political Theory and Institutions
University of Liverpool

London   George Allen & Unwin Ltd
Ruskin House   Museum Street

First published in 1975

© George Allen & Unwin Ltd 1975

ISBN 0 04 320106 7 hardback
0 04 320107 5 paperback

Printed in Great Britain
by Cox & Wyman Ltd
London, Fakenham and Reading

Preface

The chapters of this book deal in one way or another with the study of government and administration. They advocate a certain approach to the subject and hope to persuade the reader—student, practitioner or layman—that it has some claim to attention. The focus of study, it is argued, should be institutional, the method comparative, the purpose practical. I believe this to be a sensible programme for academic political science and a useful one at the same time. This, indeed, is the second underlying theme: the study of government should have a reformist intent.

The institutional focus, pejoratively described as formalistic, and practical comparisons, labelled unscientific, have gone through a period of discredit, undermined by more sophisticated methodologies, notably the behavioural revolution (to use what seems to have become an equally pejorative term in the last few years). As with all styles, however, there has been a swing of the pendulum or, better perhaps, a dialectical movement: thesis institutional and prescriptive, antithesis behavioural and value free, synthesis 'the new political science'—committed, reformist (or, innovation, revolutionary) but centring on political behaviour (or, further innovation, the policy-making process). In that sense, much of what is advocated here remains old fashioned because the emphasis is on the study of governmental institutions and their reform, on what is sometimes called institutional engineering. Of course, this is not the only way of improving society but as all new policies must be implemented through formal institutions and formal procedures (in our types of democracy at least), it is a *sine qua non* of social change.

It is equally true, of course, that this is not the only valid approach to the study of politics. The freedom of scholars to choose their own approach and the existence of a diversity of methods is an essential of our academic tradition. Pluralism, in that respect as in others, is undoubtedly a 'good thing'. To each student of politics his own political science. Arguably, however, there are limits to this principle where the expenditure of public money is involved: we can afford half a dozen ivory-tower universities, not fifty; we cannot finance five hundred political scientists and the research that goes with them without some regard to public welfare.

My concern, however, I repeat, is simply to advocate a particular view. If the style is sometimes polemical, that is partly explained by my own impatience with the fact that as political science grew more scientific, so it often became divorced from real politics and lost its political purpose. It is also explained by the defensive nature of this book. I am only too conscious of the fact that what I have to say may be considered not merely old fashioned but even naïve, ignoring as it does the sophisticated political science literature of the last decade. The tone is deliberate: exhortation is the purpose of the exercise. For the same reason there is an inevitable repetition of themes: all, in one way or another, are part of the same argument and the purpose is that argument.

As the arguments of this book have not come to me overnight, I have naturally drawn on ideas set out in articles written over a period of years. I have also drawn on my earlier research, mainly French and German, for illustrative material. Much of this has been rewritten, however, to organise it more logically, as the reader has a right to expect, and to accommodate the second thoughts an author has the right to have. The intrusive *I*—a style which as a journal editor I usually try to discourage—must be forgiven. The views expressed are my own and, lacking the faith of a scientist or even philosopher in the pursuit of truth, I remain sufficiently uncertain about them not to wish to pass them off in textbook fashion. I am grateful to the journals acknowledged in the footnotes for their permission to reprint.

Helen Moorcroft patiently transcribed illegible manuscripts, confirming that without a good secretary we would all be lost. My wife, a trained political scientist, felt that there were more interesting things to write about but kept me supplied with coffee nevertheless. My son relieved the tedium by coming to draw at my desk. I do not suppose he will find the subject any more interesting when he gets older—but just in case, I dedicate this book to Francis.

F.F.R.

Contents

POLITICAL SCIENCE

The Institutional Approach

Academics, social scientists at least, regularly discuss the nature of their disciplines, not just the perennial problems of methodology but even more basic questions of focus and boundaries. Most, at one time or another, feel a need to define their own field of study, demarcating it from other branches of academic activity. There is much to be said against this: to carve academic empires is to destroy the unity of social phenomena and stultify important research at the frontiers; it is to hinder the emergence of new fields of study (this point will be made later with reference to the difficulty of establishing policy studies within the existing university framework). Practically, there is as much to be said in its favour (and that is the purpose here). But above all, the definition of one's subject allows one to define oneself—and that is a reasonable urge.

An opening chapter is an appropriate place for one writing about the study of government to contribute his own view. An inaugural lecture is an equally good occasion for a newly appointed Professor of Political Theory and Institutions to expound to his colleagues the nature and significance of his subject as he sees it. After all, many of the colourfully-gowned academics who attend such an occasion, drawn from related and unrelated departments throughout the university, are not likely to hear another exposition of what a particular professor actually professes. The new incumbent of a chair, for his part, is forced to concentrate his mind, as perhaps never after, on his own *raison d'être*. It seemed reasonable, therefore, to start this book with an adaptation of my own inaugural lecture, delivered not so long ago, and I hope, for the reasons explained, that the reader will not think this mere *folie de grandeur*.[1]

[1] This chapter draws on 'The Importance of Constitutions', *Parliamentary Affairs* (Autumn 1966).

The study of politics is amongst the most venerable of academic pursuits. In one form or another, in the forms of history, philosophy and law, for example, it has been studied in our universities for a long time. The growth of our own profession, that of political scientists, is relatively new. New too is the claim that politics is an academic discipline in its own right, or a set of interrelated disciplines, separate from others and thus entitled to the status that departmental organisation in the university gives. The idea that departments of Politics should be established as a matter of course has only come to be accepted since the war. The crowning recognition of a chair is quite young.

Our Declaration of Independence is even now barely hallowed by time. When in the course of human events it becomes necessary for one group of university teachers to dissolve the bands that have connected them with others, and to assume among the departments of the university the separate and equal station of which the laws of science entitle them, a decent respect for the opinions of their fellows requires that they should declare the causes which impelled that separation. The Liverpool department when I was appointed to its chair, was but ten years old and I felt the same need. The Founding Fathers had no problem. They held certain truths to be self-evident. The only self-evident truth that I could see then, and can see today, is that having been appointed to a chair of Politics, it was a matter of self-respect that I should have a subject. At the risk of destroying faith in the omniscience of professors entirely (and, pleasurable to remember, there still seemed some in 1966), I had to confess that I did not really know what my subject was.

That is not a matter that would have worried my predecessor greatly. He stood in the empirical tradition of this country, concerned with practical matters rather than abstract principles, and would have preferred to get down to the business of practising political science rather than waste his time on prior definitions. He had been succeeded, however, by one whose temperament is rather different. I am, as he himself said good-humouredly, a continental rationalist at heart. I hope not an impractical one, however. What it means, in the present context, though, is an uneasy feeling that one ought to be able to define clearly the body of knowledge with which one is concerned. I lean towards the view that a field of study, to attain the status of an independent academic discipline, must have either a subject matter of its own, different from that of other disciplines, or, if not that, then a method of investigation distinct from others.

Many attempts have been made to define our subject matter.

One of the most common is to say that we should study political activity or, more fashionably, political behaviour. The difficulty is that politics, in one form or another, occurs in all spheres of life. As my predecessor pointed out in his own inaugural lecture, politics arise wherever men stand in some relationship to one another and cannot all have their way at once. There are politics in universities, faculties and departments, in student unions and student societies. We may single out those political activities which are related in some way to the state, but, he added, we shall understand even those better if we study them in relation to other examples of political activity. I do not doubt that this is true. But if we define the subject matter of our discipline as political activity, we may end by making all human activity our province. We are likely to find ourselves without a subject matter of our own, for other disciplines will be studying the same activities.

The second possible justification for an independent discipline is to have a method of study of one's own. Political studies, however, were developed in this country by historians and philosophers, on the Continent by jurists. Political scientists have continued to use their methods. More recently, even wider skills have been expected of us. The behavioural approach has become more and more popular. Its protagonists urge us to turn from the formal structure of political institutions, even from the way such institutions work in practice, and to look instead at the behaviour of individuals or groups.

I am not sure myself what the study of people is likely to achieve. It too often depends on the statistical analysis of information obtained from many individuals. In the nature of things, this can only be obtained from the man in the street or from relatively low-ranking politicians and administrators. Our real leaders are unlikely to volunteer useful information; in any case, they do not form a large enough group for generalisation. I suspect the behaviourists will not be able to tell us what makes our leaders 'tick'; they will not be able to predict how our leaders will act in particular cases. Their studies, so far at least, give us no real understanding of how important decisions, decisions that may be matters of life or death, are taken by our governments. Psychologists could make a contribution, but with even less access to political leaders than the empirical political scientist, they have to psychologise at a distance. Unfortunately, they disagree too often to offer us safe interpretations, while we are hardly qualified to assess their arcane methods. A science of political behaviour which does not deal with politics at this level seems to me rather incomplete. It will no doubt have to be supplemented by historians at a later date.

An alternative, of course, is to accept theories of the political process that eliminate the need to explain individual action and thus action in terms of the individual, Marxist-type explanations for example, to use another superficial though convenient label. The trouble with these is that they leave unaccounted the variety of decisions possible at any one time within their framework of trends. Mr Heath's behaviour in the crisis of winter 1973–4 undoubtedly differed from the likely behaviour of other possible Conservative leaders. In the long, even longish, run it may make little difference—but we live for the day and the day's decisions matter greatly to us.

But I am really concerned here with the implications of all behavioural studies, using that term broadly rather than as the name of a school, for the methods of our discipline. It requires an interdisciplinary approach which involves the integration of political science with the other social sciences, in particular sociology and social psychology. Now it is not just a possible inclination towards a tidy division of spheres of competence within universities that makes me somewhat uneasy. Indeed. I am willing to accept that such divisions are impossible in practice. But I fear that the interdisciplinary approach is likely to make us, in the hackneyed phrase, jacks of all trades and masters of none.

We already teach the history of political thought, though few of us are trained philosophers. In so far as our purpose is to show how political ideas have developed and how they have influenced political action, there is no great danger in this. Whether we really understand the inwardness of some of the thinkers we deal with in this fashion is another matter. When I wrote my examination papers at the London School of Economics I certainly had no understanding of Hegel's *Real* and *Rational*, though I could handle these concepts adequately for the purpose set. In so far as we try to analyse philosophers' systems of thought, we are clearly acting as philosophers ourselves. And proper philosophers might think this is a full-time occupation, leaving us little time to pursue other facets of our discipline.

Again, it is impossible to understand the politics of a country without a good knowledge of its history. Much of our explanation of French and German government, for example, depends on an explanation of the past. If we are not to miss important factors, or misinterpret factors we do examine, this too involves us in a considerable activity.

Much the same is true of law, though in fact few political

scientists in this country have a training, or even an interest, in this field. Yet it is quite impossible to understand American government without a knowledge of constitutional law. It is quite impossible to understand public administration in France without a knowledge of administrative law and, more important, its underlying theories.

Now we are also asked to be sociologists and psychologists. This is not just extra work for us, it is work of a far more technical nature. I doubt whether the political scientist can also be a good sociologist; I am sure he cannot be a good psychologist. I would have thought these full-time professions.

Of course, the practical scientist may concentrate on political sociology to the exclusion of other matters traditionally taught in departments of politics. He may in this way become an undoubted specialist in his field. But therein lies a two-fold danger. He may underrate the importance of historical and constitutional factors in his explanation of politics. His sociology itself may be one-sided. It is not clear to me that political behaviour can be studied in isolation from other forms of behaviour, political attitudes from attitudes in general. Politics, after all, for the great majority of people, is a minor part of life. The political sociologist may overlook valuable clues because of the limited questions he is likely to ask. It is not just that he is trying to solve only a small part of a giant jigsaw puzzle, but that he may not even have all the pieces that are required for that small part.

Until more sociologists and psychologists work in the field of politics, political scientists may be forced to do some of their work for them. I do not think there should be a law against trespass of this sort. But I suspect that trespassers will not do the best work in the end, nor am I sure that they are serving their own discipline in the long run. I am sure that it is in our own interest, as well as in the interest of others, that relations between politics and other disciplines should be strengthened, particularly in planning research. Let us suggest to others the seeds they might plant in their own fields; let us partake of their crops; but let us avoid, if we can, having to do their ploughing and harvesting as well.

Some years ago I reviewed three books which had nothing in common except that their titles indicated that they dealt with the theory of politics. They showed that a political scientist can apparently decide for himself what his discipline is to be; each can live in his own world, drawing his own boundaries around it. Virtually all our universities have established chairs of Politics. What is taught in them (even allowing for the recent democratisation of departments) may depend a good deal on their holders' own views about the nature of their subject. I wrote then, well before my own appointment, that vice-chancellors and selection committees, bearing the maxim *caveat emptor* in mind, presumably take advice about the worlds their new professors are likely to inhabit; though I doubt whether this really explains the very different characters, reputations at least, that different departments appear to have acquired.

My own rationalist temper sometimes makes me think that a standard syllabus would be a great advantage. But that would make life much less attractive for university teachers accustomed to defining their own courses. In practice, I am as willing to be as eclectic as the next man. Even the briefest glance at our own Liverpool syllabus will show that we cover a wide range of subjects and use many different methods of study. I am also a believer in academic freedom. My colleagues have different views about the nature and significance of our subject. I can see merits in such diversity. So I will try to avoid laying down the law on what ought to be taught in departments of politics. I shall try instead, and here I return to my starting point and to the real theme of this chapter, to indicate where I think a centre of our interests should lie.

I believe that the state, rather than political activity, should be the subject matter of our studies. This is a traditionalist view. Political studies in the past have generally been concerned with its nature, organisation and functions. We are now told to study the political process, political cultures, systems, patterns of behaviour. Perhaps our predecessors concentrated on the state because these new frameworks of analysis had not been invented in their time. But I suspect that they would have been horrified, not only by the jargon of modern political science, but even more by the way it is often divorced from the great themes of political thought. They would have regarded it as strange that students of politics should be more interested in the detailed investigation of what exists than in a consideration of what should be.

My own doctoral work involved me in the study of French socialist thought, and French socialist thought was largely utopian. The revolutionary syndicalists not merely had a distinctive theory of revolution, they had a blueprint of society transformed. Utopianism, meaning simply talk about the good society of the future, radical reorganisation of our system of government, is now out of fashion. There are signs of change, notably in America with the emergence of a committed 'new political science'. But the overwhelming majority of our own political scientists keep their noses firmly within the existing order of institutions. Not that I

am advocating revolutionary action here—far from it: the experience of the twentieth century shows it to be a bad bet, unlikely
to succeed, more likely to lead to reaction, or if successful likely to
end in perversion.

That should not exclude a concern with reform which goes
beyond tinkering at the margins. Perhaps political scientists are
too modest these days, perhaps too sceptical, perhaps too concerned with establishing a reputation for safe practicality. I am a
little astonished at this trend. One of the major lures of our subject
has always seemed to me to lie in the utopian element.

This may again be a matter of temperament. But it was an outlook shared by Harold Laski, the political scientist from whom I
learnt that political science was concerned with great issues and
great ideals. The chapters of his *Introduction to Politics* are entitled
'The Nature of the State', 'The Place of the State in the Great
Society' and 'The Organisation of the State', and these three
themes seem to be the essence of our subject. My chair is a chair of
Political Theory and Institutions. As these headings show, it is in
relation to the state that we can best bring the study of theory and
institutions together. A function of the political scientist, as Laski
saw it, was to suggest ways in which the institutions of the state
could be shaped in order to make the good society possible. His
great book, *The Grammar of Politics*, is a monument to that belief.

Nevertheless, it is to the continental political scientist that we
must look for a definition of political science as a formal study of
the state, based upon, though extending beyond, the methods of
jurisprudence. The reason for this is not hard to see. I believe I am
right in saying that in this country the state has no legal existence
at all. We have the Crown, government departments, local
authorities, public corporations—all have legal personality. But,
stricto sensu, there is no institution in Britain called the state that
can form the subject matter of our study. In our standard textbooks of constitutional law, indeed, there is no discussion of the
state whatsoever. That must strike the continental reader as very
strange. The European state is organised society in legal dress. It
is an institution, and it is as such that it can be studied.

In Germany *Staatswissenschaft*, the science of the state, was
developed in the law faculties and the same was largely true of
France. This was not simply an accident of university organisation.
There was much about the European state that could usefully be
studied by jurists: the law relating to the state, and the theories
underlying it, were directly relevant to the process of government.
European studies of government are often labelled formal or
legalistic by British political scientists. It is true that they often

fail to examine the way in which institutions really work, but they should not for that reason be dismissed. European government is bound by administrative law to a far greater extent than British. This law is in good measure the creation of courts such as the French *Conseil d'Etat* and their decisions are based on wide-sweeping discussions of such questions as the nature and functions of the state. In Europe at least, in other words, there can be no real division between political theory and jurisprudence.

My inaugural lecture was entitled 'The Importance of Constitu-ions', not 'The Importance of the State'. But of course it is the constitution which organises the state: the state, as an institution, is created and defined by its constitution. The study of constitu-tions must therefore occupy a central place in political science. The difficulty is that I believe, and I suspect that I am almost alone among British political scientists in this, that we do not have a con-stitution at all in this country in any meaningful sense of the word.

To quote a distinguished authority on constitutions, we use the term to describe the whole system of government of a country, the collection of rules, written and unwritten, which regulate the government. In that sense the constitution of a country is merely the observer's account of principles held, institutions existent and practices observed. British studies of the constitution are usually no more than a description of our system of government at work. It is a matter of indifference whether such books are entitled *The British Constitution* or *The Government of Britain*. In almost every other country, the word constitution is used in a narrower sense. It refers not to a system, nor even to the whole collection of rules, legal and non-legal, that define it, but to a selection of legal rules, usually embodied in a single document.

The distinction is not really between written and unwritten constitutions, however. Since 1787 the word constitution has meant rather more in America, Europe and the rest of the world than just a legal document. The American constitution actually established a system of government, constituted government, and, by the same token, gave it legitimacy. American government derives its legitimacy from an, admittedly somewhat spurious, decision of the American people, the Fifth Republic from a vote of the French people. This is not true of Britain. Our system of government, to use another hackneyed phrase, like Topsy, just growd. Its fundamental principle is the sovereignty of Parliament; and if you ask why Parliament is sovereign, you can give a histori-cal, but not a constitutional, answer. The constitutions of other countries, moreover, establish principles which the institutions they create cannot change, or can only change by special procedures. Parliament, on the other hand, can change the law at any time. The sovereignty of Parliament thus precludes the existence of any other constitutional principles.

I do not want to develop this argument but simply to make one point. In Britain, what we call our constitution is really a reflection of existing principles, a description of existing institutions: we can thus study British government quite adequately without any notion of the constitution at all, and this, of course, is increasingly being done. Elsewhere, constitutions establish principles and shape the system of government. Foreign systems, therefore, cannot be understood except by reference to their constitutions. It is fashionable to decry as formalistic such approaches to the study of government. We are told that processes are more important than institutions, political realities than legal principles. But because we are a country with no real history of constitution-making, we may underrate the importance of constitutional forms elsewhere. In the rest of the world, constitutional devices do play a part in shaping the governmental process. These devices, moreover, reflect political ideas. The study of constitutions is thus one of the best ways of linking the study of theories and institutions. To this then, the relation between theory and institutions, I shall return to in the following chapters.

There is another, more practical, aspect to the study of constitutions, and that is the study of what is now sometimes called constitutional engineering. Whether or not constitutions can actually shape the political process, whether or not the good society really depends on the well-organised state, it is a fact that constitution-making has been a major feature of the politics of this century, at least outside the Anglo-Saxon world. The modernists who would have us turn from the formal study of law and institutions to the behaviour of the man in the street, the backbench M P or the faceless official, may cause us to lose sight of an important part of political activity itself. To this theme of institutional engineering I shall also return in a later chapter.

Constitutions, important though they are, form only a small part of the organisation of the state. The argument here is more broadly that one should focus on the institutions of government, political and administrative. (Quantitatively, and even qualitatively, that means a good deal of attention to the administrative system—hence the importance attached to Public Administration as an academic subject in this book.) That formal structures and formal procedures may not correspond to reality is plain, though the discrepancy is often exaggerated by those who wish to dissolve them into behavioural patterns. That even the realistic description of a governmental system does not exhaust the whole field of political activity is equally plain and one would not wish to ignore the political forces that impinge on it. My point is simply that analysis of the formal arrangements of government, the theories underlying them and the possibilities of their reform, all in the light of their actual operation and the lessons that can be learnt from comparative studies, is a good programme for political science, academically viable, intellectually rewarding and socially useful.

At the same time, and this is its merit in the context of the present chapter, such an approach does give us a subject matter of our own. We share the study of political behaviour with the sociologists, studies of the course of politics with the historian. The analysis of governmental institutions we might expect to share to some extent with constitutional and administrative lawyers, though, in Britain at least, some distinguished authors apart, the interest of lawyers is marginal. The subject matter of these other disciplines is society, history and the law; the subject matter I recommend to political scientists is the state. If we want a field of our own, in which we can develop an expertise of our own, that field is surely the state or, to avoid misunderstanding, the organised state. It is a pity that we have no ready translation of the German *Staatswissenschaft*. Though even in Germany that term has now given way to *politische Wissenschaft*, an English equivalent would have provided a useful label for the institutional approach I wish to recommend.

The purpose, art for art's sake apart (the study of government can be interesting in its own right), is that set out by Lord Bryce in 1921, opening his *Modern Democracies*: 'Many years ago, at a time when schemes of political reform were being copiously discussed in England, mostly on general principles, but also with references, usually vague and disconnected, to history and to events in other countries, it occurred to me that something might be done to provide a solid basis for argument and judgement by examining a certain number of popular governments in their actual working, comparing them with one another, and setting forth the various merits and defects which belonged to each.' To political reform I would simply add administrative reform.

There are, of course, philosophical problems in Bryce's project. To any comparison of the merits of political and administrative devices, 'better for what?' is the obvious response. Even if one were to agree on this, it remains difficult to pull a particular institution out of the context of its political culture, even out of its narrower governmental context. The way it works depends on innumerable, sometimes almost unidentifiable, environmental factors. It is hard to say with confidence why it works well (or badly) within its own system; it is harder still to guess how it would function if transferred to other systems. But too much can be made of these difficulties, as I shall argue later in discussing the problems of comparison as a practical activity, and I shall try to illustrate how lessons may be learnt from studies of foreign experience.

Bryce, of course, refers to governments in their actual working while I have been emphasising here the need to study formal arrangements, preferably against the background of their actual working, though even this is not necessary in all cases. The reason for this, our Declaration of Independence apart, is practical. Modern political science is more concerned with 'real' processes than formal institutions or procedures. If not actually disinterested (value-free, if you will), it has nevertheless concentrated its energies on the advancement of knowledge rather than the propagation of reform. In the last few years there has been something of a change. For long, however, 'realism' led paradoxically to the ivory tower. A legalistic approach unsupported by a political philosophy does not necessarily lead to anything different. The majority of lawyers, indeed, have never been reformist. But one can well argue that a complete rejection of legal-institutional studies can easily encourage a neutralist position in political science.

Whether one likes it or not, after all, societies are governed by law and through institutions. If one wishes to improve society, one must in the last resort amend laws and alter institutions. Most changes in the governmental process can only be brought about in this way. Only the extreme optimist would pin his hope on moral exhortation unsupported by formal action, on changes in behaviour not channelled through concrete structures. Even quite limited reforms usually require formal implementation. Morale within the administration, standards of service, application to work, respect for the citizen—these can to some extent be changed by improved interpersonal relations, but even this, in turn, is likely to require some change in rules, perhaps even new forms of organisation. Changes in the political system can only be brought about in this way even by revolutionaries: only the anarchists pin their hopes on the spontaneous growth of institutions and a society without laws.

To sum up, then, the organised state offers the political scientist a field he can call his own, in which he can develop his own expertise without having to borrow too heavily, perhaps beyond his capacities, from other disciplines. This focus implies a certain formalism, a study not divorced from reality but taking as its starting point concrete institutions and prescribed procedures rather than behaviour patterns or the actual processes of government. Paradoxically, if political scientists become so interested in the real that they disregard the rational face of the machinery of government, they cut themselves off from practicality.

It is another curious fact of much contemporary comparative politics that it makes little reference to political philosophy: the philosophy institutions are *intended* to embody, the purpose they are designed to serve (and this is not the same as *function* in current usage). To compare British and American systems without reference to the Founding Fathers, the belief that governments are instituted for the protection of rights that pre-exist the state and the belief in limited government, would be inconceivable. But at a lower level foreign administrations are often studied in this untheoretical way. French administration, however, to take one example, cannot be understood without reference to theories about the nature and functions of the state. True, these have been elaborated by legal rather than political philosophers and might thus escape the notice of political scientists, but their doctrines are readily accessible in French administrative textbooks. They are doubly important, moreover, because as internalised norms they explain the actual spirit of French administration as well as explaining it teleologically. I shall attempt to illustrate this later.

But there is another reason for not disregarding political philosophy. The normative neutralism of much political science in the last decade, and some leading exponents of American behaviouralism have made a virtue of this, may reasonably alienate a growing number of students and confirm the rest of the world's tendency to dismiss ivory-tower intellectuals as irrelevant. Thus the approach I advocate also implies a reformist bent, a backing of values, if not of political philosophy in its more technical sense. If political scientists become so interested in the real that they disregard the ideal, they lose the motive for reform.

Let me conclude this chapter by returning to the peroration of my inaugural lecture. If one is to engage in the activity of constitutional engineering or, more modestly and more academically, to suggest to others the constitutional reforms they should adopt, it is necessary to study comparative government. When the constitutions of foreign countries have been examined, we shall perhaps be more likely to see, with a comprehensive view, which constitution is best, how a state must be ordered, what laws it must have, if it is to be at its best. It is with that quotation from Aristotle, the great-grandfather of our science, and broadening the field here, that I recommend the study of governmental institutions.

Theory and Institutions

While political scientists have battled in the field of theory—empirical, analytical and ideological—the field of institutions has become something of an intellectual backwater, still the focus of much research but not the centre of theoretical debate. The institutionalists generally take institutions for granted. The moderns, students of behaviour in one form or another, prefer to avoid the word if they can. There has thus been little recent discussion of the meaning of institutions as a concept of political science and, as a result, the word has often been used in a muddled way. A look at the terminology and its implications is one purpose of this chapter.[1] But other people's definitions are often good pegs on which to hang arguments of one's own, and my commentary on the language of others will also serve as an approach to my own view of the subject.

As befits the holder of a chair of Political Theory and Institutions I want to emphasise the link between the two parts of my domain, to argue for a view of political institutions as the embodiment of political thought. Institutions are often studied as if they were a form of practice—part of behavioural reality. I prefer to see them as constructs with a purpose, ideas about government translated into formal arrangements that probably do not coincide with practice—a different level of reality but no less real for that. I have already argued the importance of an institutional approach to the study of politics. We organise our government through formal institutions, not by informal agreements on how to behave,

---

[1] For a version of this chapter in which references to quotations is given, see 'Political Institutions: The Script Not The Play', *Political Studies* (June 1975).

and to make our government better, to improve its behaviour and ours, requires the reform of institutions. This, in turn, is meaningless without reference to political theory, for reform means purpose and purpose means philosophy. Unless we think of political institutions as the formalisation of values, as legal arrangements designed to shape behaviour, instead of confusing them with behaviour itself, we are likely to emasculate political science.

We often bow to Humpty Dumpty on the definition of terms, and I accept his right, yours and mine, to make words mean what we wish them to mean. Nevertheless, I was curious at the start of this exercise to see how the word institutions was used in current political science, so I took from my shelves a likely pile of recent textbooks. My first impression was the casualness with which political scientists treated the concept, in this very different from the sociologists. The danger of taking the term for granted, however, is that it may be used without any clear meaning at all.

Let me quote from three textbooks. The first says only that 'the study of political institutions' long centred on legislatures, executives and judiciaries, but as it developed the list came to include political parties, bureaucracies, interest groups and other groups engaged in politics which have a continuous existence; later there is the passing reference to 'specialised institutions or structures' which are more clearly governmental than others because their responsibilities are normally defined by a constitution. The second declares that 'roughly the same kind of institutions' can be found in most political systems; subsequent chapter cover legislatures, executives, bureaucracies, judiciaries, parties, pressure groups and electorates, and at the end we are told that 'not all political structures' have been treated in the book. According to the third, 'typical elements of the structure of a political system' are 'formal and informal institutions', with legislatures as an example of the formal, parties and interest groups as examples of the informal; later the author refers to the emergence of 'behaviour patterns or institutions'. In each case structures are slipped in as a synonym for institutions and by this sleight of hand the subject matter of institutional studies is extended to cover the field of organised group behaviour. By the time I reached the ten-page index to Blondel's *Introduction to Comparative Government* the word institution had disappeared entirely. We are given instead the broader concept of structures which can be the product of the operation of either natural or imposed norms. Despite some lapses into commoner speech, Blondel generally sticks to his word, depriving himself of the terminological distinction between formal arrangements and informal patterns of behaviour. The irony is his remark that 'traditionally, the study of the structures of government formed the core of the subject of comparative government'. In referring to the traditional approach, why not use the traditional word?

Avoidance of the word institutions may simply be linguistic fashion. Even those who wish to give a fairly orthodox description of the governmental system may feel obliged to use a more modern language. But it also reflects a way of looking at politics. I marked the following passage in a novel recently, thinking it would serve as one of those irrelevant literary quotations that so often adorn the works of political science: 'The Old World is theory, she kept on saying as we supped our cappucines, the Old World is theory, but the New World is action!' Not long ago one might have said that American political science was about action—read behaviour—while European political science was about theory—read formal institutions and philosophical values. Of course it would never have done, for the New World theorised even more than the Old, even if action was the subject of its theories. Now, in any case, the Old World is just as likely to produce action-centred textbooks. Thus a recent British political sociology text: 'What we want to do is define politics in terms of a class of actions, not in terms of a set of institutions or organisations.' That political sociology should start with behaviour is reasonable, but it is surely strange not even to comment on institutions as a sociological concept. Nor is our language much helped by the authors' use of 'the idea of organisation' instead of structures. Like structures, organisations may be natural or imposed: if people are organised in some way, that presupposes rules which govern the relationship between members of the group and the book explains that these may have evolved through the course of time or have been specifically enacted. Again, a distinction is blurred.

We are thus faced with a problem of linguistic confusion and with an anti-institutional fashion in political science. According to one writer, 'modern currents in comparative politics are clearly distinguished from their immediate predecessors by their treatment—or, more frequently, non-treatment—of the institutional fabric of modern governments; once the epitome of comparative subjects, the study of political institutions has now been downgraded, if not altogether eliminated from the discipline'. Downgraded yes, eliminated no. The fact that institutional studies are unmodern does not mean that there are not many dowdy dressers left in our profession. Nor is fashion a reliable indicator of distinction. We have the authority of George Mikes that in England even the richest peer may dress in rags.

There are contemporary political scientists, of course, who go further. For them the institutional approach is not merely out-dated, it is positively discredited. Some comment on these lines may, again, be all they have to say on the subject. In a small American volume on the state of the discipline there is a brief section entitled 'Focus on Institutions'. Up to a generation ago, it explains, it was common to think and speak of forms of govern-ment in terms of formally ordered political relationships, but much of contemporary work is devoted to penetrating the formal surface and describing and explaining how politics 'really works'. With that, the 'constitutional approach' is dismissed. Though the authors have the grace to put quotation marks around 'really works', there is an assumption that what goes on below the surface is more real than are formal arrangements. Try breaking the law and see what happens! 'Thus I prove it real', to misquote Dr Johnson. Note the further assumption that for the student of politics what happens is more important than what is intended—the real eclipses the ideal.

By contrast to political science, the concept of institutions has played a central role in sociology. And an even more confused one. While the *Grande Encyclopédie Française* of 1901 could define sociology as the science of institutions, a more recent survey had this to say:

'A malicious critic of sociology could hardly find a better way of arousing scepticism about its scientific status than by collecting the definitions of 'social organisation' on the one hand, of 'institutions' on the other, and comparing the various ways in which the relationship between these is conceived . . . It is absolutely im-possible to introduce any logical order into the present termino-logical confusion.'

Often, the sociologists use the term institutions in a way that bears little resemblance to the traditional, unthinking language of political science. In sociological tradition, indeed, it refers not to organisations, whether formal or informal, but to norms of behaviour and established beliefs. For Durkheim sociology as the science of institutions was concerned with just that: 'One can designate as institutions all the belief and all the modes of conduct instituted by the collectivity.' In my search for definitions I con-sulted the *Encyclopedia of the Social Sciences* to find 'a verbal symbol which for want of a better describes a cluster of social usages'. I turned to the more recent *International Encyclopedia of the Social Sciences* which, significantly, dealt only with *social* institutions. These 'institutions or patterns of institutionalisation' are 'regulative principles which organise most of the activities of individuals in a society into definite patterns'. How such patterns of institutionalisation differ from custom is not really clear to the unsophisticated, nor is it clear why that phrase should be used as a synonym for institutions. More seriously, the definition fails to distinguish between organisational and extra-organisational behaviour patterns, quite apart from its failure to distinguish between legally formalised and informally regularised patterns within organisations. This may not be muddled thinking but the result of a search for common denominators to describe social phenomena. But Occam's razor is two-edged—the process of generalisation must not be used to decimate our dictionary. In the study of government, as in everyday speech, we do need to refer to institutions of government in the traditional way and the sociologist does no service to the family of social sciences by impoverishing our language.

One political science textbook that echoes the sociologists declares that 'a human group becomes institutionalised when, to a relatively high degree, its patterns of membership and interaction become stable, uniform, formal and general'. It adds that in the writings of sociologists the notions of institution and institutionalised group are often used interchangeably, citing legislatures, bureaucracies, churches and family systems as examples. What an institution means here, clearly, is some combination of the norms of behaviour and behaviour patterns that characterise legislatures, bureaucracies, churches and families. The author then tells us that the concept has not proved satisfactory from an empirical point of view because it is difficult for the scientific observer to measure degrees of stability, uniformity, formality and generality: the tendency, therefore, has increasingly been to speak of organisations as these are more observable. Given the definition, I do not quarrel with the substance of that statement. It is mildly amusing, however, to note that the institutions of the traditional language of political science have been downgraded for the opposite reason, not because they are hard to observe but, formal tips of the iceberg of behavioural reality, because they are too easily observed and thus, like the iceberg's tip, tend to mislead the look-out.

The quotation above is a convenient lead in to organisational sociology. In *Formal Organisations* Blau and Scott distinguish formal organisations, 'the distinctive feature of which is that they have been deliberately established for explicit purposes', from the social organisations that arise naturally whenever men live together. In formal organisations 'the goals to be achieved, the rules that members are expected to follow . . . have not spontaneously emerged in the course of social interaction but have been consciously designed *a priori* to anticipate and guide interaction and activities'. It is this characteristic that I will stress with regard to political institutions. Of course, not all that goes on within formal organisations conforms to the blueprint. Unofficial patterns of behaviour, supported by unofficial values, are bound to develop within the formal system. And of course all are so interrelated that, in one sense, 'it is impossible to understand the nature of formal organisations without investigating the informal'. But from this Blau and Scott conclude that 'the distinction between the two aspects of organisational life is only an analytic one and should not be reified; there is only one organisation'. There is a trick here—the introduction of organisational life. Life is a whole, its fabric platitudinously interwoven, but that does not make the distinction between the formal and the informal an analytic one except for the observer of life's flow. The distinction between the formally prescribed and the informally behaved is not one invented by the social scientist for analytical reasons; it is determined by those who have, in the author's own phrase, deliberately established the organisation. Members of a governmental organisation, the bureaucracy for example, are usually clear enough that there is a substantive, not an analytic, distinction between the book of rules and what they themselves think or do. But the wrong things are being distinguished here in any case. What needs to be contrasted is the formal organisation, the prescribed arrangements, on the one hand, and all behaviour, whether formal or informal, on the other. Organisational behaviour takes place within organisations but it makes little sense to confuse it with the organisational framework. A formal organisation *is* reified: that is why some writers, unthinkingly no doubt, use the phrase concrete institutions.

A similar tendency to blur words is found in Etzioni's *Modern Organisations*. Organisations, he says, 'are social units or human groupings deliberately constructed and reconstructed to seek specific goals'. But is it really the group that is constructed? To use an analogy found elsewhere in political science, the architect designs a house and that is what the builders construct. Neither the architect's plans nor the builder's bricks are a social unit—that is the family which comes to live in the house. Construction, in other words, refers more sensibly to the formal arrangements in which a group of people operate. That these may give rise to a new social unit is true enough, but even if one were prepared to use construction to describe that process also, one could only call it deliberate in a limited sense. Just as families are notoriously recalcitrant and insist on leading their lives in ways that cannot be entirely blueprinted, so a group brought together in a constructed framework will organise its behaviour according to informal as well as formal patterns—differently, that is, from the deliberate intentions of the constructor.

Etzioni also defines organisations by the fact that they have a purpose, and on this aspect I would like to concentrate a little more. How is the purpose determined? Apparently 'an organisational goal is a desired state of affairs which the organisation attempts to realise'. Asking himself whose image of the future this involves, he rejects the leaders, or even the majority of members, in favour of 'that which the organisation as a collectivity is trying to bring about'. Presumably this means more than the tautological statement that the actual goal of an organisation is where the organisation is actually going. Is it the mysterious General Will or has the organic theory of institutions reared its head again? In fact, he means something much more mundane than the phrase leads one to suppose. In the case of a company, he tells the researcher to ask its officers what they think its goals are or to consult board minutes. Surely the purpose of a company is determined by company law and articles of association—the formal constitution, if you like—backed by a generally accepted philosophy of capitalism—conventions of the constitution? Etzioni's distinction between real and stated goals does not help matters, for here he means no more than the discrepancy between what participants say or think they are doing and what they are actually doing. But goals really pursued are not *ipso facto* the real purpose for which an institution was established. The behaviour of officials, indeed, is less likely to coincide with that intention than are their statements.

There is a confusion about ends here that needs to be unscrambled. Etzioni comments rightly enough that most organisations have a formal, explicitly recognised, sometimes legally specified organ for setting official goals and their amendment. He cites the shareholders meeting as an example. But this does not clearly distinguish goals from purpose. The purpose of an organisation is generally determined before it is constructed, indeed it is generally established in order to serve a purpose. Technically, this can be seen in the fact that articles of association precedes the company just as constitutions precede legislatures. Legislatures have a purpose: to legislate. Constitutional rules usually go further, providing for legislation by vote of a majority of the elected representatives of the people in accordance with specified procedures which ensure, for example, that rights of debate are respected. The purpose of legislation is something very different. It is seldom written into constitutions and then without much effect; only rarely is it a major consideration in the establishment

of legislatures. The point I want to make is this: the purpose of an
institution, the real goal in that sense, depends neither on what its
members think at any one time nor upon what they actually do.
The *raison d'être* of an institution is literally the reason for its
existence, not the function it actually performs, and reason in that
context is to be used in a rational rather than a behavioural sense.

My argument, then, is simply that institutions are established
(or groups organised, if one wants to use that phrase) quite
deliberately, sometimes for a general purpose, sometimes for the
pursuit of more specific goals, neither of which depends on the
values of their members, however these are formed and however
widely shared they may be. One can, of course, quote 'by their
fruits shall ye know them' against the Christian churches. But
neither the purpose of a church nor, indeed, its doctrine (read
values) is explained by examining the fruit. One has only to look
at the conflict between papal encyclicals and the behaviour, even
beliefs, of Catholic laymen to see the force of this. We cannot
understand the Catholic Church as an institution through its
members, however much we might learn about the life Catholics
actually live. More seriously, and this applies with equal force to
political institutions, we deprive ourselves of standards by confusing the two. Description of political reality, even explanation of
that reality, is not the sum of political science. Its crowning glory
lies in the discussion of ideas, in analysing the purpose of institutions, in measuring reality against purpose and in suggesting ways
in which the real can be changed to harmonise with the ideal.

I must now backtrack to the definition of institutions. The
Oxford English Dictionary has this to say: to institute is 'to set up,
establish, order, arrange, put into form'. An institution is 'an
established law, custom, usage, practice, organisation or other
element in the political or social life of a person . . . an establishment or organisation instituted for the promotion of some object,
especially of public utility, religious, charitable, educational, etc.'
This is broad enough, covering as it does laws, customs and
organisations. I have already suggested that in political science we
should avoid confusion if we stuck to some term like structures or
behaviour patterns when referring to practice and used the term
institutions for formal organisations. What I want to pick out here,
however, is that part of the definition which links the noun and the
verb: an institution is something instituted. The *Grand Larousse* is
even clearer. Its definition is *action d'instituer quelquechose, chose in-
stitué*'. It adds that in administrative law it means '*ce qui est établi
par les hommes en opposition à ce qui est naturel*', giving marriage,
family, association, foundation, government and parliament

as examples. The much earlier *Littré* was equally specific: '*tout ce qui est inventé et établi par les hommes, en opposition à ce qui est de nature*'. Thus my point, laboured above, that an institution is not a custom that grows naturally, not a behavioural pattern that emerges through the interaction of men, not a structure created by social forces; it is something invented, deliberately established and ordered, and therefore it has a rational and formal base.

This brings me back to the sociological approach. We have seen a church described as an 'institutionalised group' in so far as its patterns of membership and interaction have become stable. Stable patterns may be the mark of an institutionalised group, but that is not how a church is created. The Church of England is by law established. We may argue about who established the Roman Church, and perhaps it was not Man at all—'Thou art Peter and upon this rock I shall build my church.' Established it was, in any case, and though it sometimes describes itself as the body of the faithful, the rock was there first and the faithful came to it. And neither church, as a contemporary institution, should be confused with what its members do or think. Such confusion makes a nonsense of the very idea of a church. Exactly the same is true of marriage. How the married actually behave is a valid subject of study but it is not the institution of marriage. That, as the Prayer Book tells us, is an estate ordained by God; it is, of course, also a relationship formally organised by the laws of man. Let us not, for the sake of descriptive sociology, ignore the act of invention nor the intentions of the inventor, lest we forget that institutions have a purpose and that the purpose of description is to test practice against intention.

I can make the same point by reference to a recent textbook which focuses on the process of politics. 'The institutional emphasis' is rejected here because 'it is at once concrete and abstract: it is concrete in the sense of being concerned with the legal or constitutional properties of a particular organ of government; it is abstract in thinking of this organ almost as a Platonic form divorced from the context of the environment in which it operates.' The author is right when he concludes that the institutional approach does not permit the examination of significant aspects of the political process, but surely begging the question when he adds that institutionalists 'perhaps focus on the wrong problems—problems which even if solved would do little to further our understanding'. Should we not be concerned with what is 'at once concrete and abstract'? The fact that a process approach may itself focus on the wrong problems becomes clear a little later. The argument that institutional arrangements should be considered as

part of the environment in which activities occur is supported by
an illustration which can neatly be turned the other way. 'A
Triumph TR-3 can go more than 100 mph; when driven by a little
old lady, however, it is unlikely to move even half that fast'. But
would a student of motor cars want to know how a TR-3 is driven
on a particular occasion, or is he more likely to ask about the
machinery itself—its concrete properties—on the one hand, the
potential it was designed to achieve—its Platonic nature—on the
other? A significant aspect of politics can only be studied if
institutions are treated as something distinct from their environment and if their purpose is separated from their performance.

A slim introduction to the study of politics, which is conveniently next on my pile, does emphasise the importance of institutions and their goals. It defines an institution in much the same
way as others have defined organisation—as a group of people
working towards a common aim. That common aim can be a very
general one: legislators disagree on what bills to pass but they
agree on when to meet, on how to handle their business and on
what it is they are supposed to be doing. This picture of institutions creates two problems. It is misleading to speak of a group as
working towards a common aim when what it is really doing is
working in a common way. The distinction is not pedantic. The
purpose of a political institution is generally to conduct certain
types of business, in the case of a legislature to pass laws (I leave
aside other functions such as scrutiny and debate). The conduct of
business, rather than what members hope to achieve by the output,
is the core of their agreement. In so far as they have a general aim,
it is a very specific one—procedural rather than substantive, a
purpose rather than a goal. But there is a more serious ambiguity.
Neither the purpose nor the procedure of an institution is the
result of agreement among its members. Though they may
occasionally agree to amend the rules, in general what they agree
on is to abide by them. An institution is not created by its tenants
any more than a house, even if both alter the furniture and fittings
at intervals.

The problem raised here is reflected in the original statement
that an institution is a group of people and a subsequent statement that it 'consists of people, goals and rules'. In what sense are
people an integral part of an institution? People come and go
while the institution itself is permanent. That can be got round.
Indeed, in law, an institution may be a body corporate, consisting
of the members for the time being. But what incorporates them is
the formal rules establishing the institution: the constitution, a
law, or articles of association. It is not more realistically thought

of, therefore, as the formal framework in which a group of people work? That in so doing they will sometimes work in accordance with the formal rules, sometimes follow other patterns of behaviour, is obvious enough. That in the process of interaction they will develop a unity is no less obvious. Members of an institution can be studied as an institutionalised group, substantively as well as analytically distinct from the institution itself. In that sense we may agree with W. J. M. Mackenzie when he says that 'to each of the legal organs of the state corresponds, more or less exactly, a social system, which consists in effect of persons brought together by legal relationships, existing together in social relationships'. The House of Commons, therefore, is 'at once a legal organ subject to a hierarchy of rather strict rules and a social system'—the 'best club in London' among other things. Let me repeat: to confuse the two easily leads into a trap. The student of institutions wants to find out how men organise themselves to secure the ends they think desirable; if he concentrates on how they actually behave, he is not asking how ends are institutionalised, much less is he asking questions about the ends themselves.

It may be, as one book says, that the traditional interest of scholars in formal institutions is easy to understand because the formal structure mainly concerns the public and easily discernible aspects of governments. The Palace of Westminster stands there for all to see, the American Constitution is displayed in the National Archives. The behaviour of legislators can also be observed without too much difficulty. Other political forces are altogether less tangible. To that extent—though this should not be exaggerated—it is likely that they will be chronicled later. But even if the modern political scientist is aware of the whole range of political forces that interplay to determine politics, some remain so private that the researcher's net will miss them. Electoral studies are feasible; 'scientific' studies of cabinet behaviour are not. Through a battery of tests we can learn something about the humble citizen, but our leading politicians are less accessible. Which is the more important for the fate of the country? When we leave the field of institutional studies for the broader field of political behaviour, we run a risk not dissimilar to that of which traditional scholars are accused: a concentration on the easily discernible aspects of political life. The result is no less lopsided. But that is an aside. The point I really want to make is that the interest of scholars may reflect their belief that formal institutions *are* important in determining the way a political system operates.

The relationship between institutions and behaviour is often expressed in one of two ways and a shade of meaning differentiates them that is significant, though doubtless often unintended. The first stresses their interdependence. Thus: 'Political institutions and political behaviour must be viewed in a framework of inter-action.' Thus: 'We are concerned with the relationship between institutions and values, with how institutions are shaped by values and values by institutions in a reciprocal process of change.' The shaping of institutions is seen as a natural process, continuously in operation, not the result of deliberate amendments occasionally undertaken. In this perspective institutions and behaviour are equally dependent variables, and institutions, perpetually acted upon, are rather fluid. In the second formulation institutions are seen as independent variables at any one moment of time, and as relatively independent variables in the medium term. Thus: 'Political institutions are the framework of rules within which the actors in a political situation must operate.' Expressed in this way, formal institutions acquire a more solid existence. In all likelihood a greater influence will also be attributed to them.

The analogy of a house is sometimes used: what goes on within the house cannot be dictated by the bricks and mortar, but its structure does impose certain restrictions on behaviour. On occasion the residents may alter the exterior design, modify the interior, construct a new wing, even abandon the old and build again. But in normal times (and periods of constitutional amend-ment are brief) the house stands firm: it is not shaped by the behaviour of its inhabitants. The institutional rules within which the actors of a political situation must operate are usually pretty elaborate, far more constraining than the plans of a house, even where the architect has fancied himself as a designer of interiors and has tried to channel family life by fixtures and fittings. In constitutional democracies, that is to say in states where the law is usually obeyed (Watergate notwithstanding), formal arrange-ments are an important, and in the immediate run an independent, factor in determining the way a political system operates. I do not say that they are the most important in all cases, just as I do not say that behavioural patterns will not reshape them indirectly in the long run through formal amendment. All I claim is that they deserve study in their own right.

There is a second argument for institutional studies. Most reforms of the political system require a change in formal arrange-ments. We are governed by laws, not by men. This is not a meaningless platitude of democratic ideology. The actual work of government has to be carried out through legally established institutions, in many cases according to legally defined procedures. Changes in our way of government may require a prior change in political attitudes, but there are large areas in which attitudes alone cannot alter behaviour patterns. Nor can changed behaviour patterns by themselves, through some process of interaction, alter formal institutions: a deliberate act of reconstruction is required. The conclusion is drawn by one writer:

'Since modern governments fashion their primary activities—administrative and lawmaking—according to legal definitions, the predominance of legalistic approaches to constitutional and institutional change is quite understandable . . . Regardless of the current preference of some political scientists, the legal-institutional approach is still strongly represented among practising politicians and lawmakers . . . The student who ignores it is out of touch with the chief frame of reference of the practitioners of politics and the reality they perceive.'

One must not exaggerate what institutional change can achieve. Few institutionalists actually fall into this trap, though other political scientists sometimes create an impression to the contrary. Let me return to the author who introduced us to the little old lady with a TR-3. He accepts that few institutionalists are so naïve as to argue that formal arrangements alone can determine how a political system will operate. He lays a more sophisticated charge against them instead: institutional engineers tend to regard other factors as intervening, almost extraneous, variables which thwart the natural impact of institutional arrangements. The danger of their attitude is that it may lead them to use such factors 'to explain away cases which fail to conform to a hypothesis concerning the effect of a certain institution'. Put more simply, the reformer may blame others for the failure of his plans. The statement may have some truth, but it reads oddly in context for it actually follows the case of the little old lady. Surely she was an extraneous variable? She does explain why the TR-3 did not perform according to specification. The example is not as unrelated to politics as might appear at first sight. The sensible reformer obviously takes into account what he knows of the environment, but there is a limit to the extent to which a practical man can take into account the unexpected. A design cannot be faulted simply because it does less well than hypothesised if that occurs. Leave aside the unforeseeable, the reformer cannot even take into account all behaviour patterns that are known to exist at the time. The factors that may influence a case are incalculable in number, inscrutable in content and indefinable in relationship. To await their measuring and ordering would postpone decisions for ever. It is for that reason, of course, that practitioners, for their part, prefer to remain out of touch with the frame of reference of a political science that is too scientific.

Political institutions do have a considerable influence in shaping political behaviour as a matter of fact. And as a matter of principle we should assume this to be so if we have a practical interest in politics. The institutional approach is to that extent more realistic than others. It is also more idealistic than most. Students of the behavioural environment necessarily focus on what is, not on what might be. Critics now tell us that behaviouralism is conservative because systems analysis is static, but it is conservative also because its starting point is reality. Institutions, on the other hand, are ideal and concrete at the same time. They are the embodiment of values, a script for man to live by in the political community. How should they be designed? The political philosopher must start with man's potential, not with his current behaviour. The advocate of institutional reform, the political scientist who combines the study of political theory with that of political institutions, who seeks to determine how the state may be organised to be at its best, must have a utopian streak.

I remember, in my formative years as a student, an article on French politics in *The Listener* illustrated by a photograph of the pillared façade of the National Assembly in Paris. *Assemblée Nationale* was boldly inscribed there in gold letters, the purpose apparently to inform the volatile French, with their notorious constitutional instability, of the name and location of their chief parliamentary institution. For long thereafter I thought of institutions in terms of bricks and mortar. Our own parliament was the Palace of Westminster or, only a nuance different in that perception, what went on within its walls. The layman probably still thinks of institutions in some such way: the more concrete the image, the easier it is to grasp. For social scientists, on the other hand, an institution is obviously not a neatly labelled building. It is true that certain institutions cannot be identified by a physical shell, but some scholars use the term in a way that leaves nothing visible at all.

We have seen that the term is actually given a variety of meanings in the literature of the social sciences. It is foolish, however, to use an established word in a way unrelated to everyday usage. However clear the writer's definition, the reader will either get angry or muddled. It is no less foolish to use a word so loosely that its ambiguities confuse the writer as well as the reader. We have seen both problems. Sociologists have often defined institutions in a way that bears little resemblance to common speech; political scientists have often used it unthinkingly. There is little that can be done about this. Our vocabulary cannot be legislated. Even the august *Académie Française* is more successful in recording the use of words than in imposing its own definitions. Clarity of thought and clarity of expression apart, what is important about naming, however, is that it tends to be a way of setting parameters to the discussion of a topic. Definitions have a way of determining focus. That, indeed, is the purpose of this chapter—to suggest a definition of institutions that is really a way of looking at them which I believe useful for political science.

Let us stay with the French Assembly for a moment. One can perceive that institution in several ways. Convenient labels can be drawn from a rather hackneyed analogy with the theatre. The institution as a physical object can be thought of as the theatre itself in which the action takes place. To use the term in that way is not to trivialise it as much as those who want to study real politics might think. For the general public—the mass who do not attend any performance—it is the theatre that is readily identifiable. If one of the problems of modern democratic politics is the alienation of citizens, this is not only because of a general, and understandable, suspicion of politicians. In small part it may be because of the difficulty of recognising the institutions of government. Would local government not be more meaningful if it were all to be found in a town hall? Bricks and mortar locate an institution. They may also symbolise it. The Big Ben tower, the door of Number Ten, the scales of the Old Bailey identify an institution.

At the other extreme, there is the emphasis on the actors. This emphasis may reflect an attempt to demystify abstract institutions like the state to which it is hard to attach a concrete shell. It is more likely to reflect a legitimate interest in what the actors do: who does what to whom and who gets what, when and how. When the behaviour of a group of actors, the ways they interact, acquires a firm pattern, some talk of these patterns as if they were themselves institutions. This is commonly the language of sociologists. I have argued at length the danger of confusing people and institutions because, if one is not careful, formal institutions disappear altogether in the process. An institution like the Church of England, established by law and subject to legal rules, cannot in the nature of things be the interaction of members, nor, indeed, though that is not the point here, can a deliberate construct of this sort be the natural result of such interaction. To start with the actors, in other words, can eliminate from consideration the formal constructs that make up the world of institutions in the traditional language of political science. In some cases, of course, one can work backwards from the members to the formal rules by which they are bound, as in the case of Members of Parliament.

The fact that this is not possible in all cases, however, shows the dangers of the approach. The Crown as an institution, for example, has nothing whatsoever to do with the behaviour of the queen.

A third way of looking at an institution is to think of it as the script of a play. In that sense it has two aspects. First, the script defines much of what occurs on the stage. It is, if you like, the formal rules of parliamentary procedure. To these one might add those conventions that are more than behaviour patterns, being regarded by the members themselves as externally fixed, no less binding because unwritten. Actors, of course, have great scope in interpreting even the most detailed script: Olivier's Hamlet is not Gielgud's Hamlet. Whatever they may add to it, however, they remain bound by the text; the script, for its part, does not change as a result of their interpretation—it is Shakespeare we read, not Olivier or Gielgud. Second, a script is more than a written document, more than the formal context of action. It embodies the authors' intention, both in the stage directions and in the dialogue itself. A play—a good play, at least—has a message; it serves a purpose.

One can take the three preceding views together and say that together they make a play. A play depends on its actors (not to get bogged down, let us include the director) as well as on its author. What the audience see is an interpretation of the script. It depends also, if to a lesser extent, on the stage setting, the bricks and mortar of the institution. A political institution seen as a whole, therefore, could be taken as a complex, almost magical, fusion of stage, script and actors. There is a great temptation for political scientists to describe institutions in this way. Whether it is useful to use the term institution for this all-embracing thing, the play, is another matter. We can separate the elements, not just analytically but substantively, without much trouble. Parliament is a formalised system of rules as well as the best club in London, and the rules can be studied in their own right. Failure to make the distinction distracts attention from the script itself. Used too broadly, in other words, the term institution loses its usefulness. The ambiguities of institution-as-play create confusion and, more serious, the approach this implies can lead the political scientists along a barren path. If the play's the thing, reality as performed on the world's stage the focus, purpose loses its place.

This brings me to my central point, the reason why the theatrical analogy seems so appropriate. A not uncommon line of theatre criticism is to discuss whether the actors have played their roles in the way intended by the author. That is sometimes an almost impossible question. Some dramatists give us a clear idea of their message, George Bernard Shaw in his prefaces, for example. The enormous literature devoted to Shakespeare, on the other hand, leads one to doubt whether anyone knows that he really intended. Indeed, and that too is a relevant question for the student of political institutions, one may be tempted to ask whether he ever intended to convey as much as the Shakespeare industry assumes. Perhaps there is no message beyond that we read into his works. Perhaps the same is true of some institutions, established without much in the way of political philosophy. One can still investigate, even if the question is lower keyed, what the actors have added to the script or subtracted from it.

What I am saying, therefore, is that political institutions are not merely endowed with a script but that the script, in one way or another, generally embodies the meaning of the institution: not the function it actually performs in the political system—the question of the system approach—but its purpose. If we ask whether an institution is functioning well, we may be asking whether it plays a useful role in our system of government, useful often then meaning satisfactory to the discussant. If we use a slightly different word, however, and ask whether it is functioning properly, we mean in accordance with the intention of those who established it, who wrote the script.

The notion of political institutions as the embodiment of political theories seems an attractive one. It enables us to link the two sides of our subject, political theory and institutions. Institutions, in that light, are the script rather than the play. One can immediately think of the American Constitution and the institutions it established. The script is that of the Founding Fathers. It is their script that succeeding generations of political actors grapple with, interpret and reinterpret. Over the years they have done more than reinterpret the dialogue of course; they have changed the sets and the costumes, and they have added new business, until the play bears little resemblance to what was originally performed. Would Shakespeare recognise some of the current versions of his plays—*Julius Caesar* played as contemporary political drama, for example? Neither change detracts from the importance of the original intention. And just as, in the long run, scholars are likely to find more food for thought in Shakespeare's original texts than in contemporary interpretations, so the political theorist may well learn more from the Founding Fathers than from current practice.

I said that to define an institution in terms of its script seemed an attractive approach. A problem immediately arises, however, when one turns from countries with a written constitution to this country. We have no Founding Fathers. As every schoolboy knows, our constitution just grew. There is a temptation, therefore, to describe it as current practice or, at a somewhat higher level, as what contemporary politicians consider proper political behaviour to be. Though the emphasis is different, both appear at first sight to be behavioural descriptions. When I first put my argument about the nature of political institutions to my colleagues, using the theatrical comparison, one answered quick as a flash that in Britain we have only characters in search of an author. Pirandello's situation is in fact a neat analogy. It worried me at first. Is all one can say about the British Constitution (and this, of course, does not refer to most of our political institutions) that the actors are writing their own script as they go along? But the six characters *were*, after all, in search of an author. Put another way, even in our system of government there is the notion that there is a script to be found. Among the factors that shape our parliamentary system is the climate of political ideas. This can be investigated by the behaviouralist through the beliefs of contemporary actors, but it is possible for the political theorist to search more deeply. A. H. Birch makes the point in *Representative and Responsible Government.* 'In Britain these ideas and attitudes have their roots in certain traditional doctrines about the purpose and ideal nature of a representative system.' These doctrines were established long ago and in a very different society, but they form the common stock of ideas about British government and are continually referred to in political discussions; they cannot, therefore, be dismissed. 'They are not modern doctrines, based squarely on the facts of contemporary life, but they are not out of date doctrines either; they are traditional doctrines, and unless they are understood it is impossible to understand the nature of the British representative system and the current controversies about it.'

The British system of parliamentary government has a script in the narrower sense, the formal rules according to which it conducts its business; but in the wider sense a script is also to be found: it embodies values and it has a purpose. Commentators may well come up with different interpretations, just as, in fact, they can interpret the Founding Fathers differently. Because political theorists differ about its meaning, however, they need not conclude that an institution is meaningless. Some political scientists may take that view and concentrate instead on describing and explaining institutional behaviour. But true political discourse would be impossible if we all followed that line. The purpose of studying political institutions is above all the discussion of ends and means. That is the traditional role of the political scientist and it remains his task.

The Purpose of Institutions

One expression of academic freedom in Britain is the deliberate avoidance of anything that might look like academic uniformity. Hence, perhaps, trivial but symptomatic, the diversity of nomenclatures we adopt. We have, in British universities, departments of Government (now old fashioned), Politics (ambiguous and slightly disreputable as a title), Political Science (the standard American label, generally avoided here because it raises too many questions about whether there *is* a science and, if so, whether it is *a* science), Political Studies (conveniently avoiding these problems) and, as in the case of my own department and rather grander, Political Theory and Institutions. There may have been special motives for this choice of words; the intention, more practically, may have been to inform the prospective client that we teach Hobbes, Locke and Rousseau as well as British and foreign systems of government. Appropriately, the juxtaposition also provides me with a title for this chapter.

The study of institutions can give rise to theories about how they operate, correlations, even causal relations, based on observation and comparison. But theories can themselves give rise to institutions, can shape the way they operate. The first are the scientific theories of political science, the second are the philosophies of the politicians, lawyers and administrators. Here I intend to look at the way in which institutions embody ideas, against the background of which they must be studied if they are to be properly understood. This is particularly important in comparative studies. Seemingly similar institutions in different countries often turn out to be different in practice—and in intention—

because the 'theoretical' assumptions of those who establish and operate them are themselves different.

By way of my first example I want to look at one of the institutions—the *établissement public*—of French public enterprise. The organisation of the public sector in France was in fact my first venture in the study of administration and it was my realisation that many of the key terms in French discussions of public enterprise were untranslatable (often because they reflected concepts that had no parallel in Britain) that first made me aware of the importance of doctrine in the interpretation of institutions.[1]

Many French textbooks on government are written in legal terms. As the author of a recent British textbook on the same subject notes, though they are out of harmony with much modern political science, they are among the most professional and, within their own terms, the most satisfactory writings on politics in France. The legalistic approach may be carried too far, but it may also be condemned too easily by those accustomed to a different approach to law itself and, as a result, a different approach to political studies. It is not merely the important place legal studies occupy in French universities that explains the approach of French textbooks. That place of honour itself reflects an approach to law that places it at the centre of government and even of politics.

There is a practical reason for this: administration is more circumscribed by law than in Britain, perhaps because the rational French mind likes to define things clearly, perhaps because the French distrust the arbitrariness that we call discretion, perhaps, a concrete expression of this distrust, because all but a few decisions are subject to judicial review. In any case, formal accounts are probably less misleading than in Britain: institutions and procedures are described more fully and, on the whole, more accurately in legal terms than in Britain.

But there is a more fundamental reason for the pre-eminence of law and that relates to the nature of the subject itself as the French see it. As a recent French writer explains in the preface to an English edition of his textbook on French law, a Frenchman does not regard the law as something of interest only to lawyers. The law is not limited to litigation but is seen as a method of social organisation. This, of course, implies a very different concept of what the law is. The primary interest of jurists was not positive

---

[1] The following section draws on unpublished study, 'Public Enterprise in France', completed almost twenty years ago.

law as embodied in legislation or the rules developed by the courts: what the universities taught was an *ideal* law. This concept is difficult for the common law lawyer, who ties his subject to the work of the courts, to understand. It was seen as 'a method of social organisation', as 'the social science *par excellence,* an instrument which deals not only with conflicts in society but which provides for the ordering of relationships within society'. What is relevant here is its concerns with how the state, in all its ramifications, *should* be organised. This brings us to the importance of judicial doctrines as a key to understanding the actual institutions of the state, expressions of such doctrine.

There is another part to this. As ideal, leaders of society as well as judges, were asked to draw inspiration from the law and to give it reality. Legal thinking certainly influenced the development of French institutions. While the unwritten constitution of Britain grew with the practice of politicians, the written French constitution owes as much to jurists as politicians, two categories that often overlap in France anyway. Virtually all senior civil servants have had some, most a fair amount of legal education. In devising institutions and regulating their procedures, as in operating them, they are inclined, quite unlike their British counterparts, to think in terms of established legal concepts and the broad legal philosophy into which they have been socialised through training and work.

The public sector of French industry is extensive but grew in response to no consistent programme and there was no consistent theory, political or administrative, about how it should be organised. Various forms of organisation were adopted, though even these were not standardised. They ranged from governmental services with so-called autonomous budgets, through public corporations with administrative or industrial and commercial character, to national, mixed-economy and subsidiary companies, passing a variety of other public and semi-public institutions on the way. Some differences reflected the particular needs of the undertakings concerned, some changing ideas about the proper role of government and effective management, some mere chance in draftsmanship. This somewhat untidy situation was naturally abhorrent to the French mind, especially the legal mind, leading academically to talk of a crisis in the concept of the public corporation for example, and practically to a good deal of subsequent rationalisation. Underlying all, nevertheless, were much wider juridical concepts embodied in administrative doctrine and practice. Fundamental were the theories of the state, its relations with subordinate institutions and its responsibilities with regard to public services.

The public corporation is a creation of French administrative law of the nineteenth century, when it was employed for such institutions as schools, hospitals and asylums. After the First World War the same device was used for certain newly established industrial undertakings of the state and after the Second for certain of the great nationalised industries, notably electricity, gas and coal (railways, airlines and banks, on the other hand, became state dominated or wholly owned companies). The nature of these undertakings was quite different from the earlier institutions and a distinction was drawn between corporations with administrative and those with industrial and commercial character. On the face of it, this meant that the former operated in accordance with the procedures of administrative law, while the latter followed business practice. Their industrial and commercial character was limited in relation to the state by administrative controls, however, and in relation to the public in so far as they were *concessionnaires* of public services.

The use of the term public corporation to translate the French *établissement public* is misleading, however, and that common mistranslation shows the misunderstanding that can arise when what appear to be parallel institutions, in this case nationalised industries, are studied out of the context of their national governmental systems. German law has a more useful vocabulary, distinguishing between the *corporation* of public law and the *institution* of public law. The corporation is defined in much the same way as in Britain as a body of persons legally constituted as an artificial person. The institution, on the other hand, is established by some public authority for the more convenient performance of certain of its duties and consists essentially of designated physical assets. It, too, enjoys legal personality, i.e. the right to act in law, but this legal fiction attaches to certain of the parent authority's assets rather than to a separate body of incorporated individuals. The *établissement public* is closer to the German institution than to the German corporation of public law (the *établissement d'utilité publique* is closer to the latter).

A major difference between the French and British concepts of public enterprise can be traced, in the light of the foregoing, back to different concepts of the state. In Britain the state as a legal entity does not appear to exist. The state *as such* receives no treatment in books of constitutional and administrative law and the word itself only appears marginally, with reference to offences prejudicial to the safety of the state for example (where the word '*country*' would serve as well). Though we have Secretaries of State, ministers are in fact ministers of the Crown; civil servants are servants of the Crown not state officials; it is the Queen, not the state, that prosecutes offenders in the courts. No one authority has an inherent general responsibility for the provision of public services. Some responsibilities are assumed by the Crown by virtue of its prerogative powers. New duties are created by Parliament and are entrusted to whatever body it thinks fit: these include government departments, local authorities and a host of independent bodies such as Trinity House, the Arts Council, the National Coal Board and the universities. These last are statutory creations and subject to varying degrees of government control but they do not form part of *the* state: they exist in their own right, in the same way as the Crown and government departments on the one hand private corporations on the other. It is against this pluralist picture of a state composed of distinct bodies, each with a life of its own, that the public corporations of British public enterprise must be seen.

France, on the other hand, is a unitary state. The state as such has a legal personality. It is responsible for public services. For the more convenient organisation of some of these, it may set up a specialised institution, though it may also delegate functions to private operators who become *concessionnaires* of central or local government. In the first case, we get the *établissement public*.

The nature of legal personality (*personnalité morale*) has given rise to much debate among French legal philosophers. Much of this has centred on the question whether the personality of corporations is a legal fiction, the creation of positive law, or an objective reality, pre-existing law. On the whole, the issue is more relevant to the treatment of corporations of private law than institutions of public law. It is clear that the *établissement public* is not a legal organisation with a life of its own separate from the state. The French university, unlike the British, is not the incorporation of its members, nor is a local authority the incorporation of its citizens. It is defined as a branch of the general services of the state, even if detached from the totality of its services. The French speak in this respect of *decentralised services*, to distinguish such institutions from *deconcentrated services* like the external (i.e. field) agencies of central government ministries.

The *établissement public* is endowed with legal personality and financial autonomy. Taking these two terms at their face value, they might appear to describe the British public corporation as well. But there is a clear difference. Although the British corporation is, like the French, a creature of statute, once created it exists in its own right. The legal personality of the French institution has a lesser meaning: it arises, in a phrase used by several authorities, out of the dissection of the legal personality of the state and it thus remains a subordinate institution of the state (I shall return to this point). Financial autonomy means that its funds are distinct from the national budget and not independent of control (the same term, indeed, has been used to describe certain specialised accounts within central government).

The result of all this is an approach to government control reflected objectively in legal and administrative doctrines and subjectively in the attitude of administrators. In both Britain and France there is extensive government control, but in our case this appears as something *imposed* on the corporation and, as such, remains very much an *external* affair; there it is the natural corollary of the institution's status and takes on a more *internal*, as well as a more administrative, character. This applies even where the attempt was made to break with tradition and place the institutions of public enterprise in the realm of private law.

Interestingly, French intentions after 1944 were rather different from what transpired. General opinion was that the newly nationalised industries should enjoy the greatest independence. It was felt, on grounds of economic efficiency, that the new industrial undertakings should be left free to determine their own policy and manage their own affairs in a businesslike manner. The legislators may have been influenced by British experience, an influence strengthened by their contacts in this country during the occupation. Bureaucratic administration was to be avoided by granting the corporations industrial and commercial character and assimilating them as far as possible to ordinary industrial concerns.

Another factor worked in the same direction. The liberation brought to the front a syndicalist-inspired doctrine of the French trade union movement. This was formulated as far back as 1920: 'We do not wish to increase the functions of the state itself . . . by nationalisation we mean that national property should be placed under the control of those directly interested—producers and consumers.' The nationalised industries were not to form part of the state but were to belong directly to the nation. This was emphasised by placing them under tripartite boards of workers' and consumers' nominees and spokesmen for the general interest (mainly officials, the state representing the general interests of the nation). *Nationaliser sans étatiser* was the slogan of the time.

Everyone seemed to agree in the immediate post-war period that *étatisme* was the enemy to be avoided at all costs, meaning by this both state intervention and the bureaucratisation of management. The nationalisation laws for electricity, gas and coal were thus remarkably free from any reference to governmental control.

It may seem surprising, therefore, that the whole development in the following decade was in the opposite direction.

Neither of the intentions mentioned above was fulfilled. The syndicalist notion of control by representative boards, and with it the notion of undertakings independent of the state, was virtually a non-starter. The powers of the boards were circumscribed, virtually all important decisions were made subject to ministerial control and, to facilitate this, government commissioners were appointed to attend board meetings. The boards were also weakened by the fact that chief executives were appointed by the government, drawn mostly from the civil service and in constant direct relation with the supervising ministry. Generally members of the prestigious technical corps of the civil service, indeed, they tended to have an *étastiste* outlook themselves.

Entrepreneurial management was undermined by the imposition of a host of controls, some relating to the economic policy of the government but many not dissimilar from the general controls of public administrations. Financial controllers, agents of the Ministry of Finance, were attached to the undertakings to exercise internal *a priori* control of expenditure, and in some cases there were technical controllers representing the supervising ministries as well. Purchase and construction contracts were subjected to *a priori* scrutiny by special committees, while other committees supervised the acquisition of land and buildings. The administration of the public domain, a government service, acquired other rights. A special section of the Court of Accounts was made responsible for *a posteriori* audit. Investment, wages and prices were all made subject to elaborate controls, as were many other aspects of their activities. Where, as in the case of electricity and gas, they were *concessionnaires* of public services, there were yet further technical and financial controls. Conditions of employment were regulated by special *statuts* which had the force of law, so that employees enjoyed a status not dissimilar from that of civil servants.

There were numerous reasons for this development. Economic and political factors went a long way to explaining the nationalised industries' rapid loss of independence in the post-war years. Financial controls inevitably followed the heavy calls their investment programmes made on the national budget, not to mention the large subsidies some required. They were the obvious targets for national policies of price and wage control. Economic planning, in which the public sector occupied a key role, had the same effect. Politically, too, the tendency was to strengthen the state's grip. Paradoxically, this tended to be a conservative viewpoint, conservatives mistrusting socialist-established citadels within the state—*féodalités* as they were significantly described. Ingrained administrative habits worked in the same direction. Here, however, I want to concentrate on the influence of two judicial doctrines.

Many of the controls to which nationalised industries are subjected apply to all services of the state, others apply to private industries as well. There is a further category, however, which arises as a result of the fact that certain public undertakings provide a public service. Public services are services of general utility which require guarantees of uninterrupted operation, constant adaptation to public needs and equal availability to all citizens. Transport by land, sea and air, and electricity and gas supplies are the clearest examples. The state, in this case the central and local authorities, has a general power, duty indeed, to ensure or regulate their provision. True, the definition of public need changes over time as a result of governmental, judicial and legislative decisions, but that does not diminish the inherent authority of the state in relation to the undertakings concerned. Practically, it is translated into concessions which impose duties and organise controls. More fundamentally, it underscores the point that these undertakings, providing services for which the state is responsible, are automatically subject to its influence.

The more interesting point, because of its significance for political theory, relates to the French concept of the state. The state, writes the British author mentioned earlier, is a focus of interest, in certain respects the most important, in the study of French politics. It is vital, therefore, to know what the French mean by this term. In the *ancien régime* it was the King who was the state. When Louis XIV, said *l'état, c'est moi*, this was more than a declaration of his power (true, one can argue that the concept of the Prince was gradually replaced by that of the Crown and sovereignty institutionalised). The Revolution declared the sovereignty of the people, but at the same time it transformed the concept of the state (indeed, one can argue that it created the state as a juridical concept).

The sovereignty of the people was embodied in the state *as an institution*: the state is the nation personified in the strict legal sense as well as in political theory. Though, with the growth of democracy, another doctrine emerged, namely that the sovereign will of the people is expressed through elections and the representative assembly, this does not alter the fact that it is institutionalised in the state: the latter is the machinery of the nation to regulate matters of public concern, the *res publica*. No corporation within society can claim to rival it. It is in this respect that the term *féodalités* applied to too independent undertakings is significant. It relates, of course, to institutions in a feudal system when many corporations rival the central authority. *The Republic, one and indivisible* contrasts with the pluralist model with feudal origins found in Britain.

If one asks who owns the coal mines in Britain, that would probably be regarded as a metaphysical question. Pushed, one might be forced to say that the mines are vested in a corporation, the National Coal Board, that a corporation owns property in perpetual succession and consists, for its part, of the members for the time being of its board. Political nonsense, but there is no inclination to pursue the matter in the textbooks: perhaps it is not relevant to our practice, but it may well shape attitudes. While in France the situation is technically complex as regards the property rights of the *Charbonnages de France* on the one hand and the state *stricto sensu* on the other, as distinct legal persons that is, and jurists do not agree on some of the legal consequences, there can be no doubt about the broader question: in its embracing sense the mines belong to the state.

It is at this point that we must return to the nationalisation programme of 1945. Nationalisation without absorption in the state, the slogan of the time, was not merely a prescription for managerial efficiency. As we have seen, it reflected an ideology. That ideology was based on an attempt to separate the concepts of state and nation. It is reflected in the preamble to the 1946 constitution which declared that any undertaking which possesses the character of a national public service, or is a monopoly, must become the property of the community. The electricity and gas nationalisation law says that the capital transferred to *Electricité de France* and *Gaz de France* belongs to *the nation*. An attempt was made to translate this into practice by placing these institutions under boards representing the great interests of the nation. There was some notion of economic democracy to parallel political democracy. Thus, while representation of the national interest as such was assured by government nominees, workers and consumers nominated their own.

But these boards never acquired effective control. The trend in company law was against this for one thing: a Vichy reform, not repealed, strengthened the authority of chief executives and reduced boards to something more like supervising councils. The point here, however, is that though the distinction between nation and state has been attempted before by French jurists, it never found solid roots in French jurisprudence. One authoritative textbook explains the failure of the nationalisers' apparent intentions

by their disregard of accepted juridicial doctrines. A fundamental assumption of our public law, he writes, is that the nation
has no other personification than the state.

Whatever factors have influenced it, the status of public enterprise in France is shaped by juridical concepts that have become
part of the administrative culture. The public institutions concerned embody legal theories so broad, however, that we may
fairly call them political theories.

CHANCELLOR GOVERNMENT IN GERMANY

My second example of the importance of theory for an understanding of institutions is drawn from Western Germany and
relates to the role of the Chancellor in the governmental system.[1]
Again, the purpose is to show the dangers of underrating 'formalistic'—meaning in this case constitutional— approaches to the
study of government. In Britain, a country with no real history of
constitution-making, it is perhaps too easy to underrate the
importance of constitutional forms: such insularity may lead to a
study of government almost as one-sided as that of the constitutional lawyer.

I have already argued that constitutional devices play an
important part in shaping governmental processes and that these
devices reflect intentions, the intentions in turn theories. Typo-
logies, such as the distinction between parliamentary, presidential
and convention government, may be abstract, but they are useful
in the exposition of such theories. The real oversimplification
tends to lie not in the depoliticisation of constitutions but in the
identification of broad categories with single models, the forerunners, no doubt, but not slavishly copied in all cases. We tend
to describe the presidential system in terms of the American
model, the parliamentary in terms of the British. Within the broad
parliamentary category, a further distinction may be drawn
between German chancellor and British cabinet systems. In a
sense, informal British prime-ministerialism has been formally
institutionalised in Germany. An account of the German model
may thus add to those available for overviews of the forms of
government in the western democratic world.

In principle it is the Cabinet that determines policy and is
collectively responsible to Parliament in Britain. It is often said
that we really have prime-ministerial government; but that, on the
whole, is the result of political rather than constitutional develop-

[1] Drawn from 'Chancellor Government as a Political System and the
German Constitution', *Parliamentary Affairs* (Winter 1966).

ment. The system may properly be labelled cabinet government until a generally accepted constitutional theory about its replacement by the Prime Minister emerges. This 'collegial' form of government was generally copied in Europe. One country in Europe, however, developed a different tradition that appears to have been largely overlooked by the classificators of political systems.

Numerous accounts of post-war Germany emphasised the emergence of 'chancellor democracy' under Konrad Adenauer. Influenced by the gap between constitutional principles and the actual location of power in Britain (and a similar gap in the Fifth French Republic), students of German politics made a similar assumption. They ascribed German prime-ministerialism to Adenauer's character and political skills, the changed party system and the general trend towards a personalisation of power. Such factors played their part in making chancellor government work, but the system is firmly anchored in the German constitution itself. When democracy came to Germany in 1918 it was grafted on an earlier, chancellor-based form of executive organisation. The Anglo-Saxon political scientist's dislike of constitutional studies can lead him to miss the fact that Germany is *theoretically* intended to have prime-minister government. It was after Adenauer, when reality swung the other way, weakening the Chancellor, that there was a real gap between constitutional principles and the actual location of powers.

To bring out the specific features of the German constitution, it is well to look first at the British system. In Britain the absence of a written constitution makes it difficult to discover any hard principles about the functions of the Cabinet and the Prime Minister and their relationship to each other. No powers are legally invested in either the Prime Minister or the Cabinet as such, nor are their respective functions regulated by any formal published rules. On the other hand, it is a firm convention that the Prime Minister has the right to 'hire and fire' his colleagues. His chairmanship of the Cabinet also gives him certain powers: he calls meetings, arranges the agenda and, it seems, can sometimes decide the 'sense' of the Cabinet on particular issues. But the question is not really what goes on inside the cabinet room: whether the Prime Minister is first among equals or master of his colleagues is an internal matter. The constitutional doctrine would appear to be that it is the Cabinet that determines the policy of the government, co-ordinates the departments and controls the executive. It is an even firmer constitutional principle that the Cabinet is collectively answerable to Parliament for government policy.

There is, however, another way of looking at the constitutional position. The executive function in our system of government is vested in the Crown and one must therefore consider the relationship of Prime Minister and Cabinet to the Sovereign. According to one standard textbook, the Queen is by convention advised in all matters by the Cabinet: as members of the Cabinet, the principal ministers advise the Queen collectively. But there is an alternative doctrine, stated for example by a recent Prime Minister, that cabinet members are really the Prime Minister's agents and he alone is directly responsible to the Queen for what the Cabinet does. That may just be another way of saying that what goes on within the Cabinet is an internal matter without constitutional significance. To an extent, then, prime-ministerial government can be founded on constitutional doctrine, but it is a weak prop in the light of the continued acceptance of the doctrine of collective responsibility to Parliament.

Parliamentary government was not established in Germany until 1919, that is to say after the monarchy's collapse. The governments of Prussia and the Empire were to the end governments of the King and Emperor. Problems of governmental organisation, however, arose early in the nineteenth century when it became apparent that the King of Prussia could no longer personally coordinate the expanding services of the state. Two solutions were canvassed. Stein argued for the establishment of a council of ministers of equal rank to discuss policy, settle interdepartmental disputes and advise the King jointly. Hardenberg advocated the appointment of a single minister of the Crown with departmental heads as his subordinates, subject to his instructions and responsible to him, with neither collective nor individual access to the monarch. Elements of these two conflicting principles—collegial or cabinet (*Kollegialprinzip*) and hierarchic or prime-ministerial (*Kanzlerprinzip*)—were found in all subsequent constitutional developments. In their pure form, both are in fact rare: the *Kanzlerprinzip* held only in the Bismarckian era, the *Kollegialprinzip* is found only in Switzerland. Present-day British and German systems combine both, though in different proportions. A third principle, that of individual minister's legal responsibility for, and thus autonomy in, the conduct of purely departmental affairs (*Ressortprinzip*), logically associated with the collegial system, was later also grafted on the prime-ministerial.

A diluted version of the collegial principle was adopted in Prussia. Ministers headed the various departments of government and together formed a council. In the first half of the nineteenth century one of its members was named Minister of State, but he had no special privileges. The functions of the council itself were vague: ministers were largely independent of one another, were not bound by council decisions and retained direct access to the monarch. Eventually Minister-Presidents were appointed and these began to look something like early British Prime Ministers, though the triangular relationship between them, other ministers and the King remained a matter of personalities. The monarch's active role in government prevented the emergence of a genuine— i.e. united—Cabinet: the absence of any real parliamentary responsibility, the fact that ministers did not need to hang together if they were not to fall together, the fact that as virtual civil servants they had no links of party loyalty, all strengthened him.

It was the alternative *Kanzlerprinzip* that was adopted at federal level when the Empire was established in 1871. Considering that the King of Prussia became simultaneously German Emperor, this was a little surprising and, indeed, not entirely deliberate. At first, it was not even clear that the Empire was a 'government' in the full sense of the word. Provision was made for an Imperial Chancellor but the original idea seems to have been that he would be a high official with limited functions. The appointment of Bismarck changed the situation. The Chancellor headed the entire imperial administration which at first came directly under the Imperial Chancellery. The rapid expansion of central government, however, soon made a specialisation of functions necessary and services were organised into Imperial Offices under State Secretaries. These were not ministries and their heads not ministers. The Chancellor was constitutionally the sole responsible minister of the Empire and alone made policy. (In Germany 'responsibility' then meant, and in constitutional parlance sometimes still means today, something very different from the British usage: it is not a matter of political responsibility to Parliament but legal responsibility for the administration of government, evidenced by countersignature of government acts.) The State Secretaries were the Chancellor's subordinates: this meant that they had not only to execute his policy (as, constitutionally, in the Federal Republic today), but that (unlike the Federal Republic) he was also their superior in the day-to-day administration of their offices. No Cabinet existed.

The tendency was for State Secretaries to become more and more like ministers as time went on. Bismarck had neither the time nor the inclination to supervise departmental affairs and needed, for his part, to consult departmental heads on the formulation of policy. Some form of cabinet system might have developed had it not been for the existence of the Imperial Chancellery which made itself responsible for policy discussions and the co-ordination of services, mainstay of the British Cabinet. The early existence of a strongly organised Chancellery, compared to the relatively recent development of Prime Minister's services in Britain, effectively underpinned chancellor government in Germany.

The organisation of the executive was discussed at length after the collapse of the Empire and many distinguished academics took part in the Weimar debates. The issue, then, was political as well as administrative. Not unnaturally, great emphasis was placed on the institutionalisation of parliamentary responsibility. Hugo Preuss, constitutional historian, liberal and Minister of the Interior, was responsible for the first draft. Influenced by his study of Britain, he wanted to limit constitutional provisions to a declaration of the Chancellor's responsibility for policy and ministerial responsibility for the conduct of their departments, believing that a British-type cabinet system, under the leadership of the Chancellor but with collective responsibility to Parliament, might then develop naturally. The more legalistic views of Clemens Delbrück, a former Secretary of State and a conservative, were adopted instead. The principles he advocated were an amalgamation of the old Prussian and imperial systems.

A Cabinet, but not a British-type cabinet system, was established. The primacy of the Chancellor was maintained. He alone was responsible for the policy of his Government, both in relation to Parliament and in relation to his Cabinet. On the other hand, the constitution provided for cabinet decisions by majority vote on matters of interdepartmental concern, including fundamental policy issues such as the budget and the presentation of government bills to Parliament. Ministers were no longer to be his administrative subordinates but were to conduct the affairs of their departments under their own responsibility—though the cabinet rules allowed him to issue general directives, supervise their work and veto decisions contrary to his policy.

While these principles were reintroduced in the Bonn constitution, the arrangements for parliamentary responsibility were less successful and were not copied. Both Chancellor and individual ministers required the confidence of the lower chamber and this could be withdrawn from them. It is true, of course that a similar notion was found in Britain, but it was effectively counterbalanced by the unity of the Cabinet which led to emphasis on collective responsibility. The power to remove individual ministers may have seemed reasonable to draftsmen thinking of an earlier period in which they were not leaders of a parliamentary majority, standing or falling together, but servants of the Emperor, whose government functioned regardless of Parliament. Weimar differed from the Empire in the appointment of politicians as ministers (though even this was not always the case), rather than in the emergence of a politically united Cabinet. The situation bore some resemblance to the American system where senate approval of a Secretary of State as suitable administrative head of a department may be divorced from support for the President and his general policy: to that extent, and that is the relevant point here, it underlined the distinction between the Chancellor's and the individual ministers' responsibilities.

The Weimar constitution was an attempt to mix all three principles discussed earlier—*Kanzler, Kollegial* and *Ressort*. In the confused political situation of the time, it offered no firm anchor. There were too many parties, uneasy coalition cabinets were headed by weak chancellors, quite unable to play the part allotted them. Parliament itself had developed no tradition of sustaining governments, only of criticising them: it was often purely destructive. The President had extensive powers, including the appointment and dismissal of chancellors and the dissolution of Parliament. There was no convention that he should exercise these powers only on advice, as does the British sovereign who has similar powers; and as the President was popularly elected it was not clear whether such a convention was intended. Despite their great legal expertise, the Weimar fathers devised a constitution that embodied many uncertainties and some contradictions. With the wisdom of hindsight, it can also be seen that they ignored political realities. It was this constitutionally ambiguous position which, in the end, allowed President Hindenburg to appoint Hitler as Chancellor.

The framers of the Bonn constitution took up most of the Weimar principles, though with modifications. Constitutional devices were introduced to make the system more stable, notably by freeing the Chancellor from dependence on the President and by making it harder for Parliament to overthrow him. To these we shall return in a later section. They dropped the provision that individual ministers require the confidence of Parliament. The Chancellor alone is invested by Parliament and he alone is fully responsible to it. Only his responsibility can be enforced: the provision dealing with votes of confidence and no confidence relate only to him. The constitutional fathers were aware that effective parliamentary government means cabinet unity. This, we might think, means collective responsibility, but they were no more inclined to break with tradition in 1948 than in 1919. The parliamentary system now seems to have taken root in Germany, but in a different constitutional soil from Britain the plant grew differently. The Government is drawn from a parliamentary majority, ministers are parliamentarians, but the sole constitutional link between executive and legislature is through the head of the Government.

The constitution states: 'The Federal Chancellor determines the general policy of the government.' The term actually used, *Richtlinien der Politik* (guiding lines of policy), first appeared in the Weimar constitution as an improvement on an earlier draft *Richtung* (direction) because it seemed a little more specific, carrying some notion of directives; but it remains far from precise. There is certainly no easy way of recognising a *Richtlinie* when one meets it. Policy may be embodied in declarations to Parliament or in public statements, it may take the form of directives within the administration, but there is no constitutional requirement that it should take any form at all. In the last resort, it exists in the Chancellor's mind, fluid, elaborated as the need arises in discussion with ministers or through communications from his office. Constitutional lawyers have argued a good deal about the meaning of the term because it raises problems about the Chancellor's relations to the Cabinet as a whole and to individual ministers, as well as about their respective areas of responsibility to Parliament. While it is hard to imagine any case before the constitutional court that could depend on its interpretation, and to that extent the question is academic, it is important if one is trying to discover the intentions of the constitution.

It is difficult to define the Chancellor's *Richtlinienkompetenz* and the spheres of competence the constitution intended individual ministers to have. Most commentators agree that the Chancellor has the power to determine both (the so-called *Kompetenzkompetenz*), but arguably that is intended to apply only at the margins. At its simplest, the line may be drawn between policy and administration. It is agreed that the Chancellor's decisions must be normative in character (i.e. they cannot determine the action to be taken by ministers in specific cases). Some commentators go further and draw a distinction between the general policy of government and departmental or administrative policy, but students of public administration will recognise the difficulties in that. It is usually held, in any case, that the Chancellor must leave ministers reasonable scope in the conduct of the affairs for which they are formally responsible: it is the ministers who legally head the departments. It is an issue, again, that cannot be judicially decided because it does not fall within the cognisance of the courts (i.e. a plaintiff can go no further than the ministerial decision; neither he nor the ministry could invoke a policy directive).

What is at issue here is the *Ressortprinzip* that was a major break with the Bismarckian tradition when it was first introduced at federal level in 1919. It still applies. Ministers are now the highest authorities within the administrative hierarchy. This is the concrete meaning of the constitutional provision that they conduct departmental affairs under their own responsibility: that responsibility is legal and administrative. We come back to the constitutional intention. What is implied is a fair degree of independence within their *Ressort*.

One may ask whether individual ministers are also intended to have a political, that is to say parliamentary, responsibility. This concept is ambiguous even in Britain. On the Continent, where the approach is more legalistic, it is taken to mean not merely answerability but dismissability. The Weimar constitution, as we have seen, organised its enforcement through the individual vote of no confidence. A similar provision was found in the first draft of the Bonn constitution but, as it was dropped, it seems clear that so strict an interpretation was not intended. The situation is not so simple, however. Unlike American Secretaries, ministers are parliamentarians and attend parliamentary sessions. The German Parliament has imitated the British Question Time which forces ministers to account for their activities; they may also be forced to defend their departmental policies by interpellations which lead to full-scale debates. Moreover, motions of censure on individual ministers are not excluded. It is therefore clear that ministers are in practice answerable to Parliament. As they also take part in debates to defend the general policy of the Government, it is hard to see that they are not collectively answerable as well. While constitutional principles in Britain and Germany differ, practice, in this respect, is not dissimilar.

It is equally difficult to relate the Chancellor's *Richtlinienkompetenz* to the powers of the Cabinet as a whole. The key article of the constitution says little, but elsewhere, and in other laws, there are numerous references to decisions of *the Government*. Constitutional lawyers now maintain that this normally refers to the Cabinet. Previously the opposite was true: it was usually interpreted to mean the Chancellor or an individual minister (as in Britain, where the Cabinet does not hold any of the legal powers of the Executive). While the Chancellor has the right to make policy alone, he probably has few powers to *act* alone. Policy must be transformed into legislative proposals and a budget: the constitution is quite specific that these are to be introduced by the

Government. As the rules of procedure provide that decisions cannot be taken against the vote of the Chancellor, it would appear that he can veto his Cabinet but not act without it. One could argue that cabinet members must in the last resort accept his definitions of policy, just as the Councils of the Roman Church must accept the Pope *ex cathedra*, but that is constitutional metaphysics carried too far. It nevertheless creates some ambiguity as in theory it is the Chancellor who is subsequently responsible to Parliament for the decisions of his Government.

A practical reflection of the Chancellor's special position is the Chancellor's Office, heir to the old Imperial Chancellery, a long-established system of far more extensive services than those at the disposal of the British Prime Minister. It is well to remember the different origins of these services: the British grew mainly out of the cabinet secretariat, the German out of what was originally the sole ministry of the Empire. As executive functions were hived off, it became a super-ministry to which the other departments (mere offices at the time) were subordinate. The present changed system is reflected in the changed terminology: the old offices have become ministries, the Chancellery an office. It has nevertheless retained some of the characteristics of a super-ministry.

The great period of chancellor government was Konrad Adenauer's long term of office (1948–63). He dominated his Cabinet in a way that his predecessors in the period 1919–33 and his successors after 1963 were not able to do. Commentators generally described his regime as 'chancellor democracy'. In executive terms, it was possible to draw a parallel with the Bismarckian Empire or, indeed, with the American presidential system: his ministers tended to resemble the Imperial and American Secretaries, departmental administrators rather than participants in the policy-making process. In the light of our analysis of the German constitution, we may now ask two questions.

First, what part did constitutional arrangements play in the establishment of chancellor democracy. This is the question of constitutional engineering to which we shall return. The difficulty, as with all political studies, is that we cannot isolate the different factors in a given situation and measure their influence. The Weimar constitution also provided for chancellor government, but it proved ineffective. To some extent this was undoubtedly due to flaws within the constitution itself, but political circumstances were also very unfavourable and the constitution was not able to master these forces. The situation was very different after the last war: respect for the spirit of the constitution was high; a party system emerged that made constitutional government possible.

And yet it is undeniable that non-constitutional factors played a major role in shaping the governmental process: much can be attributed to the force of Adenauer's personality and to his political skills; something to Germany's inclination to accept a strong but respectable father figure at the time. But one cannot disregard the constitutional factors either. The problem is that of the 'hero in history'—he can only be effective if conditions are suitable. One of the conditions that made Adenauer's ascendancy possible was the German constitution: Adenauer simply used his constitutional powers to the full. (While his successors Erhard and Kiesinger were too weak to use the constitution fully, Willy Brandt was unable to do so because of a changed coalition situation.) Had these been different, his task would have been much more difficult, though not impossible, at least given a political crisis, as General de Gaulle has shown.

The second question, and the one really at issue here, is whether chancellor government was the intention of the constitution, whether the system that emerged (for whatever reasons) was in accordance with a specific theory of government deliberately translated into political institutions. That is what I hope to have shown. Adenauer himself, inclined as he was to 'lonely decisions', could justify his personalisation of power by reference to his constitutional duties with regard to policy-making. He could justify his dominance of the Cabinet by the claim that the provision with regard to parliamentary responsibility made him the sole member of the Executive to enjoy democratic legitimacy. It is true that he sometimes overstepped his constitutional role, sometimes verged on the authoritarian-plebiscitary. Nevertheless, his style of government was generally in line with the implications of the constitution. As one commentator wrote at the time: 'The most astonishing thing about the new chancellor democracy is the astonishment that has arisen as a result of the discovery of its existence.' That astonishment would have been less if political scientists had paid as much attention to institutional theory as they paid to empirical politics.

Institutional Engineering

The reform of governmental institutions is a continuous process. Sometimes the reformers' strokes are so broad that they alter the entire political perspective, sometimes so small that they can be seen only close to, within some branch of the administration. Complete transformations of the governmental system without revolution, *coup d'état* or some other catastrophe such as military defeat, are rare. Major changes within democratic systems, on the other hand, are now commonplace. In Britain hardly a year seems to go by without the introduction of some new institution (the ombudsman, for example) or the reorganisation of existing institutions (civil service, local government, national health service, to name but three). One would be hard put to quantify these in order to determine whether the pace has become more rapid, as so much else in life, but it is certainly true that a textbook on British government is now likely to be outdated in one or two major respects by the time it reaches publication. The less obvious modifications that take place all the time, important to those directly involved but observed only by the specialist student outside, would not bear counting.

All of these, in their different ways, can be described as institutional engineering, building or rebuilding government—as a whole, in large sections or small parts. The hallmark of such engineering is that it is *deliberate*, based on notions about the purpose of institutions and about how institutions work. At its best, it is the translation of normative and empirical theories into institutional form, though often it is rational only in the more limited sense of conscious action. The point I am making is the obvious one that institutions also change *themselves*, in character if not in form, as a result of changing environmental factors. The behaviour of institutions does not necessarily correspond to that prescribed in organisation charts and work procedures.

The distinction between political behaviour and political institutions is, in fact, central to the purpose of this chapter. Political scientists tend to stress the extent to which the operation of institutions, thus their character, is shaped by the behaviour of the actors involved. They sometimes give the impression that such behaviour is a largely independent variable as far as the institutions themselves are concerned, shaped instead by a host of environmental factors which together determine what is now conveniently described as political or administrative culture. I say largely independent because it is obviously not entirely unrelated: formal rules, internalised by the actors, translated in terms of this approach into norms of behaviour, also form part of the culture. But even that concession shifts the attention away from the rational link between institution-making and behaviour patterns: the emphasis is on the receptivity of the actors rather than on the direction of the stage managers. The purpose of this chapter, on the other hand, is to consider the relationship the other way round. To use the metaphor differently, institutions are not stages on which different plays can be enacted, they are scripts which include stage directions (style of administration) as well as the dialogue (administrative procedures).

I am concerned here with arrangements which deliberately set out to influence political or administrative behaviour. Two examples are taken, one from each end of the scale, administrative tinkering and constitutional transformation. The first, reform of the French prefectoral system, was intended to make administration more efficient, the second, reform of the German constitution, to ensure stable democracy. In so far as a distinction can be made, the first concentrated on procedural reform, the second on organisational. Both were designed to shift behavioural patterns. This, of course, is only one aspect of institutional engineering as a rational activity, but it is in some ways the most interesting because it does reinstate an equality of treatment in the study of institutions and the study of behaviour. It will also be noted that in both cases, though more obviously in the second, the intentions that underlie institutional reform enable one to consider the relationship between theory and institutions.

PREFECTORAL REFORM IN FRANCE

Reform of the prefectoral system was an important part of the modernisation of government undertaken by the Fifth French

Republic. The aim was to facilitate further administrative decentralisation of the functions of central government, to relieve the centre, choked by the growth of these functions and out of touch with the affected provinces, to bring decision making nearer the ground, to rationalise complex administrative structures, to ensure the more effective local co-ordination of central government field agencies as a counter to the specialisation of services that comes with complexity, to improve the local machinery for economic and land use planning and thus to promote regional development, and to bring government nearer the people. In all this the prefect played a key role and the purpose of the reforms in question here was to revitalise traditional powers he had effectively lost, though with which he was still formally endowed.[1]

This is not the place for a discussion of the prefectoral system as such. I shall return to it in any case in a subsequent section illustrating what can be learnt from foreign experience for domestic reform. Here we are concerned simply with an apparently successful attempt to change patterns of administrative behaviour by formal changes in organisation and procedure. A word must nevertheless be said about the prefect and his role in the French system of administration.

France is divided territorially into ninety-five *départements* (roughly: counties). These are basic units of administrative decentralisation (i.e. basis for the organisation of central government field services) as well as second-tier units of local self-government. In each there is a high government official called the prefect. The prefect has numerous roles. He represents the state in his department, both in a dignified sense and as repository of state powers in case of emergency. He is to some extent political agent of the Government. Administratively, he is also the chief representative of the Government and head of most government services in his area (the exceptions are, obvious enough, the judiciary and the military, less obviously the financial administration). As senior official of the Ministry of the Interior in his department, he heads the state police services and supervises the first-tier local authorities. He has broad responsibilities with regard to the security of the state and the maintenance of order under a variety of crisis situations. He has responsibilities in the field of economic planning and specific powers with regard to public works and public investment. He is the chief executive of the departmental local authority.

We are only concerned here with some of these functions. The

---

[1] The following section is drawn from 'The French Prefectoral Service Revived', *Administration and Society* (May 1974).

prefect is legally 'the delegate of the Government and the direct representative of each minister'. Several points follow. He represents the Government as a collective body (i.e. the Cabinet), as well as the Prime Minister and each minister individually. This representation of ministers is direct: lines of authority do not pass through the Cabinet or the prefect's own Ministry of the Interior. In principle he is the sole direct representative of ministers and all powers of decision delegated by them to their field services are delegated to him in the first place. Most of the decentralised powers of central government are thus brought together in his hands. At the same time, the prefect 'assures the general direction' of government officials in his department. The powers of decision referred to above relate largely to official acts with effect *outside* the administration (whether general in character or relating to individual cases), here the reference is to his position *within* the administration as head of all government services in his area (with the exceptions noted above). All lines of authority and channels of communication from the various ministries to their senior field officials run through him: he is the hierarchic superior of most civil servants in his department and directs the work of the field services.

One man represents the Government in its relations with its own field services and in the relations of the latter with the public: he acts as a focus of state power. At the same time he ties together the specialised services of the state, acting as supreme administrative co-ordinator. In other words, France has a strong system of integrated administrative decentralisation with the prefect as integrator. It is in this respect, as in so many others, entirely different from Britain.

Like so much else in France, the prefectoral institution was really established by Napoleon. His prefects were invested with the authority of the state and were responsible for the administration of the then newly established *départements*. Their powers subsequently declined, but the system was too well grounded to wither away: it survived, ready to acquire new functions when the need arose and the period of weakness was followed in the Fifth Republic by a notable revival. Some of the reasons for the past decline are relevant to understanding the difficulties inherent in the system, while the present, strengthened position can only be understood against the background of post-war developments. Important though the reforms undertaken in 1964 were, however, they largely reaffirmed the existing theory of the administrative system and principles which had simply fallen into disuse. We have here, in other words, a limited engineering exercise designed to force the actual behaviour of administrators into channels already formally prescribed.

The prefects of the First Empire had wide responsibilities in a state with considerable modernising ambitions but a relatively weak administrative structure for carrying these out (however strong in comparison to most other states of the time). A contemporary instruction to prefects said: 'Your mission extends to all branches of internal administration; your attributes cover everything concerning the public fortune, national prosperity and the well-being of the citizens you administer.' Though the will, in early days, was often there, the infrastructure was not. Their main function, however, soon became political: agents of the party in office, manipulators of elections and distributors of patronage. In the eyes of democrats, the institution was discredited. It declined for other reasons. The acceptance of *laissez faire* in social and economic matters cut much of the original purpose from under the prefects' feet. The general weakness of governments from the Third Republic onwards, reflecting unstable coalitions as well as liberal ideology, worked in the same direction. The gradual acceptance of democratic values, and the consequent depoliticisation of the prefects, eventually deprived them of importance even as manipulators of local politics. Their functions became increasingly negative. They remained responsible for law and order, which was important but not a matter which would itself give them a leading role in the life of their area. The other responsibility with which they were left was no more positive: the supervision of administration, especially local government, had a political content, it is true, but involved a large element of routine legal and financial control.

Another development is of greater importance for understanding the problems of the system in modern times. The prefect's position as administrative head of all central government services in his area was gradually undermined. In the integrated prefectoral system the prefect is the superior of all specialist chief officers of the external services representing the various ministries in his department. This does not just mean supervision, or even coordination, but includes direction: as hierarchic superior, all lines of command between the centre and the field should run through the prefect and he should hold all delegated ministerial powers. In theory, as we have said, this principle was maintained in France at all times, but the practice changed and sometimes even the principle was eroded.

The reasons were plain enough. Originally the Ministry of the Interior had a general responsibility for virtually all internal affairs and the position of the prefect as its official was administratively simple because most government activities were likely to fall within the province of his own ministry. The subsequent growth of government brought specialisation and the hiving-off of new ministries, some of which were in turn subdivided. Most established their own field services. France in fact developed an extensive system of administrative decentralisation. The great majority of civil servants work in the provinces, including many senior officials; they are organised in a series of specialised external services, each separately structured, each staffed by its own civil service corps, each headed by its own chief officer, most with a corresponding ministerial division headed by a director in Paris.

Several consequences spring to mind. It is harder for the prefect to co-ordinate, even to supervise, much less to direct, the work of officials who do not form part of his own—or even his own ministry's—staff. (The offices of the various services may be widely dispersed, reducing contacts and making day-to-day intervention difficult to organise; as members of the staff of their own ministries, officials do not depend on the prefect for their careers.) The growth of government activities and the technical nature of much of the work involved also makes the prefect's position harder. (He will find it difficult to follow what is going on and, with only a small staff of his own, may not be sufficiently well briefed to intervene; professionalism leads to a natural tendency for specialist officers to communicate directly with their opposite numbers in the capital who 'speak their own language'; the desire for quick decisions and demands of general convenience, together with the technicality of the work and the pattern of personal contacts, will lead to informal channels of communication which take the shortest route and by-pass the prefect). The prefect is not helped by the absence of any real sense of identity between the officials of different services in his area. (There is bound to be a strong sense of identity, however, within each service, locally a reflection of shared work, nationally a reflection of the way the civil service is organised: the field services are staffed by members of the same corps as the central services of their ministries and they move between the two during their careers.) Ministries are likely to develop their own interests and resent intervention by an 'outsider' in mid-hierarchy. (This is particularly true where ministries are staffed by specialist corps whose loyalties will strengthen internal lines of communication and add to the suspicion of cross-cutting hierarchies; the *esprit de corps* of the prestigious French technical corps goes further: they are often responsible for sectors of government activity and tend to regard these as autonomous

empires to be guarded against outsiders.) Over the years, ministries have frequently organised their external services on different
territorial bases. (That different services have different natural
geographical areas is commonplace and the fact that the prefectoral institution was weak at the time these services expanded
allowed the specialist corps to place their own convenience before
the needs of political and administrative co-ordination.)

The disadvantages of such 'vertical separatism' became increasingly apparent in post-war years and changes were eventually
made. Several factors combined to bring the reform about. One
was the growth of economic planning. While this led primarily to
regionalisation and the appointment of regional prefects with
planning responsibilities, it also influenced the position of departmental prefects: although designed to meet new challenges, the
notion of the prefect as animator of the economy and agent of the
modernising state can be seen as a return to Napoleonic origins.
Another was a general move towards administrative rationalisation, part of which has been to reaffirm the traditional principles
of the integrated prefectoral system and to re-establish the prefect
as effective chief administrative officer in his area. A general
administrative problem of decentralised administration is the
growing difficulty of co-ordinating an increasingly complex system
of specialised government services in the field. The need for such
co-ordination was sharpened by a growing demand for even
further transfer of decision-making powers to the field. This was
partly an efficiency demand (i.e. simplify the decision-making
process), but it was also linked to a democratisation demand (i.e.
bring government nearer to the governed).

A decree of 1955 reaffirmed the pre-eminent role of prefect as
described earlier in this section, but as no other steps were taken
to strengthen his position, this was largely ignored. It became
clear that formal statements of principle could not alter the situation and that structural changes would be needed to underpin the
prefect's authority, redirect the flow of business and thus counteract the informal lines of command that had entrenched themselves.

The establishment of de Gaulle's Fifth Republic, with its
renewal of the authority of the state, was in itself likely to renew
prefectoral authority. The restoration of executive power after
1958 gave new prestige to its representatives in the provinces; a
stronger government meant stronger prefects also, almost by
definition. De Gaulle's Government was also committed to
decentralisation, partly to rationalise the administrative system
and make public administration more efficient, but also (cf. the
abortive constitutional reform) to bring more vitality to the

provinces. While reform of the prefectoral system lay in the logic of economic and administrative needs, the Fifth Republic, unlike its predecessors, had the powers to implement it. A study group recommended a greater deconcentration of government work which would leave policy-making with the ministries but place management squarely in the hands of the field services. This meant increased delegation and the replacement of *a priori* by *a posteriori* controls. The strengthening of the prefectoral institution was only one of the measures taken, and perhaps not the most important over-all, but it was certainly a key element. Without it, further deconcentration would simply add to the vertical fragmentation of specialist services by making each more powerful in its own sphere.

Reorganisation was not planned in the abstract and imposed suddenly on the country as a whole. As one official document put it, the need was recognised 'to confront reforms which may be attractive in theory with the necessary proofs of reality'. Pragmatic engineers, the reformers chose a number of departments as preliminary guinea pigs in 1962 and, when the experiment proved successful, a general reform was decreed in 1964. The purpose was simple: to integrate government services more strongly at departmental level. In outline, this meant strengthening the authority of the prefect by concentrating powers in his hands more clearly, in particular by regulating the delegation of ministerial powers to the field more strictly; establishing an effective but light-weight system of co-ordination by reorganising his office, restructuring the flow of business and building up his sources of information; reinforcing his hierarchical position *vis-à-vis* specialist chief officers by giving him a voice in personnel matters; rationalising the distribution of work by the clearer division of responsibilities between prefectoral and other services. The field services of all ministries except Defence, Justice, Finance and Education fall under the prefect's authority. Their titles change continuously as the result of amalgamation and redivision at the centre but the areas covered are Public Works, Housing, Transport, Industry, Agriculture, Posts and Telecommunications, Labour, Social Security, Health and Welfare. For these, the decree of March 1964 laid down broad administrative rules.

The position of the prefect as chief government officer was reaffirmed. He may 'give the necessary directives to heads of services to define the general direction of their activities'. The accompanying circular added that he was to have 'general powers of animation, co-ordination and direction'.

His position as sole representative of the Government and direct representative of all ministers individually was also reaffirmed. Provisions relating to the delegation of authority were strengthened. All powers of decision transferred to the field were to be vested in him, including those transferred on an *ad hoc* basis by ministers as well as those provided for on a more general basis on laws and regulations. The problem of listing these powers, involving a mass of legislation and many authorities, was not simple and attempts to draw up inventories during the trial period were not very successful. Taken in conjunction with a move towards increased delegation, however, it meant, in the words of the circular, that prefects were to be responsible for the 'quasi-totality of powers of decision exercised in the name of the state'. What exactly is meant in context is not entirely clear but it seems to refer to 'acts' in the legal sense, i.e. having consequences outside the administration, whether regulations issued locally or local decisions affecting individual citizens (administrative acts are subject to appeal in the administrative courts). Internal affairs, i.e. organisational questions and the preparation of reports submitted to ministries for decision there, however, are adequately covered by the preceding provision which make the prefect the hierarchic superior of all the services concerned.

Clearly the prefect cannot—and should not—deal with the thousand and one daily decisions that need to be taken. Decisions must be prepared by the technically competent specialised services and his regular intervention would create an unmanageable burden of work, often merely to achieve duplication of effort. A purpose of the reform was to simplify administrative routine and the prefect was therefore to redelegate as much as possible to the heads of services. A distinction was in fact drawn between 'delegation of powers' (transfer of a defined bloc of business to a specialist chief officer who then becomes personally responsible for the decision taken, unless his authority is expressly revoked) and 'delegation of signature' (blocs of business where the chief officer signs on the prefect's behalf, but the latter may reserve affairs of a certain importance, e.g. by imposing a financial ceiling, and can intervene in specific cases by calling for papers and acting himself). In both cases, however, he was to be kept informed of all decisions taken. The fact that heads of services exercise the prefect's authority, rather than their ministries' or their own, should have an important psychological effect in shifting previous, often informal, lines of authority and should thus counter vertical separatism. Paradoxically, it could also increase the competence of specialist chief officers: the prefect is more likely to delegate now that his final authority is clearly defined, while chief officers, for their part, need not refer as many questions to Paris for decision as

before, thus benefiting from the Government's increased delegation of powers to prefects compared to its earlier delegation to
specialist field services.

To be effective, of course, more was required than the formal
regulation of power. Without corresponding arrangements for
handling business, the prefect could still be by-passed in practice,
particularly in internal matters where no formal 'decision' was
involved; even in the latter he could become a rubber stamp,
signing documents he did not really understand, based on internal
papers he had not seen. Centralisation of correspondence was the
device used to underpin his role, a method that sounds almost
trivial but which was designed to provide him with the basic
intelligence for meaningful action on the one hand, to act as a
built-in institutional check on the re-emergence of informal
channels of communication on the other. To ensure that the
prefect is informed in advance of all developments that may
involve a decision later, all incoming and outgoing correspondence
must pass through the prefecture. A special office makes copies of
all papers for the prefect's use before sending the originals to their
proper destination. This running documentation means that the
entire business of the various field services, even at preparatory
stage, is available for the prefect's use: it can be brought to his
attention by the official in charge or called for as the need arises.
The rule covered both correspondence with the public and that
which is internal to the administration. Incoming, it includes
instructions, circulars and letters from the ministries to their field
offices; outgoing correspondence is also sent to the prefecture for
forwarding, with or without his signature in the case of a decision,
to permit him to add his own comments in the case of a recom-
mendation to Paris. (Sensibly, certain matters were excluded:
those covered by the rules of professional secrecy, those of a
purely technical nature with no obvious administrative or financial
implications and those of special urgency—but then a duplicate
must be forwarded through the prefecture which alone has official
status.) Much importance was attached to these procedures and
they do seem to play a significant part in ensuring that lines of
authority flow through the prefecture.

Further provisions ensured that the prefect would have available
a wide range of information on all matters falling within his pur-
view. There is a general obligation on all services to keep him
informed about matters that may give rise to future decisions
and about developments more generally: they are bound to send
him copies of important internal papers, regular reports and
special studies for example (prefects can specify the categories of

information they wish to receive, though they are advised by circular to ensure that the burden is not too heavy). On the other side, the correspondence office in the prefecture functions as an intelligence unit as well as a filter for communications and is responsible for seeing that files are as complete as possible: it may call for papers on matters of general interest or for further information on matters with which the prefect is dealing at the time. In addition, of course, the prefect has direct sources of information through personal contacts in committees, conferences with senior officials and regular discussions with individual heads of services; if he is dissatisfied, he can at any time call in the officers concerned for an oral report.

As a further measure to strengthen the prefect and facilitate the co-ordination of policy, the prefect was made *ex-officio* chairman of all administrative committees in his department, though he may be represented by a member of his staff. There are many committees which, in addition to officials, often include representatives of the elected local authorities and sometimes of interest groups also; one observer found 150, of which at least 30 could be described as important. The system was simplified by regrouping: clearly a rationalisation of committees is a prerequisite of effective prefectoral participation, quite apart from being a prerequisite of effective co-ordination between committees.

The importance attached to economic planning is reflected in specific powers, particularly with regard to public investment programmes, including all projects financed from public funds, whether undertaken by central or local government or, indeed, by private enterprise. He was described as 'solely responsible' in such matters and must be associated in all schemes at the 'stage of conception', that is to say well before even decisions of principle are taken; at the stage of execution, his powers are more formal and thus even clearer.

Finally, the prefect's position *vis-à-vis* other senior civil servants was strengthened by associating him more closely than before in personnel matters. The problem was that he has to deal with a staffing system which is not locally organised: civil servants belong to separate corps, nationally organised and more or less autonomous in career terms. In the past, the prefect did not control posting into his department and thus had little say in the appointment of the heads of services he had to direct; he had not much more influence in transfers out, whether as promotion or to remove a man he found incompatible or judged incompetent. True, he reported each year in general terms to the ministries concerned and these reports were added to the files, but the ministries were more concerned with their own problems of promotion and staff deployment. This clearly placed the prefect in a somewhat ambiguous hierarchic position. Although the corps system remained firmly entrenched, some changes were made. The prefect was to be informed in advance of all movements of senior personnel and can thus intervene at the right moment. In this way, and through increased direct personal contacts with the ministries, he has managed to acquire a good deal of influence in staffing matters; he is better able, if not to choose his own team, at least to avoid fundamental incompatibilities, while his voice in promotion makes him less irrelevant to the specialist officer's career and thus enhances his authority.

The prefect's own administrative service, the prefecture, is obviously vital if his work is to be done adequately. This is a hybrid organisation, concerned with his work as executive of the department local authority, with his duties as representative of the Ministry of the Interior (police, elections, supervision of first-tier local authorities, etc.), with his role as co-ordinator of all other central government services and with his newer planning responsibilities. In the past, the staff to sustain his role as 'animator, director and co-ordinator of developments in his department' was minimal. The system was geared to formal supervision rather than planning and intelligence: the general staff function was weakly organised. There were other staffing difficulties. He has few elite (i.e. prefectoral corps) civil servants to assist him and the rest of even his senior staff have neither the status nor the qualifications of the senior specialist field officers. While they are competent in routine administration, they are less good at functions requiring a broad view of problems and the initiation of new policies. The pressure of daily business, in any case, was such that new functions could not easily be fitted in. Reorganisaion of offices and the provision of new supporting staff was obviously required. It is not the intention here, however, to deal with these wider problems but merely to touch on some of the questions related directly to the prefect's integrating role.

One of these problems is how to relate the work of the prefecture and of the specialist services. Despite all that has been said about the prefect's reinforced authority, the fact that officials work in separate buildings, quite likely in different parts of the town, has serious disadvantages in terms of the organisation of work and group psychology. Collaboration in a genuinely integrated administrative system depends on physical proximity, both for the convenience of routine and for a sense of identity. A possible solution is to build new centres—'administrative cities—to house them all, a solution that appeals to town planners and has obvious advantages for the public but that is rarely possible.

A more concrete problem, already discussed, is how to organise the flow of business. The answer has been the establishment of a special centralising office in the prefecture. Its primary duties are archival: it copies and registers documents and passes them to their proper destination, but its functions are not entirely passive and it is responsible for obtaining any further documentation necessary to complete the files.

A more interesting question, perhaps, is whether the prefect should have his own staff to assess matters that come to him for decision, giving him a source of advice independent of the specialist chief officers and able at the same time to watch the activities of specialist services in order to draw his attention to matters that might not otherwise come his way. In other words, should the prefecture have its own small offices corresponding broadly to all spheres of government action? The answer appears to have been no. The 1964 circular stressed that the responsibility of chief officers for technical functions and the internal management of their services should not be diminished, and that they should be closely associated in policy making. The prefect, indeed, was advised to give them his confidence. This means that specialist services should act as external services of their ministries *and* as services of the prefecture. The departmental administration should be regarded as an integrated unit: relations between a service and the prefect should be direct, not through some parallel office in the prefecture. This, of course, is implicit in the demand for a rationalisation of responsibilities and is also important if a proper climate is to be created for the exercise of the prefect's co-ordinating functions, much of which finally depends on his personal contacts with other officers.

In summing all this up, one might ask how far these institutional and procedural reforms have enabled the prefect to establish himself as the direct representative of all ministries and the effective director of all specialist services. It is clear that much depends on the men, on how they see their role and on whether they have the personality to impose it. The fact that there appears to have been a real shift in authority patterns in the departments since 1964, however, would also seem to indicate that the reforms discussed above provided the essential framework within which the prefect could assert his position.

As one might expect, the situation varies from department to department, but the general impression is that the prefect is now 'the real boss'. He directs the work of heads of services in a quite

practical day-to-day manner and intervenes extensively in decisions. He is well informed about all development, either through
the formally prescribed procedures or because in the course of his
work he has called for further explanations. He is likely to receive
a daily report from his immediate aides in the prefecture who
bring to his attention matters he should consider and as a result he
may phone a senior official or call him to a meeting. As chairman
of numerous committees, and through other less formal staff
conferences, he participates directly in a wide variety of business.

His position *vis-à-vis* the field services is strengthened by the
direct contacts he is able to establish with their own ministries. He
is likely to spend a good deal of time in Paris and in this way he
builds up personal relations with directors in the ministries as well
as with officials in the Prime Minister's office, in the planning
agencies and elsewhere. He is also likely to have good contacts as
a result of earlier periods of service in the private office of the
Minister of the Interior or some other minister and in other senior
posts in central government. This means that he can deal directly
with the various ministries, by telephone if necessary, and he is
thus placed in a strong position in relation to the heads of services
who, whatever informal contacts they may foster on the side, are
bound to use his office if they wish to contact their own ministry
officially.

The formal arrangements for the centralisation of correspondence appear to work quite effectively in most cases. Even if heads
of services maintain direct contacts with their headquarters
unofficially, they are quick to inform the strong prefect of their
action. The prefecture has become a normal channel of business,
not only between services and their ministries but also between
services within the department. It has thus established itself as a
real co-ordinating office: real lines of authority now run through
the prefecture.

This analysis has been concerned with the role of the prefect in
integrating a system of decentralised administration. The conclusion has been that the system is much more integrated than before
and that formal changes have played a considerable role in this
achievement, largely by reshaping informal patterns of behaviour.
It is a successful example of administrative engineering.

CONSTITUTION MAKING IN GERMANY

The earliest constitution-makers were optimists. They believed in
a natural harmony and in man's ability to discover by reason the
rules which would allow that harmony to prevail. The good society

depended merely on the right organisation of the state. Their first European attempt was the completely impractical constitution of 1791. The search for the right formula continued. The France of the Revolution and its aftermath was a laboratory for such experiments, a laboratory that did much to undermine man's faith in his ability to organise the good society at all. Only in America, under conditions not repeated elsewhere, did it survive. In Europe, a new realism emerged: constitutional engineering concerned itself with practical devices to achieve limited reforms. It is instructive to compare the American constitution of 1787 with the French and German constitutions of 1871; the first a political philosophy in itself, the last two *ad hoc* arrangements to regulate the machinery of government.

Only for a brief period after the First World War did the old optimism revive. Democracy was established for the first time in many parts of Europe and it was established by the draftsmen of new constitutions. The constitution drafted at Weimar for the new German republic was a classic example. Rarely can so many eminent professors of law and specialists in constitutional history have collaborated in so practical an exercise. Unfortunately, they were not practical enough. They made a number of technical mistakes which contributed to the failure of the system they established. At the same time, of course, they overrated the extent to which a constitution can speedily alter inimical political habits that are deeply ingrained, especially if these are not counterbalanced by at least a superficial acceptance of the new order and a willingness to abide by the rules of its game. They also overrated the extent to which a constitution, even the best-laid plans of men, can act as a bulwark against irrationality and violence in times of real crisis.

Most of the countries of Europe adopted new constitutions after the last war. Their draftsmen were more modest in their hopes but they believed that constitutional engineering on a limited scale, based on the study of specific weakness, could help to stabilise government and check authoritarian tendencies under all but the most difficult circumstances. The most interesting example is no doubt Germany and I intend here to illustrate how Bonn tried to improve on Weimar.

In 1948 German politicians were authorised by the three western occupying powers to draft a democratic constitution. Hoping for reunification and reluctant to take any step that might be interpreted as a final solution to the German problem, they neither called a specially elected constituent assembly nor did they submit the finished product to popular ratification: they relied on the provincial legislatures, already established, and called the final document a fundamental law rather than constitution, a piece of verbal metaphysics that appeared significant to the participants and has been seriously analysed by commentators since. The possibly transient nature of the new constitution, matched by desire for the immediate recognition of reacquired statehood it would nevertheless give, eased agreement.

The founding fathers drew on earlier traditions of the Weimar Republic, which was itself a reform, rather than a transformation, of the governmental structures of imperial Germany. There was little inclination to adopt an entirely new model, a presidential system on American lines for example, or a system of assembly government as established—though only on paper, in the eastern zone. In that sense, they were less innovative than General de Gaulle in 1958. At the same time, it was the disasters of the past that were uppermost in their minds. Much of the debate was concerned with analysing the failures of the Weimar constitution, much ingenuity spent on devices to improve it: the result has sometimes been called an anti-constitution to Weimar. Attempts were also made, however, to prevent the establishment of another dictatorship by provisions that went beyond the elimination of technical weaknesses in the old constitution.

While earlier European constitutions were generally coloured by near-utopian hopes for the future of mankind, the Bonn constitution had a more negative, though also more practical, character: it was designed to correct mistakes of the past rather than to usher in a new era of popular democracy. It showed its pessimistic distrust of the people by eliminating Weimar provisions for the direct election of the President and the institutions of popular initiative and referendum, and its distrust of the popularly elected majority in Parliament by introducing a system of checks and balances, including the judicial review of legislation. What the founders hoped for was a period of stable democratic institutions which would allow for the growth of a genuinely democratic political culture.

At the same time, they were influenced by the western Allies' ideas of democracy. The constitution-makers were in fact instructed to establish a federal republic, partly because the allies, notably the French, did not wish to see the re-emergence of too centralised, thus too strong, a German state, partly because the Americans found it difficult to conceive of democracy without federalism. Other notions were picked up by the Germans themselves, the link between MPs and constituents from Britain for example, the constitutional court from the USA. These influences have an additional interest here because they relate to the points

I made earlier about the relationship between theory and institutions and the reference in my opening chapter to the importance of comparative studies in the activity of constitutional engineering.

A first step was to safeguard the fundamental democratic order against abolition from within. It has to be remembered that Hitler not merely came to power legally but that the Nazi regime subsequently functioned within the Weimar framework, amending it out of all recognition, it is true, but, formally speaking, never breaking its continuity. The principles of democracy, federalism and the 'social' state were declared immutable (beyond a further statement that private property should serve the public welfare, no body was given to the last of these phrases and it never had any clear meaning). At the same time, prominence of place was given to an extensive Bill of Rights and these rights were protected more effectively than before to prevent their suspension or, more dangerous because less dramatic, their gradual hollowing out: details, including sensible limitations, had inevitably to be left to ordinary legislation but their essence cannot be touched. The influence here, direct experience apart, was American democratic theory and Catholic theory of natural law. The constitution-makers declared, as did the American Founding Fathers, that man had rights prior to the establishment of the state and could not be deprived of them by its institutions, not even by a democratically elected majority in Parliament. The problem, of course, is that it is easier to organise the negative protection of rights by allowing a constitutional court to strike down contrary legislation than it is to ensure their legislative implementation. Although the constitution states that rights are directly binding ot legislature, executive and judiciary, little can be done if Parliament fails to give them clothes.

An innovation was the establishment of a special court as guarantor of the constitution. The Weimar draftsmen had not considered one necessary; there had been some talk of judicial review but the socialists suspected the reactionary character of the judiciary and preferred to trust the popularly elected legislature, while the conservatives believed that a good legal system had its own self-implementing force and for that reason wished to maintain the separation of law and politics. Both views proved wrong. At the same time, the New Deal record of the American Supreme Court counteracted a previously unfavourable impression. The new constitutional court has one of the most extensive jurisdiction of any in a democratic state. It can invalidate actions of the legislature or the executive if these conflict with the rights of the citizen. It also arbitrates in conflicts between organs of the state, including federal and state governments, and thus helps to protect the federal character of the republic. In these two ways, therefore, it can determine the concrete limits within which the governmental institutions operate. It also has novel powers in relation to political parties to which I shall return.

The obvious point has already been made that these functions are to some extent negative: the question has been asked whether the court could direct Parliament to enact legislation giving substance to promised rights, but realistically it has declined to take this course. On the other hand, it has taken the climate of opinion into account and has avoided formalistic interpretations by developing a sociological jurisprudence which takes into account facts well beyond those a British court would be likely to consider relevant. On the whole, it has followed a sensible middle path, maintaining its independence, handing down some important decisions, without allowing itself to become the final arbiter of German politics. Its authority is respected: no decisions have been evaded, or attacked as vitriolically as in the southern states of America. One commentator adds that 'its jurisdiction has undoubtedly contributed to the deepening of the idea of the liberal democratic constitutional state'.

The constitution created a federal state or, better, re-established a federalism that had been virtually destroyed during the Nazi era. In this, therefore, it followed German traditions (although, in the nature of things, it could not base itself on many of the old states) as well as Allied dictates. The division of powers between federal and state governments was in fact the major issue during the constitutional debates. In addition to a short and obvious list of exclusively federal powers, there is an exhaustive list of concurrent powers in which, however, federal legislation enjoys priority. At the same time, the execution of most federal policies is placed in the hands of the state governments. In this system Germany differs from other federal countries, a distinction sometimes being made between German 'horizontal federalism' (line drawn between federal legislation and state administration) and 'vertical federalism' (line drawn between areas of legislative competence with parallel federal and state administrations). Though not new, this was a convenient way of combating the 'obsolescence of federalism' detected earlier in America by combining nationally uniform policies with localised administration.

The role of the states is ensured by the fact that they employ most of the civil service. They also have exclusive legislative powers in the important field of education (*Kulturpolitik* was always a sensitive matter for denominational reasons) and they

control the police. Experience again taught the advantage of keeping these functions out of central government hands. The state's
financial resources are guaranteed. Finally, their position is
strengthened by the reintroduction of another traditional federal
element into the central government system itself: the upper
chamber of Parliament is not an elected senate but represents the
state governments. This is not merely a variation of checks and
balances but a sensible provision where the states have actually to
administer the laws passed by the Federal Parliament.

Probably the most changed institution was the presidency. The
Weimar President was directly elected for a period of seven years,
a period longer than Parliament, and could thus claim a democratic legitimacy. This put him, as it put President de Gaulle and
Pompidou, in a strong position *vis-à-vis* the head of the Government who at best emerged from coalition negotiations in the
corridors of Parliament and at worst was imposed from outside.
The President was invested with considerable powers under the
constitution: he appointed and dismissed the Chancellor and other
ministers, he dissolved Parliament, he was Commander in Chief
of the armed forces, he could legislate by decree in emergencies
(and this included periods of parliamentary stalemate, defined as
legislative emergencies). While the Crown in Britain has similar
powers, it has long been accepted that these are exercised only on
advice. This was not the case in Germany and Field Marshal
Hindenburg modelled himself on the Emperor he had served.
Faced with a Parliament that had no traditions of parliamentary
government and that was hopelessly divided by a multi-party
system, it was only on the basis of presidential powers that the
country could finally be run. Leaving aside the question of what
forces stood behind the near senile President towards the end, the
last years of the Weimar Republic saw not only legislation by
decree, but the appointment and dismissal of chancellors and the
dissolution of Parliament without any reference to an elected
majority: it was thus, indeed, that Hitler came to office.

The President is now elected by an assembly composed of
federal and state parliamentarians. His functions have been
reduced to those of a dignified representative of the state, though,
as in Britain, he can also 'warn, encourage and advise' the Government (as an ex-politician he is rather more likely to do so) and, if
he so wishes, can exercise a similar 'moral magistracy' in relation
to the public (to use a term sometimes employed during the Fourth
French Republic). What formal powers he has must be exercised
on government advice. Some, however, were removed entirely. No
provision at all was made for emergency powers, so misused,

though bitterly contested legislation subsequently reintroduced them. The armed forces were brought under the civilian control of the Minister of Defence to prevent the re-emergence of a 'state within the state'.

The Chancellor was strengthened by this dismantling of presidential powers, some of which he inherited, He became the undisputed head of the executive branch of government, ending any possibility of a dual executive, the ambiguities of which, though in different form from Weimar, now beset the Fifth Republic. We have seen in an earlier section that the Chancellor has traditionally been a strong figure *vis-à-vis* the rest of the political executive (i.e. the Cabinet). The constitution reaffirms his responsibility for the policies of the Government and his answerability to Parliament. Some ingenuity, on the other hand, went into devising novel provisions to regulate his relationship to the elected chamber in order to stabilise governments after the appalling record of Weimar.

It is sometimes said that the constitution-makers sought to create a 'rationalised' variant of parliamentary government and it will be remembered that this phrase was also applied to the constitution of the Fifth Republic which, on the face of it, if not in practice, was more concerned with stabilising executive-legislative relations than with strengthening the role of the President. The instability of Weimar governments was due partly to the multitude of parties able to form many different coalitions or no coalition at all (an attempt to deal with this through electoral reform is discussed below), partly, as we have seen, to the absence of any tradition of party support for governments emanating from a parliamentary majority.

The lower chamber has now lost much of its power to overthrow governments, particularly by the joint action of extreme left and extreme right, agreed only on disruption as in Weimar. The new device, much praised at the time, was the constructive vote of no confidence: the chamber can only vote a Chancellor out of office if it votes for a successor at the same time. The idea, of course, is to prevent purely negative action, while forcing the parties to take responsibility for the formation and support of a government. In fact, the simplification of the party system has made this provision largely irrelevant, though it was tried once, unsuccessfully. The risk to governments between elections is now, as it might be in Britain one day, that of a small Liberal party holding the balance of power and changing front. It is hard to judge, in any case, whether the new provision would really have been effective in a multi-party situation: obviously a divided Parliament can make the life of governments difficult to the degree of impossibility even without a vote of no confidence, while the provision that the Chancellor can call for a vote of confidence and dissolve if he fails to obtain it merely prevents the *interregna* that sometimes occurred in the Fourth Republic.

Other reforms of the parliamentary system were undertaken that cannot be discussed here, though it is worth mentioning the introduction of a Question Time in imitation of Britain. It should not be thought, finally, that the German Parliament is really weak: that is always a relative matter and in its ability to influence the legislative process it is probably more effective than the British. Nor was it the intention of the constitution-makers to undermine Parliament. Quite the opposite. In stating that popular sovereignty is expressed—and only expressed—through elections, it clearly intended to establish a representative, that is to say a parliamentary, democracy.

The electoral system was regulated by law rather than by the constitution, but it is relevant here. The main problem was to prevent a reoccurrence of the splintered party system of earlier days. No serious consideration was given at the time to a British-type electoral system as an alternative to the almost perfect proportional representation of Weimar. The reasons, tradition and notions of fairness apart, were obvious: it was not clear then that a two-and-a-half party system would emerge and 'first past the post' elections could have given a party with a relatively small proportion of the total vote a majority (no party, moreover—and they all approached the problem with their own interest in mind—could at that time predict who would come top of the poll). The simple solution was to retain proportional representation but to limit its effect by imposing a hurdle of 5 per cent of the total vote, below which no seats are obtained. The number of parties represented in Parliament dropped from the original twelve to three in 1957 and has not increased. It is hard to assess what influence electoral engineering has had, however. The polarisation of voters into two major parties can be attributed to many factors, including Adenauer's success in establishing the Christian Democratic Party as a broad anti-socialist front and the later success of the Social Democratic Party in broadening its appeal by shedding its Marxist image. There is also a bandwagon effect: once a party looks as if it is able to obtain an effective majority, politicians tend to join it to obtain office and voters forsake other parties in order to vote 'usefully'. Social, cultural and economic divisions have become simpler, depriving some sectional parties of their base.

The 5 per cent clause (which psychologically tends to be higher as electors may fear to waste their votes when a party approaches that figure) nevertheless has some effect. It does make it difficult for new parties to establish themselves. This, of course, can be a good thing as well as a bad, in keeping the extreme right National Democratic Party out of the Federal Parliament for example. Success might have forced conservatives and socialists to continue their 'grand coalition' as the only possible democratic majority, thus depriving the country of an alternative government, an essential element of democracy itself. Failure to secure representation, on the other hand, has contributed to its decline: it has been deprived of a platform that would keep it in the public eye, while even potential supporters, next time round, may be reluctant to risk another wasted vote.

Another aspect of the electoral system is worth mentioning and this relates once more to lessons of foreign experience. The British, instructing the Germans in democracy after the war, made great play of the link between M Ps and their constituents. This clearly depends on direct elections in single-member constituencies. The Germans adopted what looks like a complex hybrid system. The citizen has two votes, one for a candidate in a single member constituency, the other for a party list: half the members are elected by each procedure, but the second vote is decisive because the lists are used to bring total representation to the correct proportional figure. Ingenious though this is, it appears to have little effect. True, it produces occasional evidence that a particular candidate is more or less popular than his party, though the difference is usually marginal. The main purpose has not been achieved: there is no significant difference in the relationship between the two sorts of M P and the body of citizens.

Finally, we come to the constitutional provisions relating to political parties and these, too, are new. Germany is one of the few democracies where parties are regulated in this way. Partly, this reflects what we might consider a somewhat legalistic approach. Having been told that parties are an essential element of democracy, indeed the essential element in forming the political will of the electorate and thus in translating popular sovereignty into representation, they felt it desirable to write this fact into the constitution. The Weimar view, supported by the courts, was that parties were private associations and thus not subject to outside control. Now that they have been 'constitutionalised', some theorists believe that they have been raised to the status of constitutional organs. This relatively abstract argument, though it might have had practical consequences in terms of constitutional court intervention, has not been accepted.

What has been accepted is that parties should be subject to special rules because of their significance, though the law of implementation did take some twenty years to pass. The constitution laid down that the organisation of parties must be democratic in character. There could be two views of this, parallel to the two views of democracy itself, popular and representative. The latter was adopted: officers must be democratically elected and candidates democratically selected. Much importance was also attached to the financing of parties and accounts must be published showing the source of funds. While this is intended to prevent hidden subsidies and thus hidden pressures, supporters can obviously disguise their contributions by channelling them through intermediary organisations. To prevent the dependence of parties on the support of large interests and to equalise the chances of those with no access to such funds, provisions were also made for state subsidies. These could be justified by the educational role parties play in a democracy, but there has been much litigation about this, as about the right of individual contributors to claim tax exemption.

The other leg of the constitutionalisation of parties was the prohibition of anti-constitutional parties. Here, again there was a lesson of the past: after the failure of the 1923 Munich putsch, Hitler determined to obtain power legally, through the electoral system, using the constitutional order to defeat it from within. This was to be made impossible. The dangers of communism were obviously also present in the minds of the draftsmen. The constitutional court, on the application of the Government, can now disband parties that pursue anti-democratic aims. Only two parties have been banned in this way, a neo-Nazi party in 1952 and the Communist Party of Germany in 1956, the latter after a four years' trial which involved the court in a study of history and a study of political theory (how communist parties *actually* behaved in the past and what the *true* aims of Marxism are, even when the Communist Party appeared committed to activities within the law). Hailed originally as a positive achievement, this part of the constitution soon gave rise to doubts. The effect of banning a party might be to drive it underground and make it more dangerous; martyrdom might win it new supporters; breaking the electoral barometer might disguise the extent of opposition within the country. The prohibition of successor organisations, or even the pursuit of such a party's aims by other means, had unexpected consequences and led to serious restrictions on the free expression of opinion. As a result, when a *détente* with East Germany became possible, the Government made no attempt to take a new only slightly renamed, German Communist Party to court.

The issue did arise in 1968 with respect to the National Democratic Party but the Government felt that there was insufficient evidence against it to win a case: the party had learnt the need to maintain a formally democratic front. It would have been harder, in any case, to ban a party that had already won representation in state legislatures and was thus 'democratically' legitimated. It would be virtually impossible to ban established parties if they were to move to an extremist position. As neither of the two banned parties were a real threat—neither could pass the 5 per cent hurdle— the value of this provision is doubtful. By making parties adjust, even if only superficially, to democratic methods and goals, it may nevertheless prevent the spread of anti-democratic propaganda. But there is an important flaw in this, not to be foreseen by the constitution makers: in contemporary Germany it is the 'extra-parliamentary opposition', in the main without proper party base, that offers fundamental opposition to the existing order from the left.

It is hard to say how successful the constitution as a whole has been. There is no simple *post hoc propter hoc* in political science. A party system has emerged that looks not dissimilar from the British, but for reasons only partly connected with the electoral arrangements. The result has been stable governments which have not required the protection of the 'constructive vote of no confidence' clause. Two parties were dissolved because of their undemocratic aims, but neither was a threat and both have successors which are tolerated. Further points of this sort could be made. The constitution has nevertheless given Germany a workable system of government. There have been major constitutional controversies, about electoral law reform, the regulation of party finances and the introduction of emergency powers for example, but these have been contained, as have party conflicts, within Parliament and within coalition cabinets. The process of government has been as orderly and, notwithstanding a number of scandals, not less democratic than elsewhere. Even allowing for a ready acceptance of the new regime after the catastrophe of defeat and the revelations of Nazi evil, after allowing for a relatively indifferent public satisfied by economic prosperity, this is still no mean technical achievement against the background of German parliamentary history.

If the constitutional framework has effectively channelled the processes of government, the question remains whether it has had much impact on the country's political culture. The Weimar Republic was a democracy without democrats. What of the politicians of the Bonn Republic and, more important in the long run, its citizens? The constitution, at the time of its making, was not an expression of prevailing political norms: it was imposed upon a chaotic society by a political elite supported by the occupying powers and it was never put to the formal test of popular acceptance. The man in the street was not much interested in any case, overwhelmed as he was by the daily problems of survival. He may still have been the deferential-authoritarian citizen of imperial days at heart, if not a Nazi, but, politics discredited, many fell back on the slogan *ohne mich*—'don't involve me'. And it is still true that the symbols of the new state do not arouse much enthusiasm: there is none of the veneration for flag and constitution found in America.

But has the constitution had an educational effect? This was after all a second intention. In the behavioural language of a recent textbook that treats the governmental system in behavioural fashion: 'By establishing exemplary norms and roles sanctioned by constitutional law and by endeavouring to prescribe future relationships, the framers sought to reshape the political culture in conformity with their image of a stable and democratic order.' The fact that the constitutional order is almost universally accepted, even if the reasons have sometimes been negative, has contributed as much to the stability of the political system as has the effective structuring of state institutions. The high electoral turnout, among the highest in western democracies, is an indication of this acceptance, though it also reflects a dutifulness that predates democracy. All this may, nevertheless, conceal ingrained deference to authority, nationalist attitudes, non-participation in everyday politics coupled with the possibility of a relapse into irrationalist mass politics—all far removed from the ideal civic culture. A serious crisis may show weak attachment to the existing order and the democratic way of life. We cannot tell, opinion surveys notwithstanding, how deep the roots of constitutionalism have sunk until the system faces a really serious challenge. This, in any case, is not quite the same question as whether the constitution itself could avert its own collapse in such a crisis. Neither is an experiment that can be laid on for the political scientist.

What is undoubtedly true is that the constitution has given Germany a period, longer than that of the Weimar Republic or the Third Reich, in which democratic norms *could* gradually establish themselves. And, more to the point, it embodies devices which are likely to prevent minor crises from escalating to major catastrophes, just as it prevents the gradual erosion of democracy within the continuity of its order. That is probably all a constitution as such can do and that is the sensible purpose of constitutional engineering.

Comparison as
a Practical Activity

The wary writer covers himself in advance as best he can against
the most obvious lines of criticism. Let me say, therefore, that this
chapter is not intended to break, or even blunt, a lance in the
methodology debate of comparative politics, nor is it put forward
as a contribution in its own right to the science of comparative
politics.[1] The intention is much simpler. I want to argue that there
are practical forms of comparison which the political scientist can
use when in a less than scientific mood and that useful ends can be
served by such practical activity. A plausible argument to forestall
the critic, but probably sensible, is that the case for an unsophisticated approach to comparative politics should be presented in an
unsophisticated way. Put another way, it may be that to be practical one should sometimes be naïve.

The study of foreign governments forms part of what is generally
called comparative politics. The word 'comparison', however, is
used in different ways and this—often unconscious—ambiguity
lies behind much of the criticism levelled against their more old-
fashioned colleagues by the practitioners of the new science
of comparative politics. 'Not truly comparative', their work is
dismissed, 'description without pattern, thus no sums and no
answers', or, in more stylish terms, 'mere juxtaposition of facts
lacking a conceptual framework, thus allowing no hypotheses to
be tested or deduced'. Methodology is fashionable, of course,
but often enough the moderns are justified in their critique. On
the other hand, just as often they are not. Students of comparative
politics—there is no patent on the title—may legitimately have

[1] Revised version of 'On Comparison as a Practical Activity', *Government
and Opposition* (Winter 1972).

their own, quite different purposes when they pursue their subject.

In fact, three distinct modes of comparison can themselves be compared. They serve different purposes and it is a shame, therefore, when one is undermined by methodological criticism more appropriate to another. All three serve useful functions.

The purpose of comparison may well be to do no more than describe two or more phenomena (objects, persons, places, events, institutions). If I say 'one of my children is dark, the other fair', I am making a comparison but nothing beyond the description need be implied, certainly no value judgement and probably no theoretical deduction either, beyond, perhaps, a reflection on the diversity of life. Comparison, in the layman's use of the word at least, need involve no theorising and therefore no theory. When two returned holidaymakers compare notes, what they are generally doing is simply to alternate two accounts of the phenomena they have observed, and that may be all they want to do. Run together, however, this gives us comparisons such as 'in X we had sunshine but in Y it rained, in X the beach was sandy but in Y there were pebbles. . . .'

Sometimes, when the tellers are also prepared to listen, the purpose of the conversation may be to form a judgement: which is the better place to book for next year? But I would stress that there is no reason at all why the purpose of the comparison should necessarily lie in the conclusion. The purpose, and the interest, of several accounts may well lie in the fact that the tales are different. They can only be different by comparison to something, even if that something is no more than our direct experience. In the last resort, therefore, there is a legitimate form of comparison that is essentially stories about strange places (people, events, institutions) told for their own sake.

Now, this is equally true of political science. As often as not, when we compare the government and politics of Britain, France, America and Russia (to name only the standard textbook four), the primary intention is to tell four stories. There is nothing wrong with the country-by-country textbook so long as its major aim is this. We may study countries X, Y and Z because they are important world powers, because they exemplify different political values, because there is something about their politics that makes them interesting (or interests the writer), because the material is available, or for a host of reasons—the reasons behind the choice do not alter the fact that our appreciation is enhanced by that simple form of comparison, the awareness of difference. We do, in fact, like to see how countries differ without having to postulate a scientific urge to theorise about the differences observed. The tourist's enjoyment of French wine may be increased by (though certainly not depend on) his comparing it with English beer; the fact that Clochemerle is not Muddlecombe adds to the study of French politics in the same way. Some political scientists, while allowing all this, would nevertheless maintain that a simple, country-by-country approach is not scientifically comparative and might add that such textbooks (or courses) should be labelled 'foreign governments' to make this clear. Well, there is not all that much in titles—Humpty Dumpty had the last word there—and one need not argue so long as one remembers that even straightforward, consecutive description of different systems of government is a form of comparison.

In fact, a fair number of country-by-country books (or series) do not leave the reader entirely to his own devices; they do not expect him to make his own *ad hoc* comparisons on the basis of points he happens to notice and remember, much less do they expect the probably unmanageable feat of a global comparison based on general impressions of entire political systems. Material is organised accordingly to a pattern or 'conceptual, framework' (this must surely be the most overworked term in the political scientist's vocabulary today). Apart from facilitating comparisons, the ordering of material may have a theoretical spin-off: similarities and dissimilarities may allow the writer, or lead the reader, to draw theoretical conclusions. It is true, of course, that these conclusions generally precede the writing: material is organised according to a pattern that will show what it is intended to show. This approach rarely works convincingly. The conceptual framework of scientific-sounding section headings is often a façade behind which each writer simply tells the story of the country he knows well, not perhaps in the order that he would naturally choose and not perhaps with the emphasis he would otherwise give, but a fairly straightforward account nevertheless.

The only way to overcome this problem entirely is to abjure country divisions altogether and to organise the material on some other basis. This may be the way forward for the teaching of comparative politics as a special science if—and it is a big *if*—the student is already thoroughly familiar with the politics of several countries. Otherwise it has serious drawbacks. By eliminating countries, one disintegrates the seamless web of politics, oversimplifies the untidy multiplicity of relationships, ignores the nationally unique and leaves the student with no real grasp of how a political system operates. He may end with a series of generalisations as abstract as those of mathematics. Politics, however, is not like that: it can only be understood by a feeling, intuitive in the last resort, that comes with the study in depth of a number of systems. The comparativist may try to get round this in a small way and will illustrate his generalisations (about the relationship between electoral and party systems for example) by reference to the experience of certain countries. The chances are that such examples, torn out of context, will be grossly simplified and perhaps not even true. The innocent student must take them on trust, however, if he knows nothing else about the countries concerned, and that is not the best way of teaching any subject. All this would probably not be challenged by even the purest exponent on the non-country, conceptual-framework approach; he might argue, indeed, that there are two different subjects that ought to be studied simultaneously.

That may well be the point here. The study of foreign countries is interesting in its own right and inevitably involves the participant in a form of comparison; over and above this, it is didactically important as the only path to understanding how political systems tick and is a necessary check on the claims made by purer comparativisits.

The last paragraphs have been something of a digression and I would now like to return to the main theme, the uses of the word 'comparison'. In a second, hardly less simple sense, we may compare in order to evaluate. Which is the better holiday resort, the prettier girl in a beauty contest, the most suitable applicant for a job, the most efficient institution for some purpose? Note, again, that nothing very scientific need be implied in this mode of comparison. Once the criteria have been defined—if explicit definition is required—there may be some question of determining proper units of measurement (sunshine hours, vital statistics, typing speeds or academic qualifications), but there is no need to probe below the surface. The question 'why?' (why does the sun shine more frequently in place X than in place Y, why has girl X a better figure than girl Y?) need not arise. Climatology will confuse the holidaymaker and physiology the judge of beauty queens: for the purpose of their comparisons the superficial data is sufficient in both cases. Causal explanations may become relevant, of course, if, having considered whether an institution in country X performs a particular function better than a similar institution in country Y, we go on to ask whether the institutional arrangements of X can be transferred successfully to Y. But that is a separate issue and its difficulties need not get in the way of comparative evaluation even in the field of political institutions; indeed, the more practical of us will probably only want to consider the transferability of a foreign institution if, by simple comparison, it seems worth transferring in the first place.

That definitional problems can arise even in such non-explanatory comparisons is obviously true and a good deal is made of this by the methodologists. In comparisons at this level, however, such difficulties are often irrelevant: those making the comparisons know well enough what they are looking for. If they do not, definition may be impossible: if the meaning of criteria is analysed too far, some questions wrong-headedly become unanswerable (beauty contests would become almost impossible if we had to define a pretty girl and quite impossible if we had to justify that definition). In other cases probing may show that different observers are not using the same criteria because they have different purposes in mind (different job specifications, for example, in the case of members of a selection committee). This is likely to emerge when the list of suitable measurements is drawn up and can often be resolved. If it cannot, there is no cause to despair: every observer can legitimately make his own comparisons so long as his criteria are stated, and his findings can be used by others to the extent that they seem relevant to whatever purpose they have in mind themselves.

How is the comparative efficiency of a series of institutions to be measured? 'It depends on what you mean by . . .' is the obvious answer to a question of this sort. Efficiency can mean different things, a surprising number of different things, in fact, if one goes on repeating the question. The bigger the question the more obvious the difficulty becomes. Undergraduates are taught early that it is meaningless to ask which electoral system is best: 'for a working majority or fair representation?' is a standard reply, and if fairness is the criterion, do we mean numerically or in terms of power (is it fair that a proportionately represented minority party should hold the balance of power?). The dangers are most obvious when we come to the traditional big question of political science: which country has the most democratic system of government? It was loose, often implicitly value-laden use of such terms that partly justified the attack on unscientific comparisons. Generally, moreover, such questions naturally raise the 'why?' issue. There may be some satisfaction for the political scientists of the country that comes top—or near the top—in a league table of governments measured according to some standard of democracy (that they may be tempted, unconsciously one hopes, to choose winning criteria is another matter), but the purpose of the comparison is usually to discover why one system works better than another.

This level of comparison is not at issue here, however. At levels more modest, for example the protection of citizens by administrative courts or parliamentary commissioners, it is not too difficult to agree on measurements of effectiveness. It is only the dedicated methodologist who makes discourse impossible; the sensible man carries on meanwhile as best he can, making practical comparisons and acting on them, often, practically enough. Let us revert, therefore, to the more manageable problem of comparing specific institutions rather than entire governmental systems. One is commonly told that one cannot take institutions out of their national environment for this purpose, any more than goldfish out of a bowl: both depend on their environment for their existence.

Environments, of course, are likely to differ. Broadly enough defined, indeed, they are bound to differ—all other things cannot possibly be equal. Even a circumscribed environment, the administrative subsystem in which a particular governmental institution operates for example, includes a myriad of details which cannot possibly be the same in each country, nor, taken in such detail, can they differ according to a simple pattern, so that any attempt to compare a number of systems in all their aspects must inevitably lead to endless permutations. If that is one trouble with environment, there is another that can make equal nonsense of the concept. Environment itself is infinite: everything is interconnected, the entire world a seamless web. If one wishes to play absolutely safe, to neglect no factor that might possibly influence the working of an institution, one must search the entire social and political order of the country concerned and then go beyond the frontiers of the nation.

The comparison of phenomena in their environment, taken too seriously, is an activity literally without end. The purpose of a *reductio ad absurdum*, of course, is to show the need for compromise. In practice, perfection is impossible and crude tools are, in any case, not just better than no tools at all—they are often better than tools which are too fine. Common sense may allow us to limit the environmental factors that need be considered. Indeed, for certain purposes of comparison—if we are comparing how things are organised, for example, rather than why they are as they are—this is relatively easy.

Nevertheless, it would seem sensible to compare institutions in countries that are roughly similar rather than pick countries which differ so greatly that what emerges is a study nine-tenths ecological and only one-tenth focused on the starting point. If we stay with the example of administrative institutions, a marked tendency in recent years has been to compare exotic countries with cultures quite alien to our own. One has only to look at the work of the comparative administration movement in America—certainly a spearhead of comparative studies—to see this. That there were good reasons is beyond doubt, some practical (the needs of technical aid administrators), some theoretical (an interest in the methodology of comparing whole systems), and the achievements are not in dispute, but the contribution has been academic rather than useful.

If the starting point—the purpose—of comparison is to see how the institutions of one's own country can be reformed, and it is my argument that this should be a major interest of political science, then one would do well to concentrate on systems where a reasonable number of other things are likely to be more rather than less equal. This is a plea, in other words, for more comparative studies of West European institutions.

Despite all the differences between the cultures in which their administrations operate, West European states have much in common: advanced (complex and industrialised) economies with considerable mixed-economy elements; urbanised societies with relatively high levels of education, high standards of living and extensive social services; liberal–democratic politics with party and interest group participation in policy-making and with formalised protection of citizens' rights; legal–rational administrative systems with large and highly qualified bureaucracies subject to a wide variety of parliamentary and legal controls; extensive state intervention in economic and social affairs as a result of their complexity, the expectations of the public and the acceptance of considerable responsibility by the bureaucracy itself. These countries also have many broadly similar problems of administrative reform: rationalisation of an increasingly complex and over-extended administration at the centre; decentralisation to meet the demands of democracy as well as the needs of efficiency; planning for economic growth and balanced regional development; training of civil servants in new techniques; reform of Parliament to retain its control of the administration; protection of the increasingly administered citizen; further participation of citizens in policy-making.

This brings us back to our second mode of comparison of similar institutions. Even if we compare how things are, rather than why, there is another difficulty the critic may raise at this stage. This is the 'are you sure you are comparing like with like?' question—basically, the now well-worn structures and functions point.

If one compares institutions, one should not forget, though only the very absent-minded are likely to, that they may have different functions: the Mayor of Clochemerle is very different from the Mayor of Muddlecombe not simply because he is a Frenchman, operating in a French political environment, but also because, formally, he has a very different role to play in the governmental system of his country. If our main interest lies in the function (how are certain things done in countries X, Y and Z?), then perhaps we will have to isolate different institutions in each case. But I would stress that it does depend on what the focus of our interest is, and that may be either structures or functions. A seaside resort, a spa town, a ski village and a cultural centre perform rather different functions, and the intending holidaymaker would not be gathering the most useful information if he simply compared sunshine hours. On the other hand, they all form part of the tourist industry and it may be useful to compare the different needs they serve—i.e. the different functions apparently similar institutions perform. It is fair enough to point out that the American Congress is not the British Parliament; they play different roles in their respective political systems and some of these roles may be played by institutions other than Parliament in Britain and other than Congress in America. But both are legislatures and it is of some interest to compare what they do, i.e. to start with the structures and look at their functions, rather than the other way round as so many modernists advocate.

In any case, and this is really the point here, there are all sorts of internal arrangements that can be compared without overmuch worry about the environmental factors that determine their role. To stay with Congress and Parliament, some of these arrangements, the broad outlines of their committee systems for example, will fall outside this category. Many procedural details, on the other hand, are only marginally affected by the broader differences of political function and some, at least, should be transferable. It is exactly such technical studies of a limited field that may prove of immediate use to those concerned with feasible parliamentary reform. Political scientists have tended to fight shy of such humdrum research but it is worth noting that this has been the approach of practitioners' bodies such as the Inter-Parliamentary Union, presumably with practical intent.

Different starting points can thus lead the students of comparative politics to different questions. (*a*) What types of institutions perform similar functions? (*b*) What types of function do formally similar institutions perform? (*c*) In what different institutional ways can the performance of a particular type of function be organised? (*d*) in what different ways can a particular type of institution be organised?

All-important is the researcher's purpose. Now, it should be remembered that at this stage I am still really discussing the second simple sense of the word 'comparison', the evaluation of alternative institutions rather than the construction of explanatory theory. This is generally a limited exercise with some practical intent and involves questions (*c*) and (*d*). An example of question (*c*) might be 'in what different ways is economic planning institutionalised in countries X, Y and Z?' An example of question (*d*) is 'in what different ways is the work of the legislature organised in those countries?' Or, to take another example, one can first compare (question (*c*)) the different ways in which citizens are formally offered redress against maladministration in Western Europe—the ombudsman versus *Conseil d'Etat* debate—and then (question (*d*)) compare in technical detail either the ombudsmen or the administrative courts of a number of countries. Essentially, one would be describing a number of institutions, how they are formally organised and how they work in practice. What one wants to know, of course, is which arrangements are the most effective and whether they are transferable.

I have already noted the difficulties this may raise. The first can be avoided to some extent if the writer leaves evaluation to the reader: 'here are descriptions of different holiday resorts—compare them and choose the one that suits you best'. This may often be the most practical thing to do, in a piece of commissioned research for example. Alternatively, one can avoid the definitional problem by adopting criteria of effectiveness that suit the purpose in hand: how good is an institution at achieving whatever it is that we—as reformers—would like to see achieved. Often, quite adequate definitions are inherent in the institution itself: the effectiveness of a ski resort lies in the adequacy of its slopes (one can, of course, add the *après-ski* facilities as an additional measure); the effectiveness of an ombudsman lies in the extent to which he obtains redress of legitimate grievances (a difficulty here may be that his powers will vary according to the constitutional-political order in which he operates, but even then one can ask how efficiently the internal organisation of the institution allows it to deal with those matters for which it is responsible). In simple terms it is not as difficult as some make out to ask whether function A is performed better by institution x in country X than by institution y in country Y.

If one system appears to work better than another, several questions obviously follow. Are there differences within the institution that might explain their relative performance (organisa-tion, procedure, personnel)? If a plausible explanation emerges on the basis of internal differences, we may feel justified in ignoring differences of environment as an unnecessary complication. If not, we must bring the environment into our study and, if we are to complete our work in reasonable time, we must decide where to draw the limits. Common sense and some general acquaintance with the government and politics of the countries concerned will usually tell us well enough. So, however, will the study of the institutions themselves. The question 'what environmental factors are vital to the working of a particular institution?' can be trans-lated into two other questions: 'what formally external factors are in fact internal to the working of that institution?' (environmental inputs can often be treated as internalised forces); and 'what external factors are important to the effectiveness of its outputs?' (these can often be treated as a prolongation of the institution).

Having answered these questions as best we can, we come to the point that really interests the practical student of comparative politics as distinct from the theoretician: if institution x in country X performs function A better than that function is performed by institution y in country Y, would institution x also perform better than y in country Y? Here, where environmental factors become really important, we come to the second difficulty. One cannot wait for perfection in science, however. All the grains of sand on the environmental beach will not be counted and classified in our time. If the political scientist is to say anything useful, he is bound to jump gaps, judging for himself what factors are important, estimating those that have not yet been measured and balancing those that, even if quantifiable and quantified, cannot be measured in compatible terms.

This is an argument for looking at institutions in countries which have already been well studied. If one wants to compare British and European experience in some area of administration, it is probably sensible to look first at France. More is already known about French administration than about the administra-tion of other European countries. It should be easier, therefore, for the foreign observer to make sense of a French institution by placing it in its wider context than would otherwise be the case. Students of comparative politics are constantly urged to increase the number of countries studied, to diversify their interests in order to provide a wider range of data as a basis for broader generalisa-tions. This may be useful to those who want the data to construct grand theory, but it brings with it the danger of knowing less and less about more and more. The case for building on strength, for studying in further depth those countries we already know well, can be argued with equal force.

If an institution depends on its environment, the more known about that environment in advance, the better. It is easier to move from the wider system to the particular than vice versa: the student who starts with an institution and tries to move outward may, despite what has been said above, and especially if he starts *tabula rasa*, miss some important factors, misunderstand others and never see the picture whole. That apart, and concentrating on the particular institution in focus, there is the question of the availability of data. Where little is available, as is the case in too many countries, one can, of course, make a field trip to gather the material oneself. Indeed, many specialist studies are the product of such one-off investigations. That this is a time-consuming method may seem an unscholarly objection, but it is not irrelevant. Few have the time to spare, particularly at a given moment, and a study based on secondary sources is better than no study at all; that such sources may be more accurate than data collected by a newcomer to the field, though uncharitable, may be an additional reason.

Comparative studies do not lose their practical value if some of the problems raised above are virtually ignored. At the lowest level, though not a level to be despised, one can look at foreign experience to see whether there are any devices that might not have occurred to the domestic reformer if his knowledge were limited to his own national experience. This is a mode of comparison that involves no more than a juxtaposition of stories. Stories can stimulate thought. New ideas must come from somewhere.

One can go further, however, still at this level. A study of how— and how successfully—another country has tried to solve problems similar to one's own is bound to have some value, even if the lessons of foreign experience are only suggestive. In our present state of knowledge, to repeat a point I made earlier, the field of administrative engineering remains a practical art and such simple comparative studies do not come off much worse than domestic studies in the scientific value of the conclusions that can be drawn.

I now revert to my opening and the third purpose of comparisons. This is the truly scientific purpose of establishing hypotheses about political systems, in whole or part. It is not entirely clear that the term is used in this context as the ordinary man would use it. What the comparative political scientist is doing when he acts 'scientifically' is to say: similar performance can be observed in cases a, b and c and in cases x, y and z—what features have a, b and c in common, x, y and z in common, and in what do the two groups differ? From such correlations hopefully one moves to explanations. Of course, the subject is much more complicated than that, but the point is simply that in much of fashionable comparative politics the real interest seems to lie less in the actual comparisons than in the generalisations. If comparative politics is to be a science, and in so far as the core of science lies in explanation, this is reasonable enough. All I have argued is that there are other, perfectly good modes of comparison which are not scientific in that sense but which are just as interesting and probably of more immediate use.

An illustration of the tendency of others, however, to take a more exclusive view and equate comparison with causally based generalisations may be given. 'Comparative politics is concerned with significant similarities and dissimilarities in the working of political institutions and political behaviour' says the author of a recent overview of the discipline, echoing the consensus of the approaches he describes. The definition is somewhat arbitrary. Comparative law, for example, is concerned with differences between the laws of several countries, not *significant* differences where that word is used, as here, to mean signifying something for the explanation of similarities and dissimilarities in various systems rather than important in itself. I have already argued that comparison and comparative politics need not concentrate on differences relevant to the construction of general theories. The comparative lawyer needs to know foreign laws for practical purposes or, if that is not a comparative activity, conceivably because he seeks ideas to reform domestic law. In that sense, I would also query the word 'working' in the quotation. Comparative law concerns itself not only with the working of laws, but with laws as such, their formal content. Comparative government can legitimately do the same. Formal differences may be interesting in their own right as alternative ways of organising things, regardless of how they work in practice.

Where 'scientific' comparative politics does offer comparisons, moreover, the focus is often on entire political systems or on large subsystems such as the bureaucracy. This can only be handled intelligibly by gross abstraction, hence the concern with conceptual frameworks which too often provide contrasting models that are intellectually stimulating but empty of content, a legitimate pursuit of scholars but not a very practical activity. Much has been written in recent years about the nature of comparative politics, treating the subject at this third level. I get the uneasy feeling, however, that, if one measured the output, one would find the space devoted to methodology and model-making quite disproportionate to that actually describing the phenomena compared (to be fair, I am not talking here of the many excellent single-country studies set in a conceptual framework: they, however, have their own drawback in that most researchers seem to feel honour-bound to use their own framework, thus vitiating their contribution to the development of a scientifically based comparative politics).

There was a time, not long ago, when comparative politics was described as a subject in crisis. It soldiered on to its present, probably stable, state of sophisticated confusion. I have in my study a long shelf of recent books devoted to issues in comparative politics, and these are only a random selection that came my way of a much larger output. True, there is a great deal of repetition in *readers*, but even so there is too much. So much attention can only be paid to methodology because it fascinates a group of scholars. I do not buy the argument that so extensive and complex a debate is the necessary preliminary to the real work of research and comparison. Theoretically, it might be so, but I suspect that many of those involved are not even pure scientists, they are pure methodologists at heart. I cannot see why one should expect the majority of students or, indeed, of political scientists to be more than marginally interested.

The more I see of the output, the more sympathetic I feel towards the defenders of the pre-Fulton civil service with its preference for the literate over the numerate. What one misses in so much modern comparative politics—and not just in the methodology, but in its application—is an interest in the phenomena studied. Data is gathered because the researcher wishes to construct a theory, not because he is interested in the government and politics of the countries he passes through with his survey. That may be unfair, of course. Perhaps the interest is there, even the knowledge of real life politics, and it is only the methodology, the way the material has to be presented to the reader, that prevents the researcher from communicating what he really knows. But that makes the situation even worse because so much is wasted.

I have been suggesting that there are broadly three modes of comparison. A simple analogy from the world of art, bearing in mind that analogies are never quite accurate. I can line up a number of paintings in an art gallery in order to decide, by comparing them, which would look best on my wall. This is a simple, entirely untheoretical mode of comparison. I can compare the works of several painters, note similarities and thus determine who influenced whom (or at least hypothesise). This, broadly, can be thought of as middle-range theory. Finally, I can study a variety of paintings in order to discover some general principles of art, perhaps by isolating what all great paintings have in common (begging, of course, the criterion question of greatness). This is grand theory. Grand theory in political science is very much art for art's sake. It is too general, or too incomplete, to be of much help in the sorts of practical comparisons I have discussed earlier.

Middle-range theory would undoubtedly make it easier to decide whether institution x would still work well if transferred to country Y. But it would have to be hard theory, sufficiently comprehensive and sufficiently detailed, and the data would have to be available to make unnecessary the sort of jumps mentioned before. One can think of no field of political science in which this is really available.

The author already quoted asks whether comparative studies allow us to predict—and answers yes: in some cases and to some extent. Some things can be predicted 'with far better than random chances of being correct'. He adds, honestly, that 'the areas to which this applies are not very useful in terms of application'. That is true enough. Usefulness apart, some of the most important questions of politics, notably the behaviour of governmental leaders, are hardly amenable to rigorous study: dictators will not collaborate with opinion surveyors and even if they did the results would not be statistically significant. Individual decisions that determine war and peace find little place in the framework of comparative politics. Even those areas which seem amenable to generalisations, political stability for example, offer little encouragement. A 'better than random chance' that the political system of a foreign country is stable is not much of a basis for practical decisions. The history of our lifetime is a catalogue of disasters and many, I suppose, had a less than random chance of occurring.

If limited predictions in limited areas are all that comparative political science can offer, it might as well drop its scientific pretensions because we can do as well without. Other methods of study provide results no worse, some might think better because more realistic. This, of course, is recognised by practitioners. 'A measure of the primitive stage at which political science still finds itself as a useful predictive or applied science is the negligible employment in government service of political scientists as such compared with others.'

It would be different, of course, if there was any likelihood that greater certainty would come once the methodological debate was concluded and a massive theoretically orientated programme of fact-finding completed. But even if political scientists were ever to agree long enough to achieve this, even if research councils were to pour money into the enterprise, how far would we advance in the foreseeable future? And yet this academic approach must not be denied. Progress, in science as in other fields, has nearly always been the result of faith and has, itself, often been quite unpredictable. It is always easier to criticise than to innovate. In this country, more than most, we already have too many anti-intellectuals, hostile to the development of theory, even in the field of political science. Perhaps—just perhaps—a dose of methodology might inspire one or two students so that a future generation of political scientists will have some names to match those of the United States.

The burden of the present argument is that—fortunately—the limitations of science do not matter as much as some committed modernists might think. The purpose of this chapter, in any case, is not primarily to knock grand theory or even the rigorous approach of the scientific political scientist. Indeed, in a later chapter, lamenting the state of public administration studies in Britain, I emphasise the need for more theory in this field, not for its own sake but as an underpinning for practical courses in administration for administrators and as a help to those concerned with problems of administrative reform.

What is also needed, however, is the diversion of some energies into simple—theoretically simple-minded, if you like—comparative studies, practically orientated. Even single-country studies of some particular institution are useful in this respect, if comparisons are made *en passant* by the writer or can be made without too much difficulty by the reader for himself, and illustrations of this approach will be given in the next chapter.

As political science has become more scientific it has, in an odd way, had fewer and fewer useful things to say. Too self-conscious about the philosophical problems of linking prescriptive to empirical statements, it has often abandoned overt prescription altogether (that, of course, is not to deny the hidden values embedded in much of contemporary political science, but hidden values are not much use as guide-lines to reform). Over-intellectual, it has concentrated on the development of theories too grand for practical application (few countries are thinking seriously of changing their entire systems of government, and the sort of crisis situations in which they do are not conducive to consultation with political scientists). Alternatively, too obsessed with quantification, it has concentrated on what is quantifiable regardless of its practical use (voting behaviour is undoubtedly important, but as psychologists have shown it to be largely fixed, they cannot be said to be working in a field where they have useful policy advice to give: indeed, they are largely ignored by those who manage election campaigns in Britain).

The theme of my argument, then, and I will return to it, is that scholarship has a two-fold duty: the advancement of science and the relief of man's estate. The two are often linked, but the link may take too long to work out and—no less true because hackneyed—in the long run we are all dead. What we need meanwhile is simple studies of specific foreign institutions, explicitly or implicitly comparative, topics chosen for their contemporary usefulness, and this, again I hope will underline the subsequent illustrations. If we are concerned with the decentralisation of governmental functions, for example, as was the Royal Commission on the Constitution recently, then let us look at the experience of a number of foreign countries not too dissimilar to our own. The way they arrange things will surely throw some light on what could be done here. The emphasis, to repeat a point already laboured, probably needs to be old-fashionedly institutional because the reform of government nearly always depends on a formal change in institutional arrangements.

To recapitulate, therefore, I suggest that there are three levels of legitimate comparison in political studies. First, there is the simple juxtaposition of foreign-country accounts, often absorbing in their own right just because they are different from us, important in that as citizens of the world we should know something about the internal politics of major powers, pedagogically essential as background to conceptually based courses. Second, there is the straightforward descriptive comparison of specific institutions with relatively unsophisticated evaluation and perhaps some thought about transferability, the purpose essentially practical but none the less the traditional purpose of political science, namely the improvement of one's own system of government. Third, no less important but no more, there is the comparison that is intended to develop scientific theory.

The plea I am making is simply for an acceptance of all three modes and, above all, for an acceptance by academics of their social responsibilities. Their research should be chosen more frequently for its usefulness, not at the cost of their political beliefs but sometimes, perhaps, at the cost of their scientific principles. Perhaps, then, they would come to be employed by government services. Even if not, they would have made the contribution they can.

Lessons of
Foreign Experience

'And *other* countries,' asked the French gentleman when it was explained to him that Britain was blessed over all others in its constitutional arrangements, 'they do how?' Mr Podsnap's answer is well known. 'They do, Sir, they do—I am sorry to be obliged to say it—*as* they do.' That sorrowful view was understandable in the past, though the foreigner, thinking it a little peculiar that providence should favour so small an island so exclusively, may never have been entirely convinced. The mood has changed and for one reason or another we now often look wistfully abroad ourselves: it is our turn to ask 'they do how?' and wonder whether there may be some lessons in their manner of doing.

Some of the interest in foreign experience is connected with the 'What's wrong with Britain?' debate running from the 'Suicide of Nation?' issue of *Encounter* in 1963 to the *Spiegel* issue entitled 'Chaos über England' a decade later. The contrast with apparently more successful governmental arrangements was brought out in Brian Chapman's *British Government Observed* and Andrew Shonfield's *Modern Capitalism*. Controversial literature aside, a fairly practical interest, notably in French economic planning, had already developed. Later, of course, there was the Scandinavian ombudswagon which we joined with the establishment of our own Parliamentary Commissioner for Administration.

Two major recent inquiries into the working of British government took some foreign experience into account. The Committee on the Civil Service actually sent some of its members to visit France, Sweden and the USA and their impressions appeared as an appendix to the 1968 Report. These were generally favourable and the Report itself claims to have been influenced by what they

saw. There were many complimentary references to the French
civil service throughout, for example, though to be fair to earlier
writers these looked more like the by then established anti-
conventional wisdom than the fruit of original observation.
However that may be, many of the recommendations clearly bore
the stamp of foreign experience. The Royal Commission on the
Constitution, for its part, commissioned research on various
aspects of federalism, regionalism and administrative decentralisation in France, Germany, Sweden and the USA and these studies
were published as research papers. Much of the information was
summarised at appropriate points in the body of the 1973 Report,
with some sign of interest but almost no enthusiasm. Though
'Lessons from Abroad' was actually used in one place as a sub-
heading, the general verdict was 'alien to our tradition'. To that
extent, at least, the commissioners were not following Mr Podsnap: they saw that things were done well enough elsewhere but
felt that little of it was transferable in practice, even theoretically
desirable, in the context of our own way of government. This
difference between the two reports may partly reflect their different
scope: civil service organisation may be more easily comparable
than wider constitutional arrangements (though, in fact, some of
the Civil Service Committee's recommendations had constitutional
implications). The composition of the two bodies, the attitude of
members, the role of personalities and the way the two reports
were written may have had some influence. Another possible factor
—and it would be interesting to speculate further about this—
is the existence in the one case of a literature of *haute vulgarisa-
tion* and a background of ideas 'in the air', not matched in the
other.

The purpose of this chapter is to look at how the academic
studying foreign institutions can try to contribute to this stock of
ideas. Over the years I have looked at a number of institutions—
in Germany the Federal Railways, the Chancellorship and the
Military Ombudsman, in France public enterprise, the civil service
and the prefectoral system—primarily to describe, but also to
explain their character by reference to their environment and to
the theories underlying them. Where the purpose was not also
explicitly to draw comparisons with Britain, these inevitably
emerged: the explanation of foreign institutions, indeed, almost by
definition involves explanation of why they differ from our own.
I also found myself making at least passing comments on the wider
relevance of foreign systems.

In two cases the intention was clear. The first was the study of
specialists in the French civil service, part of a volume I edited on

the role of professionals (as compared to generalists) in Britain, Australia, France, Germany, Sweden and the USA—this was commissioned by the Institution of Professional Civil Servants, presented as evidence to the Committee on the Civil Service and later published in book form with a general conclusion about specialists and generalists in government. The second was the study of the French prefectoral system, requested by the Royal Commission on the Constitution as a case study of integrated administrative decentralisation and published by it as a research paper. These were in no sense comparative studies in the 'scientific' meaning of the term. The focus in each case was a single foreign country, though in both cases I did try to work out a wider analytic framework. The real purpose of the paper on the French prefects was to see whether any useful ideas emerged from foreign experience (the judge of usefulness not being myself), without too much concern for problems of transferability, though I did add that the study of how—and how successfully—another country had tried to solve a common administrative problem should be at least suggestive with regard to what can be done elsewhere. The paper on the French civil service, on the other hand, was clearly prescriptive in intention—not just because it was commissioned by an interested party but because it dealt with a matter about which I had firmly held and long advocated views of my own.

The present chapter looks briefly at these topics. There is no pretence that they are chosen for any reason other than their availability: this is not a textbook on comparative institutions and there is no need to cover the ground comprehensively, though in fact a fair variety of subjects are covered. What I hope to do is to illustrate the approach advocated in the last chapter, to show what can be learnt from comparison of institutions as a practical activity. This manner of illustration is practical in another sense because it draws on the workshop of one academic. The autobiographical note is not, therefore, I hope, as irelevant as it might otherwise sound.

PUBLIC ENTERPRISE

Things have changed too much in Britain and in France to make the specific conclusions of my early study of French public enterprise reliable today: some, indeed, are no longer relevant. The major impression, however, and that has not changed, is that similar functions—and the operation of railways, the mining of coal or the distribution of electricity cannot really be so dissimilar across the Channel—can be organised in very different ways from those to which we are accustomed. Obviously enough, this reflects the different governmental frameworks into which they fall. And yet, in these industrial and commercial undertakings one might expect internal factors, technological and managerial, to out-weigh the administrative environment and impose their own common patterns of organisation. That is not the case under-lines the importance of administrative cultures in shaping even public enterprise.

Though some of the forms of organisation and control deve-loped by the French may well appear transferable as discrete bits of machinery, because they are adapted to their environment they are less likely to work so efficiently in another context. But that is not my point here. What I want to stress is that there appears to be no overriding logic of organisation that is internal to public enterprise. That, again, may appear obvious enough, but it is worth remembering that much of the British debate about proper forms of organisation for nationalised industries was conducted rather as if there were such a logic. For example, administrative or parliamentary controls that reached too far into the enterprise were avoided because of the doctrine that one cannot have efficient management if there is always someone looking over one's shoulder. That was a bit of introspective reasoning which could have been tested against foreign experience—and found a false generalisation.

While it may be hard to draw lessons from one system that are directly applicable to another, one can—as I suggested earlier—look at foreign devices without much regard to their context, or even their record. There is nothing wrong with the sort of com-parative study that is merely fishing aboard for ideas, abstracting institutions from their environment, even taking them at their formal face value, to see whether they suggest new ways of arrang-ing one's own system. The points made in the foregoing paragraph become relevant here. Comparative studies also lead one to look with a fresh eye at the assumptions underlying domestic arrange-ments. The simplest lesson of foreign experience is that there are probably more ways of doing things, even within the con-straints of one's own system, than one might otherwise realise. One need not ask whether major changes are desirable, indeed that may be a matter of politics: what one can try to show is that they are not necessarily impossible. As the range of the possible is seen to be wider, a more flexible approach to reform should develop.

The wide range of French nationalised industries is worth

mentioning in this respect because it seems to indicate that there is no limit to the *sort* of undertaking that can be nationalised successfully. That there may be limits to the extent of nationalisation in any particular sector if competition is to be maintained is another thing, though even this can be organised by competing state enterprises. The Renault motor works, the French Line and another major shipping company, the *Crédit Lyonnais* and other great deposit banks, and half the countries insurance companies are in the public sector without it making very much difference to their performance either way: the customers are probably not even aware that they are dealing with public enterprise and they, for their part, are dealt with no differently than by private competitors. It appears quite possible to nationalise such undertakings without serious repercussions, either internal or external, if the main purpose is a simple transfer of ownership to the state rather than industrial reorganisation. One might have expected bank depositors, as a relatively conservative section of the community, to move their accounts to the private sector but there was virtually no reaction to nationalisation. True, the issue of nationalisation is not used in France as a form of product differentiation for a two-party system—in that sense the political context is different—but that probably does not alter the underlying point.

The wide range of institutional forms adopted for the public sector, mentioned in an earlier chapter, is equally relevant. The state tobacco monopoly, for example, is run on near-civil service lines and does not appear to leave the French smoker particularly unsatisfied. More interesting here is the fact that some nationalised industries were transformed into public corporations while others retained the status of state-owned companies. *Electricité de France* is the former, *Air France* the latter. In France this legal distinction appears to make little difference to how they operate, but clearly this need not be the case. There are obvious advantages in the use of company form to clothe nationalised industries, not least that it makes the technical process of nationalisation much simpler, possibly reducing it to a mere transfer of share ownership and avoiding the need to draft new statutes. Interesting, too, are the experiments in mixed economy companies with private and public shareholders, the latter including the state, local authorities and other nationalised industries.

The extent to which public corporations are seen as services of the state has been discussed earlier. This attitude has spilled over to the relations between government and other forms of public enterprise. The public sector tends to be used with less diffidence as a prolongation of public policy. Extensive supervision is accepted and some of this is internal to the undertaking: it does not appear significantly to undermine the efficiency of managers, whatever the effect on policy. The advantages and disadvantages of each device can be argued but some at least would repay study. There are obvious advantages in attaching financial and technical controllers to each enterprise, working within—and with—the enterprise. The presence of government commissioners at board meetings may facilitate communication. The attempt to co-ordinate purchasing and construction contracts in the public sector through a formal committee system is interesting. Other examples could be given. From different points of view, one could look at the notion of representative boards, at the complex system of formalised workers' participation, at the role of national consumers' councils, and even at the role of the parliamentary committees in the Fourth Republic.

There are practical and historical reasons why certain services are administered by government departments in this country, while others take the form of public corporations. The rationale of the distinction is not always clear, though the recent transfer of Post Office from one sector to the other was an attempt to apply some logic. It was the fact that similar functions can be organised in different institutional ways which led me to look at the German Federal Railways, run on modified civil service lines.[1]

The first German railway was opened in 1835 and the next fifty years saw the parallel development of public and private enterprise. It must be remembered that Germany then consisted of numerous independent states with different policies. The rapid expansion of railways strengthened economic ties and brought the citizens of the various states closer together: by contributing to the unification of Germany they early acquired a political significance. Against the wishes of Bismarck, railways remained a state rather than central government matter when the Empire was established in 1871, but he did nationalise the Prussian system. This move was closely linked with his decision to promote industrial expansion by the establishment of a protected economy and was also intended to strengthen the military position by allowing for the rapid mobilisation and deployment of troops. By the end of the century all lines were state controlled. From early days, therefore, the railways were intended to serve the purposes of the state. They also served the public, of course—but here, too, it was clear that from the start they were seen as public utilities rather

[1] Drawn from my 'German Federal Railways—A State Administered System', *Parliamentary Affairs* (Spring 1964).

than as commercial undertakings. Another obvious point is that this nationalisation took place before the halfway house between public administration and private enterprise had been discovered: there was no alternative to civil service administration in the public sector. Both traditions have survived.

The Bonn constitution and the subsequent Railway Law made no fundamental change. The *Deutsche Bundesbahn* is the responsibility of the Federal Government. It is administered as a separate unit but its status is little more than that. Technically—and untranslatably—it is a *Sondervermoegen*, a 'specialised property', assets separated from other property of the state, receipts and expenditure not part of ordinary government funds (this has certain legal repercussions and repercussions for parliamentary-budgetary procedures). Though it can act in law, sign contracts, sue and be sued, issue bonds in its own name, and thus looks to the public like a corporate person, it has no such identity: it is a service of the Government. Unlike the *établissement public*, unlike any term the French would employ even of such state-administered services as the tobacco monopoly, it is a *Bundesbehörde*, a federal public authority, executing state functions and thus exercising state authority. This is symbolised by use of the national flag and the federal arms. It is also reflected in use of the terminology of public administration: the railways levy dues, for example, rather than charge fares. Indeed, the non-industrial staff are civil servants. If railways administration is part of the public service in this sense, the railways operate a public service in another sense also: they have a public utility character (*gemeinwirtschaftlicher Charakter*, roughly equivalent to the French *service public*) which may override ordinary commercial considerations.

The *Bundesbahn* nevertheless has organisational characteristics that might lead one to confuse it with a public corporation. It does not form part of the Ministry of Transport. It has its own board and chief executives legally responsible for the management of affairs. The Minister of Transport is not part of the administrative structure; he is not, as the German would say, an 'internal organ' but an outsider with powers of control. The situation thus differs from the postal service which also forms a *Sondervermoegen* but which is administered by a government department under the direct authority of a minister. Although railway staff are described as *direct* federal officials (*unmittelbare Bundesbeamte*), this is true of their personnel status rather than of their position in an administrative hierarchy. The highest authority for ordinary civil servants is a minister (he is ultimately responsible, for example, in disciplinary matters); in the railways this position is taken by the management and the minister cannot give orders directly to subordinates as he can to his own staff.

The limits of this organisational separateness become clear, however, as soon as one looks at the powers of the minister. He has, in the first place, wide powers of direction to ensure that the railways operate in accordance with the economic, financial, social and transport policies of the government. This is not quite the same as the power to issue *ad hoc* directions in Britain, presumably where a conflict has arisen: in the German situation it is taken for granted that the railways work within the policy defined by the Government. Most board decisions of any importance are subject to prior ministerial approval and all other decisions affecting the interests of the state or the *Bundesbahn* can be suspended by him pending a cabinet decision. He has specific powers with regard to staffing to ensure the unity of the civil service and the application of its regulations and must also approve senior appointments. He can object to tariff changes and can impose changes which he considers in the public interest so long as the Government covers subsequent losses; he also has some say in the operation of services. Finally, he has general powers of supervision to ensure that the railways are administered in accordance with regulations (this of course, applies to all forms of public transport), that rolling stock and installations are maintained and that account is taken of technical developments (acting on behalf of the state as owner of the assets). He may for any of these purposes instruct his own officials to inspect the offices of the *Bundesbahn* or employ *Bundesbahn* officials for the purpose: his functions may be exercised by internal controls compared to the rather more external relations found in Britain.

The Railway Law states the broad principles according to which the service is to be administered: it is to be operated on commercial lines in a manner that serves the interests of the national economy. Reference to commercial principles in the law does not mean that the railways are to be run like a business in the sense that all but exceptional services should pay for themselves. It refers to methods of accountancy and, within the limits imposed by civil service organisation, to managerial techniques. The Law does, however, also say that there should be an overall balance of accounts and to that extent losses on services of public interest should be covered elsewhere. The key phrase, however, remains the national interest and that is a matter for the Government to determine. Attempts can be made to meet obligations imposed in this way by raising charges in areas where government policy is not involved, but if this cannot be done there is no alternative but government subsidies: a drastic pruning of services to eliminate losses fits neither into the law nor the underlying principles of state service.

In fact, the railways have been consistently used as instruments of policy. Freight rates have served all sorts of purposes. So have passenger fares: at one time something like half the tickets issued were at reduced prices, not for commercial reasons (e.g. to increase traffic) but as deliberate subsidies to sections of the community—the *Bundesbahn* has been described as the largest welfare organisation in the country. There is something to be said for this approach: if the railways do form part of the federal administration, it is not illogical that they should be used to promote government policies in the same way as other services of the state. This certainly increases the armoury of weapons which the Government may use to influence economic development and promote social welfare. Subsidies, of course, are the price. The 'Beeching' solution, however, was rejected from the start on grounds of political theory. Allowing for that, the record appears not to be a bad one. A recent English book on the social economy of Germany points out that West Germany has retained a larger rail network than Britain, carrying more passengers and much more freight. It is also, it seems, 'unquestionably the most comfortable system in the world'.

The *Bundesbahn* has its problems, just as British Rail. I am not suggesting that our problems can be solved by copying the philosophy, or even the administrative principles of the German institution. The purpose of the foregoing was to show just two things. A commercial and industrial undertaking can be managed as efficiently (some would say more efficiently) within an entirely different organisational structure to that to which we are accustomed. In such a structure, seen, that is, as part of the state, it can more easily pursue very different (some would say more useful) policies.

CHANCELLOR AND OMBUDSMAN

The constitutional bases of the German system of chancellor government have been described in an earlier chapter. One of the points I made at the end of the original study was the obvious one that as the functions of government become more complex and urgent, the need for adequate machinery to ensure the continuous formulation of overall policy becomes ever more apparent: cabinets and cabinet committees are no longer adequate for this purpose. Things have changed in Britain and they have changed in Germany, each moving away from its constitutional ideal type. The move to prime-ministerial government in Britain has continued. Edward Heath had something of the Adenauer style in his relations to other members of the government, so this is partly a question of personality, but there were also institutional changes that strengthened his position, notably the establishment of a 'think tank' (technically in the service of the Cabinet, but it is not hard to see here and in other developments the beginnings of a real Chancellor's Office). In Germany, on the other hand, coalition government clearly weakened Willy Brandt's position, so that in practice he did not have the sole responsibility for policy the constitution allotted him. This does not make it less interesting to study German arrangements for the policy-making and co-ordinating functions of government. These can be examined from a technical point of view, as organisational and procedural elements in the machinery of government, without too much worry about how they are affected by the personalities involved or changes in the political environment.

There is no room for such an exercise here, but the point can be made that German doctrine about the Chancellor's powers and the existence of long-established Chancellor's Office *do* provide the constitutional framework into which such arrangements can be fitted. This brings me to the second point I made at the conclusion of my original study. Modern democracy requires clearly organised political responsibility. This is more easily fixed on one man than on several. The trend to prime-ministerial or presidential government appears to be general. The German constitution provides for it. By this I do not mean that it is always a fact—the exact distribution of power is bound to fluctuate for a variety of reasons and so is the extent to which Parliament and public see the Chancellor as personally responsible for the policy of his Government. What the German system provides is a theory which matches the trend towards a 'personalisation' of power (to use a hackneyed and somewhat ambiguous phrase). In Britain, where we have to wrestle with the meaning of constitutional principles, disengaging these, as often as not, from practice conveniently described as convention, the situation is altogether murkier. Perhaps, in continental legalistic fashion, underpinned by political theory, we should be rethinking, in order to define more clearly, the proper relationship between Prime Minister, Cabinet, Parliament and people.

The literature on ombudsmen has swollen beyond measure. The German ombudsman differs from the common run, however: he is a soldiers', not a citizens', defender. That is an area to which we have not yet thought of extending our own system and to that extent a look at the German experience may be interesting.[1] As one might expect, the institution was copied from Sweden where a second—*Militieombudsman*—was appointed as a result of army reforms in the nineteenth century. The question of an ombudsman for civil affairs did not really arise in Germany: the citizen is protected by an old-established network of administrative courts, to which was added some elements of parliamentary control over administration. When a conscript army was re-established, measures were taken to guarantee soldiers their constitutional rights and machinery was devised to protect them against abuse of authority. As we shall see, this was similar in part to the machinery that exists to protect civilians and civil servants. In the light of German experience, however, an additional safeguard seemed desirable. The idea of an ombudsman was first raised by a Member of Parliament who had taken refuge in Sweden during the Nazi period and several other members subsequently went there to study the institution. When adopted, it formed part of wider reforms and something must be said first about these.

For obvious reasons, the German constitution of 1949 contained no provisions for armed forces. It was not long, however, before the Federal Republic was pressed to contribute to western defence. Fears of German militarism led to proposals for a European Defence Community of which German troops would form an integral part and a treaty to this end was ratified by the German Parliament—but rejected by the French. The constitution having been amended to permit the re-establishment of armed forces and the reintroduction of compulsory military service in 1954, more detailed amendments were made in 1965. Back-benchers of the government parties joined with the opposition in demanding that the political control of the army should be constitutionally defined and the rights of soldiers constitutionally protected before any build-up of forces started, and—a reflection of the influence of the German Parliament, sometimes underrated—imposed their wishes on a reluctant Government.

Mirabeau had coined the phrase that Prussia was not a country with an army but an army with a country, and this description remained to some extent true of the Empire. In the Weimar Republic, on the other hand, the army had tended to become a state within the state, neither master nor subordinate of the Government but a rival to it. This was possible constitutionally because the Commander-in-Chief was responsible directly to the

---

[1] Drawn from my 'Parliamentary Commissioner for Military Affairs in the Federal Republic of Germany', *Political Studies* (February 1964).

President who exercised supreme military authority, by-passing the Cabinet: the Minister of Defence had only limited administrative functions. As the officer corps was largely hostile to the democratic republic, this arrangement had unfortunate results. The politicians of the Bonn Republic were determined to ensure primacy of the political authority: the armed forces were to be controlled by the democratically chosen Government of the country, responsible to Parliament; military policy was to reflect political aims and not some supposedly non-political national interest determined by the army itself. The Minister of Defence now exercises supreme military authority. In the Ministry of Defence—as part of the 'civilianisation' of military policy—many key positions were occupied by civil servants, while the senior military commander was downgraded to the relatively undistinguished status of Inspector General.

Strengthening the position of the minister was one way of strengthening parliamentary control. So was the establishment of a special defence committee of the popularly elected chamber. This differs from most other committees in significant ways: it has constitutional status where others owe their existence to the rules of Parliament; it continues to function in the parliamentary recess; unlike the legislative committees, it has supervisory and investigating functions, and considerable powers to this end which may be exercised on the motion of a quarter of its members. It is part of the Parliamentary Commissioner's duty to aid it in its work.

At the same time the legislatures were determined to counteract militaristic tendencies within the army itself. In the past officers had developed an outlook which separated them from the rest of society, forming a caste with its own rules and ethos. At a lower level, the army had acquired a reputation for exceedingly harsh discipline: soldiers were trained, often brutally, to the 'obedience of corpses'. The new army, by contrast, was to consist of specially trained and equipped civilians doing a particular job of work and the phrase 'citizens in uniform' was widely accepted. Numerous measures were taken to implement this concept and to ensure that soldiers remained fully-fledged members of society. Some of these —by far the least successful—were designed to educate officers and other ranks for democracy. The Parliamentary Commissioner has a duty to evaluate and report on the education activities of the army.

The Bonn constitution declared that the dignity of man was inviolable and laid down a catalogue of basic rights. These were to apply to members of the armed forces, though with necessary limitations. What it does not allow, as *did* the Weimar constitution, is infringement of human dignity for the general purpose of military training (the so-called *Manneszucht* or instilling of soldierly qualities). These rights were confirmed in the Soldiers Law which stated that soldiers had the same rights and the same duties as other citizens, subject only to specified restrictions justified by the needs of military service (e.g. aspects of the right of assembly and the right of collective petition). Officers may only give orders compatible with international law, the constitution, the ordinary law of the land and military regulations. Within these limits, the soldier has the duty of obedience, comradeship, truthfulness and secrecy. He may not engage in party political activities while on duty and must be of good behaviour while off duty. In return—and this is additional to his rights as a citizen—he has rights with regard to pay, maintenance and welfare, and may take action against the state in the same way as a civil servant if he considers himself unjustly deprived. The Parliamentary Commissioner plays a role in all these fields.

Another fundamental change, reflecting the civilianisation of the army, is to be found in the organisation of military justice. The military criminal code covers all the more serious offences that may be committed by soldiers (mutiny, desertion, disobedience) and, against them, by officers (abuse of power of command or of disciplinary powers, mistreatment, degradation of human dignity). Cases under the code are tried by the ordinary criminal courts. Prosecution is the responsibility of the ordinary public prosecutors' offices and they are bound to prosecute in all but trivial matters if the evidence is sufficient (this is the German version of the Rule of Law, much stricter than the British): an aggrieved party may appeal against their failure to act. Military disciplinary regulations cover lesser offences and these are dealt with by superior officers or military tribunals. The latter are parallel to the disciplinary tribunals for the civil service and appeal from them lies to the federal disciplinary court. Disputes arising out of the soldiers' 'employee' relationship with the state (pay, grading, promotion, leave, pensions) are dealt with by the ordinary administrative courts in the same way as civil servants. The military career is thus assimilated as far as possible to the civil service career. It is one of the duties of the Parliamentary Commissioner to keep an eye on the administration of military justice and report on its working.

The constitution declares that anyone may appeal to the courts if he feels that his rights have been infringed by a public authority and this right is enjoyed by members of the armed forces like anyone else. The constitution also states that everyone has the right to address requests or complaints to the administrative authorities or the legislative assemblies (this is the right of petition). Individually, soldiers may petition Parliament. Elaborate provisions of a more practical nature have also been made in the military complaints regulations for cases in which recourse to the courts is not possible or appears undesirable to the complainant. The soldier may address a formal complaint to his superior officer and, if he obtains no satisfaction, may take the matter further up the hierarchy; he may by-pass hierarchic channels and go straight to the Minister of Defence; he may address himself to the Parliamentary Commissioner. The law on soldiers' representatives further provides for the election by officers, NCOs and other ranks in each unit of representatives enjoying the confidence of their fellows, a mild version of a shop steward system.

An important place in the constitutional amendments of 1956 was taken by the establishment of a Parliamentary Commissioner for Military Affairs. He was given a dual role: to protect the 'citizen in uniform' and to assist Parliament in supervision of the armed forces. He was, therefore, not merely to be a 'complaints man' but to exercise a broad watching brief on developments in the army, reporting to Parliament (and thus public) on the trends he discerned. He is elected by the lower chamber without prior debate (this to prevent his position from being undermined in advance by public discussion of his acceptability). Only two qualifications are required for the office: a minimum age of 35 and at least one year's military service. It was made clear in the debate that a professional soldier was not wanted, rather a 'man of character' (the Parliamentary Commissioners actually appointed were in fact senior ex-officers, but their military service lay in the past and they had not reached the highest ranks: they were certainly not senior 'establishment' figures).

There has been some discussion about the exact status of the Commissioner. While much of this appears academic to the British observer, more concerned with the reality of functions than with theoretical problems of law, it should be remembered that Germany has constitutional and administrative courts which may be called upon to settle such disputes. The original debate appeared to centre on the constitutional statement that he safeguards the rights of soldiers *and* assists Parliament: the suggestion was that he acts as a wholly independent constitutional organ in the first capacity, as a dependent agent of Parliament in the latter. The subsequent law on the Commissioner's office, however, clearly made him an officer of Parliament. In practice he is an officer who may sometimes act on directives but generally uses his own discretion on Parliament's behalf. There is another way of looking at this. Though elected and removed by Parliament, once appointed he is a civil servant and, as such, comes under the authority of the President of the lower chamber. This must not be misunderstood: he is not a simple subordinate, carrying out the latter's instructions. The President's supervision relates to administrative and financial matters (thus the Commissioner's budget forms part of the budget of the parliamentary administration); it is also concerned with the good conduct and application to duty of the Commissioner and his staff. His position in this respect is not very different from that of judges who come under the administrative supervision of the Ministry of Justice without this necessarily impairing their judicial independence. This question, too, is not as academic as it may sound as a fair number of administrative disputes have in fact arisen. It does mean, however, that his status is lower than that of the Swedish counterpart. More useful practical questions relate to the organisation and work procedures of his office but these are too technical to be treated here.

It is hard to define the Commissioner's *general* powers of supervision and report. The law itself states that he may conduct investigations as soon as he becomes aware of a breach of rights or of the principles of moral and democratic leadership. This narrow interpretation has never been maintained. In 1961, for example, the Commissioner explained that he saw himself as the eyes and ears of Parliament, with a duty to keep a finger on the pulse of developments in the army and, where necessary, to recommend administrative or legal reform. This leaves him considerable initiative in the problems he deals with, as he is not tied to the receipt of complaints, and allows him to make recommendations that go well beyond generalisations arising out of the investigation of specific cases. His reports, in fact, are in part reports on the state of the army (though it has now been laid down that he should not comment on military policy as distinct from matters such as morale, discipline and welfare).

His more concrete duty, of course, is to protect individual members of the armed forces. He may undertake tours of inspection and ask for complaints or he may receive these from the complainants themselves. There are two limitations in the latter case: complaints must be made by an individual and not a group, and they must not be anonymous. The Commissioner is bound by rules of secrecy (though there are practical limitations on this as matters cannot be dealt with effectively unless the responsible authorities are informed); complainants are guaranteed that there will be no punishment or discrimination against them as a result of their action (though the courts have held that abusive generalisations are not genuine complaints within the meaning of the law and therefore do not entitle the soldier to immunity). The Commissioner has extensive powers of investigation: he can, for example, demand any information he requires, including the sight of files, from either the Minister of Defence or from any subordinate authorities, including military and civil offices, officers and officials. He is also entitled to request the aid of other authorities, the same interauthority co-operation that all public authorities are bound to give one another. He cannot, on the other hand, compel the attendance of witnesses or require evidence under oath.

When we come to look at his powers of enforcing redress, however, we find that they are virtually non-existent. It is reasonable that he should not be able to give direct orders to the military authorities who are the subject of complaints, but he cannot even institute legal procedings under the procedure outlined earlier: in this respect his powers are markedly inferior to those of the Swedish ombudsman. In practice he has two possibilities: he can communicate his views to the Ministry of Defence or the commanding officer concerned or he can pass the matter to the public prosecutor's office. The former course of action is the most common and can, of course, be relatively informal. Often it is enough to bring an issue to the notice of a sufficiently high level in the military hierarchy for the army to rectify the situation of its own accord. Otherwise the Commissioner must rely on his powers of persuasion and for this reason it is as important that he should be *persona grata* with the officer corps as that he should have the confidence of the rank and file and of Parliament. All else failing, he could report to Parliament, either in a special report dealing with a single incident or by bringing up the case in his annual report. This has not been found necessary, however, and the cases that have been described in his reports have been included anonymously to illustrate his work or give concrete examples of the general problems found.

There is a steady flow of complaints. Interestingly, in view of the original purpose of the institution, relatively few relate to the infringement of basic rights or of the penal and disciplinary codes. The issue of what constitutes degrading treatment, and thus an infringement of the inviolable dignity of man, nevertheless remains a real one. Even if the principle is broken on occasion—and there have been notorious cases reported in the Press—much of what a

British NCO would regard as normal is probably illegal in Germany and can be dealt with by the courts as well as the Commissioner. A large number of cases, on the other hand, deal with what can be described as conditions of employment questions. Some are career problems (promotion, professional training facilities); others are welfare problems (married families' housing, food and accommodation, recreation facilities, leave arrangements). Another category relates to the organisation of service activities (excessive drill or guard duties). It will be seen that the rights the Commissioner may be called upon to defend are far reaching. If one takes together the soldier's rights as a citizen in uniform and his rights as an employee of the state, it is clear that almost any complaint about life in the army can be brought to the Commissioner's notice.

It is hard to assess the success of all the changes described here. The character of the German army has certainly changed. True, notorious cases have been reported and there is a running criticism of military attitudes—but this must be seen in perspective. In comparison to the German army before 1945 improvement is so obvious as to require no comment. More interesting, though harder to make, is comparison with the armies in other western democratic states today: impressionistically, at least, the German soldier is in a not unfavourable position. There are similar difficulties in assessing the work of the Parliamentary Commissioner. The office has been beset by personal troubles and there have been a number of scandals. Because so much depends on one man, this is a case of a piece of machinery which, unlike most others, *does* depend rather heavily on personalities. It nevertheless has considerable credits. The annual reports, though sometimes controversial, largely because their scope has been so much wider than originally intended, have performed a useful function in stimulating public debate. The 'complaints man' function has been able to remedy a surprising number of individual grievances. Something like half of the complainants' wishes have been met in whole or part as a result of the Commissioner's intervention. The case statistics make those of the Parliamentary Commissioner for Administration in Britain look trivial.

I can conclude this section with the concluding paragraph of my original article which seems no less relevant now than when I wrote it. The German soldier is formally well protected against abuse and not badly protected in practice. A variety of post-war reforms have contributed to this. Complaints are bound to occur. This lies in the character of military service which will never be wholly agreeable. Means have been found, however, for dealing with legitimate grievances. It is true that the German army had an unfortunate reputation for harsh discipline and failure to respect the dignity of its soldiers in the past. That particular period of history is now past and a different political climate prevails. But there are always dangers of abuse. These exist in all armies and lie to some extent in the nature of military organisation. Germany has at least learnt a lesson from its terrible experience. It has now gone much further than its former enemies in establishing a democratic order in the military field. Perhaps it is the turn of its former enemies to learn some lessons from more recent German developments.

SPECIALISTS AND GENERALISTS

The specialist *versus* generalist controversy has been an agenda item in all discussion of civil service reform. The problem was a serious one in Britain before Lord Fulton's Committee on the Civil Service surveyed the problem and has by no means disappeared as a result of subsequent measures. As Anthony Sampson wrote in *The Anatomy of Britain Today*, the conflict between amateurs and professionals runs through many British institutions—more than on the Continent or in America—but it has its most troubled frontiers in the civil service. I expressed my own views on the subject—somewhat polemically—in an article based on a talk to the Institution of Professional Civil Servants.[1]

The challenge of the future, as the Institution's evidence to Fulton pointed out, is the challenge of technology. Our economic problems, serious though they were then, and even more serious though they are today, must be short-term problems if we are to survive at all. In the long run, the improvement of living standards, material and social, will depend on the application of new techniques. This requires more than know-how: it will depend in turn on a new spirit of enterprise in public administration as well as the private sector. Much of the now somewhat-dated literature on our failure to meet the challenge of the second half of the twentieth century pinned a degree of responsibility on the civil service, its failure to understand the new world into which we have moved, its wrong advice, often due to lack of expertise, its failure to give advice at all, its reluctance to act on its own initiative and take on the development function which nowadays must partly come from the permanent element in central government, due again to

[1] The following paragraphs are drawn from my 'Specialists as Administrators' in *State Service* (Journal of the Institution of Professional Civil Servants) (February 1967).

a lack of technical knowledge or even an interest in matters technical. It seemed reasonable to ask, therefore, as did the Fulton Committee, whether there were any ways of changing the structure of our administration in order to improve the quality of the decisions taken within it and, equally important, the interest in technical development, the commitment to modernisation and the willingness to lead which the critics had found abroad, notably in France.

I then argued two things. First: in so far as the functions of the higher civil service lie in the field of policy-making, advice should be given to ministers by men who have a personal commitment rather than men who see themselves as only the servants of a minister or the co-ordinators of other people's policies. The generalist, I suggested, is by his background, training, career choice and extra-mural interests less likely to have this attitude towards the field he administers—transport, health, education—than a specialist whose life is in some way bound up with the subject of his career choice. The second point I made was that the separation between policy-making at the centre and the management of services on the ground was a bad one, as was the separation at the centre between generalist administrators and specialist advisers. Such division of functions produces an inefficient management structure and, because of their limited background, inefficient managers as well. My conclusion was that many directorial posts should by definition be occupied by specialists, using that term broadly enough to include economists and engineers, for example. This is very different from merely opening such posts to 'the best men', regardless of previous career. I would not suggest, of course, that the most highly qualified engineer should *ipso facto* be appointed: administrative and technical expertise are both factors to be taken into account—but senior policy-making and managerial posts require specialists with administrative skills rather than men with administrative skills some of whom may incidentally have a specialist background (and an unrelated one at that).

The case against the traditional generalist seemed to me quite strong. The world in which government has to move today is so complex that the man of general culture cannot simply 'use' the specialist. The doctrine that the expert should be on tap but not on top is absurd. There is little point on turning on a tap if one cannot understand what comes out (the self-confident all-rounder, who has misunderstood without realising it, is as dangerous as the unsympathetic all-rounder). In any case, it is not just a question of asking for advice: one has to know what sort of advice to ask for, what the problems are, and surely the specialist is more likely to identify these as part of his work. If the expert can put this advice into language comprehensible to the lay administrator, he can presumably be understood by ministers and public without their intervention; if he cannot, that is not an argument for the generalist but an argument against the current education of the specialist. The common criticism that he lacks a sense of political and administrative reality, of the art of the possible, if true, is less likely to be the result of his specialism than of a back-room career which has deprived him of early managerial experience. Indeed, much the same can be said of administrators who live their lives in the ministerial corridors of Whitehall: this divorce from reality is likely to deprive *them* of the managerial skills and political insights which they accuse the specialists of lacking.

The case for the specialist, however, is not simply the negative one of generalist failure. The positive argument goes back to my starting point. The need for expertise is growing and so is the need for action: specialists must therefore be in the right place. Not that any sort of specialists will do. Professional skills must be combined with administrative and political skills; they must be underpinned by a sense of purpose and capped by initiative. Educational background and career patterns must suit the man to the role. The Fulton Committee bought part, though only part, of the 'state of Britain' literature. Its dramatic opening about a nineteenth-century civil service facing the task of the second half of the twentieth century set the tone. It did appear to have been impressed by the quality of French civil servants, using them as a foil to the British. We may turn, therefore, to a brief survey of specialists— the 'professionally qualified' civil servants, as we would define them— in France.[1] It may be possible to learn something, even after the Fulton reforms, from the comparisons that emerge.

It would be misleading, of course, to describe French civil servants out of context. Their position must be seen within the general structure of the service, that within the governmental framework, particularly the work they have to do, and that again against a background of accepted ideas about the duties of the state and the role of its servants. This is not to contradict the point I made in an earlier chapter about limiting the number of environmental factors in practical comparisons. Some of the wider differences are relevant here because they may indicate that civil service reforms should not be considered too narrowly when undertaken.

While much has changed in Britain since the days of the 'night-

[1] Drawn from my chapter 'France' in the book I edited for the IPCS, *Specialists amd Generalists* (Allen & Unwin, 1968).

watchman' state, France has a far older tradition of state intervention in all spheres of national life. Its civil service was established against a background of active government, responsible for the development of public services. The two countries are now much closer in their ideas about the proper functions of government, but to that extent France did not have the problems of adaptation that faced Britain. This holds particularly true of the philosophy into which young entrants are socialised.

Nevertheless, central government is still responsible for the management of a much wider range of services in France than in Britain. The Ministries of the Interior, Education, and Public Works (by whatever changing name) have field administrations parallel to those, more familiar in Britain, of the financial and postal administrations. British ministries, by comparison, are more concerned with policy-making in areas where executive responsibility is left to other bodies or, negative side of the coin, with regulatory and supervisory activities—with 'office work' rather than technical operations in the field. The French civil service is thus much larger and, though France is thought of as a centralised state, the great majority work in a complex network of 'external services' of central government departments. Many senior officials, with considerable delegated powers, serve in the provinces. As they are responsible for the management of specialised services, they are themselves specialists. The position is not unlike that of the local government services in Britain (in fact responsible for many of these activities) with their professionally qualified chief officers. As we shall see, many of the field services are the responsibility of specialised civil service corps: the fact that it would be very difficult to direct them from the centre except through senior members of the same corps partly explains why key posts in Paris are also filled by specialists. France, in other words, shows a greater structural continuity between central policy-making and control and the management of services on the ground. While this may run contrary to some of our ideas about local self-government, it does bring experience of technical problems and contact with the public to the centre through regular movements of personnel.

There are also marked differences between the two systems of higher education which affect the character of their civil services. The French state has long accepted responsibility for the general education of its officials (as distinct from induction, job training and short specialised courses). Members of what are the senior generalist classes in the French system will have read law and/or political science at the university before receiving a full-length

post-entry education at the *Ecole Nationale d'Administration*. The
higher education of the most important specialist classes, on the
other hand, takes place entirely within a state system. The *Ecole
Polytechnique* gives a general scientific undergraduate education
to civil service cadets. Its students go on to a postgraduate school
for more specialised training in a branch of engineering (e.g.
mining, civil, aeronautical, telecommunications). They are
educated, in other words, as state servants. The experience is not
only formative in that respect: the closed educational system
establishes bonds between contemporaries that extend to past and
future generations of the schools, strengthening the *esprit de corps*
of each group.

While the universities are open to all who matriculate, the *Ecole
Polytechnique* takes only a limited number each year by stiff
competitive examination. There is little scope, therefore, for
entrance into the elite public service at the end of an undirected
university career as in Britain: the young Frenchman has to make
his choice earlier. As the prestige of the state schools is generally
higher than that of the university faculties, however, and taking
the certainty of employment at the end together with considerable
opportunities for subsequent transfer to private enterprise, the
service is likely to recruit the best school leavers. There is not the
danger of losing the best university talent that opponents of
'preference for relevance' fear in Britain. There is, moreover, a
sense in which career patterns are more flexible than in Britain and
this is really more important in the context of the present discussion. France has never had the 'vocational' separation between
public administration, business management and technology that
one has tended to find here. The civil service has always placed
engineers and other specialists in key administrative posts; private
enterprise has long recruited civil servants for top management.
The educational system helps to make this possible. The schools
do not focus on the science-for-the-sake-of-research of so many
British universities, nor on its opposite, the practical technician's
training of our technical colleges: their purpose is to give the
student a general understanding of science and technology, some
practical specialisation, combined with some knowledge of law,
economics and management. They recruit students who do not
intend to remain specialists and educate them as all-rounders on
that assumption. Their career patterns facilitate the dialogue
between government, industry and research, preventing some of
the friction that can arise in Britain between these groups as a
result of their different backgrounds and thus different values.

The French civil service is divided horizontally into four classes,

A, B, C and D, the highest of which is responsible for policy-making and direction. As it includes virtually all with some form of higher education, thus virtually all professionals, it is much larger than any British equivalent. A consequence is that all its members do not enjoy the same status: there is a fairly clear distinction between those in the prestigious corps, basically graduates of the *Ecole Nationale d'Administration* and the *Ecole Polytechnique*, and the rest. This brings us to the corps, the basis of civil service organisation. All civil servants are appointed to a corps when they enter the service (with some exceptions for mid-career promotion) and their normal work lies within it; even when posted elsewhere they remain attached to their corps and it is through it that their careers are organised. Each corps is governed by its own rules specifying its size, entrance qualifications, methods of recruitments, and similar matters. This makes for a less flexible service than even pre-Fulton Britain as regards promotion upwards between classes; it might also appear less flexible as regards lateral movement in that members remain attached to their own corps when posted to other branches of the service—but that does not prevent such postings. On the other hand, it does strengthen the sense of corps identity and this is important in defining members' sense of purpose.

The rules of the corps may also define its 'mission'—the general field of state activity for which it is responsible. In the context of the present discussion this applies particularly to the most prestigious, generally the oldest, of the technical corps which have their spheres of competence defined less in terms of civil service positions than by sectors of national life. The civil service thus has a vertical as well as a horizontal structure but the organisation of government services can only be understood by reference to the former. A prestigious technical corps is supported by a secondary corps of class A engineers, class B technicians, and other personnel in classes C and D. This system unifies the field services and links them with Paris. It has some drawbacks: ministries that have several corps-based services are internally less unified than they might otherwise be; corps rivalries for spheres of competence may cause difficulties between ministries. Against this may be set the fact that a single corps may have a competence wider than those of the ministry to which it is attached, thus establishing useful inter-ministry links. A major contribution of the system, in any case, is that the responsibilities of the 'mission' of the corps further strengthen the sense of responsibility of its individual members.

Let us take as our example the *Corps des Ponts et Chaussées*, the civil engineers, founded in 1716 and long responsible for the 'public works' concerns of government in a very broad sense of the term. Its services form the main field services of whatever ministry or ministries are responsible for public works and transport (frequent reorganisation of ministries makes an up-to-date statement difficult). As such, it has direct or supervisory responsibility for roads and road traffic, rail transport, navigable waterways, docks and harbours, lighthouses, airports and their installations, urban infrastructure including water supply, drainage and sports facilities, school and hospital building. But its duties are wider than those of the ministerial divisions it represents. In principle, functions can be divided according to sectors of the economy or the type of work involved. While the division of functions between ministries tends to follow the first principle, the *Corps des Ponts et Chaussées* bases its claim on professional competence in virtually all fields of civil engineering. Its services co-operate (though not easily) with the Ministry of Agriculture whose rural engineers have similar responsibilities in rural areas and with the Ministry of Construction (if not amalgamated with Public Works) in questions relating to housing and town planning. They supervise the production and distribution of electricity on behalf of the Ministry of Industry. They also act at county level on behalf of local government and co-operate with the communal authorities.

More important from the point of view of this discussion is the fact that the 'vocation' of the corps is officially described as covering technical and scientific functions on the one hand, functions of an administrative, economic and social nature on the other. In the field, the work of members is only part technical; much is managerial, financial and even political (in their relations with elected local authorities and other local interests). To quote an official statement again, they enjoy great independence in their area and participate actively in the life of the country, with a wide range of contacts and considerable discretion; they participate in the work of economic planning and regional development. They are also likely to spend periods of time at various stages of their career in policy-making sections of the ministry and can aspire to the highest directorial posts there. In addition, the corps acts as a pool of elite officials for service in a wide range of capacities, administrative as well as technical, throughout the government service. There are excellent opportunities for transfer to the highest managerial positions in public or private enterprise, often on extended leave. On the other hand, those who wish may pursue scientific research in the laboratories of the service. This wide range of opportunities gives the corps considerable appeal. It tends to recruit men who are interested in administration, or planning and development, rather than scientifically minded engineers who may develop such interests in mid-career as in Britain.

It is impossible to describe a standard career pattern for engineers of the corps. They are likely to get their first experience in the field services and then move between Paris and the provinces at a variety of levels. In the ministry they may occupy staff and line functions at junior and senior levels. The best will end in very senior posts indeed. At the time the study was undertaken they held the following key positions in their own ministry: high officials charged with defence questions and international relations; Commissioner General for the Building and Construction Industries; Secretary General for Civil Aviation; Directors of Divisions for Roads, Ports and Navigable Waterways, Airports, Personnel and Accounts; Head of Economic Affairs Section. In other ministries they headed the Electricity and Gas, the Housing and Construction, and the School Building Divisions. They represented the government on the boards of public enterprise and sat on numerous councils and committees. Yet others were appointed as directors of nationalised industries, including electricity, gas, railways, airlines, Paris airport. Finally there were those who had moved out to influential positions in private enterprise, including the chairman of the Federation of Road Industries.

Now the point of all this is that we have here examples of specialists serving as administrators as a matter of course, on the basis of preference for relevance, rather than simply being eligible for such appointment in competition with generalists. While members of the corps can become real specialists if they wish, even concentrate on research, most are involved from the start with the management of services which, though described as technical, are really economic and even social in character. This applies in their early days in the field services where they are responsible for the legal, financial and personnel aspects of work as well as the technical, and where a certain political element is bound to enter in addition. As they move up the hierarchy, they reach the policy-making and directorial levels of central government. One cannot say, of course, that similar careers could be followed in Britain. The British science graduate who enters a specialised class may be a very different sort of person from the start. This may reflect his education, however, or his early post-entry experience, rather than differences in innate ability or aspiration.

This leads one to a more general comment. The French have never made the separation we have had in Britain between a hierarchy of administrative posts, responsible for policy and direction, and a specialist hierarchy with advisory or technical functions. Indeed, the specialist–generalist division of functions, as applied here, would seem strange to them. At most levels, particularly in the field, it is obvious what work requires administrators with a technical background and posts are generally restricted to qualified personnel by the rules of the service. This is less true in the ministries themselves, whether at relatively junior level in policy-making sections or at the highest directorial level— and here posts are more open: there are few rules, seniority apart, about the specific qualifications required for appointment. Nevertheless, as we have seen, a considerable share of all directorial posts are held by members of the great technical corps. This is sometimes explained by 'colonisation', a customary right to certain posts, strengthened by an old-boy network. But there are more practical reasons: specialist knowledge and experience.

Experience is important, as we have seen, because central divisions also manage field services: familiarity with their work and close links with their personnel are an obvious help. Specialist knowledge is important because most ministries are organised on the assumption that technical and advisory functions are generally linked to administration itself. It is true that there are line and staff posts. The line of command goes from the minister to the heads of divisions and through these to subordinate sections at the centre and to the heads of field services; certain inspectorates, the minister's private office and a variety of other posts, even entire research and planning sections, may be thought of as staff functions. But all these posts may be filled by members of specialist corps who serve in different capacities at different stages of their careers. The heads of divisions are to an extent their own advisers; they are also the minister's chief advisers, though they may share this role with inspectors general, usually even more senior members of the technical corps, or with his private office: there is no Chief Scientific Officer or equivalent. The organisation of advice poses few problems either on specific technical issues or on long-term policy—much is interspersed in ordinary administration. In so far as an attempt is made to distinguish a purely administrative line function, significantly it is regarded as subordinate, restricted to questions of finance, law and personnel, and handled by officials of lower status.

All bureaucracies have their own internal problems and France is no exception. The French civil service nevertheless seems to have avoided some of the problems that faced Britain at the time of the Fulton review and that may not have been solved yet, notably the place of the professional in the system. What lessons can be learnt from the French way of doing things is another matter. The extent to which civil service systems must be seen against a wider background has been stressed, yet it is not impossible to copy some aspects. What can be said, in any case, is that it appears possible to organise administration in a way that raises fewer problems about the relationship between generalists and specialists than the British.[1]

Let us raise a broader issue, however. In the sixties discussion of the French civil service tended to centre round the theme of technocracy. French planning was much admired at the time, and its apparent success was attributed to the technocrats of the civil service. I tried at the time to profile these men, largely by impressionistic generalisations about their outlook.[2] The purpose, however, was primarily to raise more general questions. One was the relationship between civil service attitudes and wider cultural factors. Another was the extent to which elite civil servants could be thought to form a class with a common outlook; if so, whether it was the ruling class (as the word technocracy implies), a ruling class among others, or whether individual technocrats were members of a more diffuse power elite. A third was the question of leadership: where, within a country, do the centres of initiative lie? And is one political system more likely to develop modernising classes than another? More specifically, was the French system better adapted to modernisation than the British because of its civil service?

Evaluation of the merits of different systems raises the question: better for what? The fact that civil services play different roles in different countries may be intentional. In the present day, however, one might be tempted to make the criterion that broadly employed by the Fulton Committee: is one more effective in promoting economic development than another? There is no obvious way of isolating the contribution of the civil service from other factors. One may nevertheless feel that the French technocrat (to stay with the now almost discredited term) has been more effective than the British generalist.

If this is true, it leaves one with a number of problems. Are the technocrats dynamic because they are experts? One's first inclination—and it is a point I made at the start of this section, is to

[1] For a discussion of the general problems of the relationship between specialists and generalists see my concluding chapter 'Agenda Item' in *Specialists and Generalists* (Allen and Unwin, 1968).

[2] 'French Technocracy and Comparative Government', *Political Studies* (February 1966), from which the following paragraphs are drawn.

suppose that they are committed to expansion by virtue of their very choice of career, their training and interests. Engineers will naturally want to build bigger and better power stations, and progress, to adapt Lenin, if not electrification, is largely natural gas. But the French technocrats are inspired by other motives as well. There is the motive of personal power which partly explained the expansion of some public sector empires. There is the French civil service tradition. Many of its members are committed to active government because they are formed in the traditions of the public service state. What has happened in France is not simply the 'managerial revolution'—a take-over by experts. The administrative elite are the heirs of Colbert and Napoleon: it is not because they are technocrats that they have obtained power; they have become technocrats in order to excercise the power that has always been considered rightfully theirs.

We could not simply copy the French, therefore, by altering civil service structures. We live in a different society with a different culture. Technocratic leadership or, less dramatically, the influence of specialists, depends objectively on the organisation of the French civil service but subjectively on its values. In so far as they are part of a tradition built up over the centuries, they are not likely to be readily transferable. But the educational system and wider career patterns also play a role, probably more important. That is only to say, of course, where it has often been said by those seeking an antidote to our 'stagnant society', that we need to change our own educational system and, with it, our criteria of appointment to key posts, junior and senior, in public administration and private enterprise, if initiative and expertise are to be combined and relations between government, industry and research to be improved. We need to think more widely, in other words, when considering civil service reform.

In any case, it is worth concluding with Fulton on senior French officials. 'They were lucid, expert and possessed the confidence that comes from the achievement of high responsibility combined with a certainty that one knows one's subject as well or better than anyone else.' Commenting that our own scientists, engineers and other professionals did not get the full responsibilities and corresponding authority they ought to have, they attributed this partly to the fact that they were equipped only to practise their own specialisms: 'A body of men with the quality of the French *polytechnicien*—skilled in his craft, but skilled, too, as an administrator—has not so far developed in Britain.' And thus 'in making our proposals, we have been influenced by what we have seen of

the role of specialists in France'. Some lessons of foreigr
were learnt. Can more be learnt from the same sourc

INTEGRATED ADMINISTRATIVE DECENTRALISATION

There are many ways of decentralising the functions of government. They run along a scale from the constitutional division of
powers in federalism, past the statutory devolution of powers to
elected local authorities, to the administrative delegation ot
functions to the field services of central government. Whether a
country has federalism or not, and regardless of the extent of local
government, there is bound to be a good deal of administrative
decentralisation. In this respect West European states face
broadly similar organisational problems. One of these is how to
extend the decentralisation of functions: negatively, to relieve the
centre, increasingly choked with work as government intervention
grows; positively, to bring administration nearer the problems of
the increasingly administered public. Another problem—and a
consequence of the first—is how to ensure the regional co-ordination of services: negatively, to counter the increasing specialisation
that comes with complexity; positively, to facilitate effective
economic and land use planning. Demands of democracy combine
with demands of efficiency, if not for regional or local self-
government, then at least for the greater influence that comes with
bringing even central government decision-makers nearer the
people. The Royal Commission on the Constitution was concerned
with this question as well as the possibilities of federalism in the
United Kingdom, and among the studies it commissioned was my
own on the French experience of integrated administrative decentralisation.[1]

The decentralisation of functions presupposes the existence of
decentralised governmental institutions. Obviously all governments require a network of administrative services outside the
capital, though their extent varies a good deal from country to
country. Such decentralisation can take a variety of forms. Field
services can be more or less extensive as regards their number and
the density of their organisation; they can be more or less powerful,
depending on the seniority of their staff and the degree of authority
they are given. In their simplest form they may be little more than

[1] The following is drawn from my 'Integrated Decentralisation: Models
of the Prefectoral System', *Political Studies* (March 1973). For a fuller
treatment of the French system, see also my *The French Prefectoral System:
An Example of Integrated Administrative Decentralisation* Royal Commission on the Constitution, Research Papers 4 (HMSO, 1973).

branch offices of their ministries, staffed by subordinate personnel and responsible only for the routine execution of centrally made decisions. The other end of the scale entails a genuine transfer of administrative authority to senior officials with substantial services in the field.

The intention here is to look at a strong system, one that is solidly organised and has decision-making, as well as executive, functions. Even at this end of a scale, different systems can be found. Decentralised administration is likely to be functionally organised, that is to say each ministry is likely to have its own field services, though at the other end of this scale it is possible to have a unified field service acting on behalf of all ministries. Somewhere between the vertical decentralisation of specialist services and horizontal decentralisation to a single all-purpose service, there is a point of overlap where horizontal co-ordination is imposed on vertical structures. This is the integrated model of administrative decentralisation and forms the subject of the present study. The intention is to consider the ways in which a strong system of integrated decentralisation can be organised.

Such a system may be called an integrated prefectoral system, taking prefect as a convenient title for the central government's chief representative in the county, province or whatever territorial area is used as the basis of decentralisation (governor in Spain, *Regierungspräsident* in Germany). In its ideal-type form, the system has a number of characteristics which distinguish it from other forms of decentralisation: the prefect represents the state in his area; he embodies the authority of the Government as a whole and of all ministers individually; he is the senior official in his area and the hierarchic superior of the chief officers of individual ministries; he is part of the chain of command and main channel of communication between capital and provinces. This of course is the French system as we have described it earlier.

Why use France as a model? A good answer is that more is already known about French administration than about the administration of other European countries. It is probably easier, therefore, for the observer to make sense of the French prefectoral system than would otherwise be the case. It can conveniently be placed in a wider context of French government.[1] Priority goes to France by rights of history as well as for reasons of convenience. The prefectoral system was one of Napoleon's most effective legacies to France: together with the *Conseil d'Etat*, it is one of the most widely copied of French institutions in Europe and elsewhere.

[1] Cf. F. F. Ridley and J. Blondel, *Public Administration in France* (Routledge & Kegan Paul, 2nd edn, 1969).

But France is more than the *pays d'origine*, it is the *pays-type*. There are probably as many prefectoral systems now as there are countries that have prefects. Though the data is missing, it is most unlikely that any two are exactly the same. The French model is probably the best case of an integrated prefectoral system and thus a classic example of a strong solution compared to other, less co-ordinated and generally weaker models. It is strong in another sense too, and this relates not merely to the prefect's role as integrating officer but also to the range of other functions he performs as representative of state and government.

Even more relevant, perhaps, is the fact that the French system was reformed in the last decade—in 1964, to be precise—essentially to reaffirm its traditional character, but also to rationalise and strengthen the institution in practice. The fact that an administrative device has shown weaknesses, been examined and reformed, provides a useful series of foci for study. The reforms took two lines, related to the two forms of prefectoral strength mentioned above. The prefect was strengthened both in regard to the wider affairs of his area, notably in the growing planning responsibilities of government, and in his role within the administration as chief officer of all field services in his area. What these challenges were, and how they were met, has been related in an earlier chapter.

The intention here is only to suggest a number of 'models'. The quotation marks are deliberate and the word is used with no theoretical significance whatsoever. To some extent it is an analytic exercise, showing the different sorts of functions (and combinations of functions) prefects can perform and the different ways an integrated system can be organised. These models may be left as a series of recipes—a cook book for administrative reformers to choose from—and, like most recipes, one cannot really tell how they will taste until one has tried them. No one doubts the extent to which the form of institutions depend on their environment, the way they work even more so. Nevertheless, a check-list of alternative methods is a necessary prerequisite for any discussion of reform, if only as a way of clarifying the mind and reminding oneself what possibilities there are, so that each can be considered at least briefly against the background of one's own situation and one's own needs.

The French prefect has almost innumerable responsibilities, some general in scope and others specific, some very important and others minor, some largely personal and others a matter of administrative routine. More is involved than a range of functions, however; the prefect fills a number of basically quite separate roles, related in the French system, it is true, but notionally distinct and, what is more relevant here, not all are necessarily related elsewhere. Some are inherent in the notion of a prefect as representative of state and government in his area, some are a vital part of an integrated system of decentralised administration in which the prefect acts as co-ordinator, but a third group might well be organised on a different basis altogether. Not all these roles, much less the multitude of specific functions, need be brought together in one man. Various combinations are possible and a number of models can be constructed.

To do this, however, one must first list briefly what the broad roles of the French prefect are and a framework into which most functions can be squeezed is suggested. Labels are given which may carry sufficient connotations to make them readily identifiable, but it should be remembered that these are not based on any classification that is legally or administratively recognised in France:

Lord Lieutenant. The prefect is the formal representative of the state in his area. In this role, he partly resembles the Lord Lieutenant in an English county. The 'dignified' representation of the state is not very important in itself, though there are ceremonial functions, but—in Bagehot's language—it clearly adds lustre, and thus authority, to his role as representative of the 'efficient' parts of the government.

Regional Commissioner. This label is borrowed from the provision for Regional Commissioners in wartime Britain. As representative of the state, the prefect is the executive authority of last resort in his area, exercising prerogative and statutory powers and controlling the legitimate use of force in time of emergency. He is responsible for internal and external security: crises in which he may be required to act include war, civil disorder, general strike and natural catastrophe.

Political Agent. The prefect is also the delegate of the Government (a notional and not very satisfactory distinction between state and government is made here). As its representative, he has political functions. In one sense his political role was more important in the past: 'eyes and ears' of the Government, reporting on the state of local politics, manipulating elections for the party in office. In a more important sense, today, he has open-ended functions that are essentially political but not necessarily partisan. His general responsibility for the administration of his area matches the responsibility, undefinable in advance, of central government itself: there are many problems he must solve by his personal authority rather than on the basis of legal powers.

Director General. The prefect is the head of all central government services in his area. The implications of this have been spelt out earlier in the book. As holder of all delegated powers and hierarchic superiors of all specialist chief officers, he is far more than a co-ordinator *primus inter pares*. It is essential to remember, at the same time, that the specialist field services of the various ministries are structurally distinct: the prefect is chief officer of a co-ordinated rather than unified organisation.

Chief of Police. The prefectoral service is the field service of the Ministry of the Interior and the prefect has responsibilities as representative of his own ministry. As such, he has his own staff and is a specialist officer in his own right. A major responsibility is the untranslatable 'police function' of French government which, in British terms, has two really quite distinct aspects: the enforcement of law and order through the state police forces of the area; and a very wide regulatory power that covers the good order of the community under the blanket of public safety, public health and public morality.

Tutor of Local Government. The second main function of the Ministry of the Interior, and thus direct prefectoral responsibility, is the supervision of local government (in French, more expressively, *tutelle*).

Planning Commissioner. Responsibility for economic and land use planning, though not part of the traditional model of the prefectoral system, is a function of growing importance. It has two facets: the prefect has specific powers with regard to public works and public investment programmes, and a wider brief to stimulate economic growth and deal with economic problems that may arise in the private sector, often on the informal basis of personal influence (here one returns to the political role).

Country Manager. Finally, the prefect is chief executive of the elected local authority at the county level and chief officer of the country's own services. In this case he is not acting as agent of central government at all.

The roles listed, we can discuss the issues that arise out of their combination and the possibility of limiting the mix while remaining

within the ambit of an integrated model of decentralised administration.

It is clearly possible to separate out the Lord Lieutenant function in all models. The separation between constitutional head of
state and political executive at the centre can be maintained by the
appointment of constitutional representatives in the provinces with
decorative functions. Whether there is a need for such a person is
another matter: would one invent a Lord Lieutenant of the
County in Britain if history had not bequeathed us one? Size and
regional diversity—ethnic, linguistic or religious—might make a
difference: a gesture to regional personality might be desirable. In
British terms one could not see a civil servant prefect acting as
representative of the Queen. In a republic the situation may be
rather different. The trend in the Fifth Republic has been to
identify head of state and head of government in order to enhance
the executive authority. If someone is to exercise prerogative
powers in times of crises, his authority is likely to be strengthened
if he represents the state itself and not merely the Government of
the day.

It is possible to separate out the Regional Commissioner and
Political Agent functions. Some countries would think neither
compatible with membership of the civil service. Clearly, there
may be cases where a Regional Commissioner is required who can
take political or quasi-political decisions. In relatively small and
homogenous states, however, this is not likely to be so except in
moments of exceptional crisis when *ad hoc* arrangements can be
made. The political function can often be dealt with in the capital,
generally by ministers or at least by civil servants who are their
immediate, day-to-day collaborators. In the British context, and
even allowing for the gradual erosion of the doctrines of ministerial responsibility to Parliament, it would be hard to see a
prefect representing the Government in the open-ended French
manner without some basic change in constitutional principles.
The question hinges, nevertheless, on the definition of politics.
The distinction between politics and administration lies less in the
substance of the matter than in the eyes of the beholder: politics,
in the last resort, is what the public considers political and for
which it holds politicians responsible. If it is prepared to accept
civil servants in areas of controversy, in the settlement of distur-
bances for example, then wide 'political' discretion may be left to
the senior officials on the spot. Equally, if field officials are to show
personal initiative in such matters as economic development, they
are bound to have some political characteristics.

The need for the Lord Lieutenant, Regional Commissioner and

Political Agent functions, then, depends on several factors. One is the size of the country and the development of its communications: the extent to which it is technically possible for the capital to make its presence felt quickly and effectively in the provinces. Another is its internal political stability and its external security: the extent to which it is necessary to maintain a strong representative of central authority in the provinces to counter dissidence or to organise civil defence. Where the state lacks underlying unity, the 'dignified' presence of its representative may be as important as his effective powers. Crisis situations may arise in all states, but a stronger case for prefects may be found in developing and multinational states with weak lines of communication and low political integration. The French prefect is now given a modernising role in the economy as well as the stabilising, public-order functions, and in this his role may well be relevant to stable, industrialised societies.

The Director General function can only be eliminated at the cost of having an unintegrated system of decentralisation. In this case field services are organised on strictly functional lines, each depending directly on its parent ministry: delegation of powers, lines of authority and channels of communication run directly from the capital to specialist chief officers. In such a system the prefect may enjoy precedence as representative of the state, but he is responsible only for the functions of the Ministry of the Interior. This is pure vertical separatism with co-ordination at the centre only by inter-ministry and cabinet committees. If the prefect's special status is recognised, however, there may be formalised local co-ordination with the prefect as *ex-officio* chairman of committees, but no more than *primus inter pares*. It is also possible to have a system which, though formally integrated under a prefect-Director General in theory, actually functions in an unintegrated manner: there are many organisational reasons why prefects should be by-passed by specialist services in practice and we have seen that this was often the case in France before the 1964 reforms.

Organisationally the prefectoral service is linked to the Ministry of the Interior. There are good reasons why it should be so. Before other specialist ministries were hived off over the years, it was responsible for most domestic affairs. It retains a general responsibility for internal administration, for the machinery of central and local government in the field, and it is thus appropriate that the prefect as chief administrative officer should form part of its structure. Its responsibility for political supervision of the territory, maintenance of law and order, and control of local government—the major functions for which the prefect is directly responsible—

is another obvious reason. A different consideration is where the centre of gravity of the prefect's multiple roles is intended to lie: whether the Ministry of the Interior is the proper base for a service that is intended to play an increasingly developmental role in economic, and possibly social, fields may be questioned. The fact that the prefect represents the entire Government might lead one to organise a prefectoral service that depends on the Prime Minister's office rather than on one particular ministry, but that would be difficult unless the Prime Minister's office was large enough to provide the necessary underpinning at the centre.

It is possible to vary the substantive areas for which the prefect is responsible as a specialist chief officer himself. In the unintegrated system the enforcement of law and the maintenance of order, with the supervision of local government, is likely to constitute the bulk of his work. Is it necessary in all integrated models that the prefects should perform the Chief of Police function? In so far as it is linked with wider responsibilities for the security of the state, and if its scope is so broad that it is likely to have political implications, then there is clearly much to be said for entrusting it to the most senior officials in the field. The other characteristic of the French police concept is relevant here. Direction of the active police is linked with exercise of the administrative or regulatory police function. This covers so wide a field, however, that it is really a general government concern. The situation may look different elsewhere, in Britain for example, where the Home Office has neither this range of duties nor the same established system of field services. In a different political culture a 'policeman' may not appeal as chief officer of all government services. It is possible to reorganise the system without destroying its integrated character by having another specialist chief officer— a Chief Constable—under the prefect, who could, however, retain the security powers of last resort as well as the regulatory powers.

Is it necessary that the prefect should act as Tutor of Local Government? In continental Europe this function came under the Ministry of the Interior because of its general responsibility for internal administration. This, again, is not the case in Britain where the control of local authorities is primarily concerned with financial and technical questions, rather than questions of politics or public order. Depending on the emphasis, it may seem reasonable to separate this function out. Even in Britain, however, it is worth noting that one ministry was given overall responsibility for the affairs of local government rather than entirely disintegrating responsibility on a functional basis between the technical ministries. There is much to be said for unity of this sort and the prefect is, after all, the co-ordinator of specialist services.

Should the Planning Commissioner function be the personal responsibility of the prefect? As with the previous two roles, this is partly a matter of the way in which central government is organised. In France economic and land use planning is the responsibility of two Commissariats with general staff rather than executive functions. If there is no Planning Ministry (by whatever name) with its own field services, the prefectoral service may seem a reasonable place to locate new planning functions; if planning is regarded as an interministry responsibility, the prefect as representative of the whole Government is the natural correspondent in his area. There are other arguments. Planning is essentially a co-ordinating activity and, in an integrated system of field administration, the prefect is the co-ordinator. The case is strengthened if delegated powers relate mainly to public works and public investment, i.e. to planning decisions within the administration, because only a Director General could impose such controls on specialist chief officers. Against this, it can be argued that planning requires professional expertise, and thus really a specialist service under its own chief officer, to do it full justice. A different situation could well have arisen in France if the Ministry of Finance and Economic Affairs had taken responsibility for planning and had reorganised its field services as a result, or if the Ministry of Industry (as it used to be) had developed its own field services. In Britain, with the Treasury on the one hand and two super-ministries (Environment, Trade and Industry) on the other, it is perhaps easier to visualise a prefect as *ex-officio* chairman of a number of inter-service and advisory committees. In the last resort, the role of the prefect as planner also depends on the extent of state planning and the extent to which this is decentralised.

Another possibility is that the prefect could be a Director General without any portfolios at all. In the absence of established structures, supported by tradition, this seems a sensible solution. It would avoid the difficulty of naming the representative of any one ministry to direct the work of other ministries. It would leave the prefect free to concentrate on the general direction of affairs without the burden of additional duties. In such a model, the prefect would presumably be attached directly to the Prime Minister. His position *vis-à-vis* other chief officers would then more closely resemble that of Prime Minister *vis-à-vis* other ministers, the prefecture would more closely resemble the Cabinet Office.

A different sort of question is whether all field services should come under the prefect's supervision in the integrated model. Some exclusions are self-evident. Defence is one case, though there are bound to be links in so far as the army has responsibilities for internal security, either by the provision of supplementary police forces or in contingency planning for civil defence. Justice is another obvious case. For less obvious reasons, largely traditional, education is also excluded in France, though it is a central government function and teachers are civil servants: the county's chief education officer does not come under the prefect's jurisdiction in matters relating to staff, teaching methods and school management, as distinct from planning questions such as the construction of schools. For other reasons, the services of the Ministry of Finance are excluded: the revenue services because they are quasi-judicial, the public accounts services because their function is to control the executive. This means, however, that the ministry's chief officer in the county, the Treasurer-Paymaster General, is not a subordinate of the prefect. This is not entirely satisfactory. True, most of the Treasurer-Paymaster General's existing services have legitimate claims to autonomy. Whatever the arrangements for planning at the centre, however, much real power is likely to gravitate to the ministry responsible for the budget and such a ministry should have field services which can be effectively integrated in the prefectoral model. The participation of Finance would seem an essential precondition for any decentralisation at all, *a fortiori* for a co-ordinated system.

The last of the prefect's roles listed, and different from others, is that of County Manager. There is no *a priori* reason why an integrated prefectoral system should include local government services. If it does, the model involves a rather different form of integration from that discussed so far, in this case between central and local government services. In the French system, this has two aspects: the prefect is the chief executive of the county local authority and, in practice, the county uses the field services of central government on an agency basis to provide certain of its services. This system has certain advantages, largely administrative. It is a form of rationalisation, permitting easier co-ordination and probably greater efficiency in the use of staff and materials; it facilitates central control by making it internal rather than external. Against this are the obvious disadvantages: internal control may be resented by an independently elected authority; the fact that the chief executive's tenure of office does not depend on his council may cause friction; and there may be a blurring of responsibilities. In the British tradition of government, such integration would appear undemocratic to say the least.

From the functions that may be exercised by a prefectoral-type official, we turn to the ways a prefectoral-type system may be organised. The focus, however, is on the prefect's role as Director General, as it is this which is central to an integrated system of decentralised administration.

Consider first the prefect's position in relation to the heads of specialist services in his area. Two ideal types can be suggested:

(1) *Prefect as Chairman.* He is simply the *ex-officio* chairman of co-ordinating committees, *primus inter pares*, and has no direct control over specialist chief officers and their services.

(2) *Prefect as Director General.* All chief officers are his direct subordinates, he is in direct, everyday control of all services, and these are organisationally integrated in his office.

These are two ends of a spectrum and different solutions are probably possible all along the line.

At the extreme end of the unintegrated scale, of course, there may not even be an official with a status sufficiently different from others to give him precedence; indeed there may be no comprehensive system of committees, and services may be entirely unlinked. Somewhere before reaching the prefect as chairman position, one can notionally mark a point where links are provided by interservice committees which are not merely consultative but have some powers of decision: this is collegial authority.

Towards the integrated end of the scale, the prefect may have direct authority over chief officers but the specialist services are separately organised for everyday purposes: here the prefect directs services as an outsider. This, of course, is the French position and is responsible for some of the difficulties in obtaining effective integration.

There is also a half-way house solution in which chief officers may be directly responsible for certain areas of their work but come under the authority of the prefect for others: here there is divided responsibility. Responsibility could be divided in the financial services between general administration and individual decisions of a quasi-judicial nature, or between teaching and capital expenditure in education. The career management of civil servants, separated out in the French as in most other systems, is another example, though in this case division is between the prefect and other central government offices.

The French prefect's position as outsider links with another way of looking at the problem of integration, namely in terms of the internal structure of field services. In a given area, these may by organised in two ways:

(1) *Federal Organisation.* Each service is organised separately, with

its own staff and offices. In the extreme case, with the prefect as chairman only, this would not be an integrated system. Services may be linked, on the other hand, at the top only by a prefect whose control remains more or less external to the organisation.
(2) *Unitary Organisation.* This is the single office, common staff solution. The field services of all ministries are brought together in a unified administration.

Another way of looking at this is to ask whether field services are organised primarily on vertical or horizontal lines: functionally, emphasising their specialist character and their links with the centre, or geographically, emphasising their common interests and local character. In the first case they are organisationally the extension of separate ministries, whatever the lines of authority may be; in the second they form a single service, locally organised. The unitary service, which may be called the integrated administration model, goes well beyond the French system. It probably requires different staff arrangements, based on locally rather than nationally organised personnel. There are obviously advantages and disadvantages in both cases. The emphasis may shift somewhat from the vertical to the horizontal if there is a change of emphasis from national uniformity of standards to planning on a regional basis, from policy-making by ministries at the centre to policy-making at regional level.

Finally, we may look at the relationship between the specialist field services and their own ministries, other field services in the area and the general public. Again, there are two models:
(1) *Direct Lines.* Lines run directly from the field services up to the ministry, across to other services, and down to the public. In its extreme form this is the vertical separatism of the unintegrated system of decentralisation.
(2) *Funnelled Lines.* The prefect is the director of all services and all lines run through the prefecture.

Lines between capital and field involve a variety of relationships and they may well be treated differently even in the largely integrated system. Different arrangements may be made for the delegation of ministerial powers of decision affecting the public and the delegation of powers with regard to the internal management of services. In both there may be some division of responsibility between prefects and chief officers, perhaps according to the importance or technicality of the matter. There may also be different arrangements for the flow of information and for personnel matters. While clear hierarchical lines of authority are sensible in the case of decision-making and management, channels of communication may well develop less formally, especially in technical matters (where these are direct, but the prefect is kept informed, one may get duplicate lines). Personnel matters are often treated differently and here the prefect's role may be essentially consultative.

One can ask whether communications between field services within the area have to run through the prefect's office or whether matters can be dealt with directly by those concerned. This, of course, raises the general administrative question of inter-service liaison in mid-hierarchy.

Finally, there is the relationship between field services and the public. Are all decisions affecting the public and all communications with the outside world to be channelled through the prefect? If so, are they in his name? Here, again, many variations are possible. Some lines may be funnelled and others not: a distinction may be drawn, for example, between formal decisions and other communications or between important and less important matters.

The French prefectoral system has adopted strong answers to most of these possibilities. To recapitulate: the prefect represents each minister individually and all ministerial powers are delegated to him in the first place; he is responsible for the general direction of all services and is the hierarchic superior of all officials (though personnel questions are, as elsewhere, something of an exception); all lines of authority and all channels of communication (with reasonable exceptions) run through the prefecture. Field services, however, remain organisationally unintegrated except at the top.

To return to the different ways of organising a prefectoral system, it would be tempting to assume that there are close links between the main variables noted so that a number of standard models can be constructed, notably the two 'pure' cases:

Co-ordinated System	Integrated System
Prefect as Chairman	*Prefect as Director General*
Federal Organisation	*Unitary Organisation*
Direct Lines	*Funnelled Lines*

A fully unified, single-office system is only possible if the organisation of field services and their staff is largely divorced from the ministries, and if integrated multi-service organisations are established locally, presumably with their own staff. A half-way solution is possible if all offices are housed in a single administrative centre—the 'Administrative City'. The various services may still retain their identity but the prefect is able to intervene much more effectively if he is on the spot, in direct, day-to-day contact with their internal business.

This brings one to the French model, which is not in fact a pure type, i.e. not at the end of a possible scale.

> *Prefect as Director General*
> *Federal Organisation*
> *Funnelled Lines*

Given the problems of technical specialisation, the obvious needs for close links between ministries and field services whatever the prefectoral system and staffing policy, this seems the most practical solution.

Variations of emphasis with regard to the prefect's role are possible even in this model. One relates to the extent to which he subdelegates his authority to his subordinate specialist officers. Clearly, this will make a real difference to the location of power, the work of the prefecture and the extent to which individual services can retain their everyday autonomy. Another is whether officers with delegated powers are allowed to act in their own names or must do so formally 'on the prefect's behalf'. This, too, may have important repercussions on organisational behaviour. The French system has been discussed in an earlier chapter. We may thus distinguish between integrated systems with limited or extensive delegation of powers by the prefect.

Variations are also possible in the extent to which the prefect directs specialist services as insider or outsider. This is partly a question of whether he can participate effectively in the work of services below the chief officer level and is largely a matter of informal organisational patterns. Clearly, his opportunities will be limited if his office is physically separated from the services under his control, and he will most certainly appear as an outsider to their staff. It is almost inevitable in the federal system.

A similar question is whether the prefect is actually regarded by all central ministries as their direct representative and is himself integrated into their own structures. This involves formal arrangements of the sort discussed (delegation of powers, channels of communication, consultation on personnel policy), but it also means informal arrangements, notably the personal contacts the prefect has with senior men in the capital.

If one is thinking of imposing a prefectoral-type integration on a system previously unco-ordinated, or if one wants to move along the scale from the simple co-ordinated model noted above, the easiest solution is probably:

Prefect as Director General-Outsider
Federal Organisation
Funnelled and Direct Lines

This would allow for direct communication between ministries and their own services except in important matters of general concern, though in all cases the prefect's office might be kept informed by duplicate copies. It would also permit the delegation of some decision-making powers direct to chief officers, notably in technical or routine matters, perhaps with the prefect's right of intervention held in reserve. Personnel policy could be left to the ministries concerned or, where applicable, a central civil service office, though some weight would be attached to the prefect's recommendations. Such a model permits maximum flexibility. It has some disadvantages, however. The prefect as outsider may find it difficult to keep his finger on the pulse of activities unless the flow of business is as well organised as in France. This means the establishment of an effective co-ordinating structure within his office. He may also find it difficult to establish his personal authority. The special status given to prefects over and above their role as Director General may well be relevant here. The model has a different sort of drawback from the point of view of the public, which loses the benefits of a single-office focus in its dealings with the administration.

It will be seen that one can easily descend into a game of permutations. Though the purpose of the main part of the study for the Royal Commission was to show how the French prefectoral system worked, the intention of this analytic part was to show that different models were available if the reform of decentralised administration was under debate and to raise questions about the alternatives. While answers are bound to depend on more concrete factors, it is useful to have a framework of possibilities. The French experience shows one solution that is not just theoretically possible but actually works. Some lessons could be drawn from this, I concluded, but it was well to remember that models other than the French might be considered.

Not unexpectedly, however, the Royal Commission found the prefectoral concept too foreign, however organised. It asked itself, if no more extensive system of devolution were to be adopted, whether a prefectoral system would have value in the regions of this country and whether it would be acceptable. It replied that, although it might well be valuable, there was no way of overcoming the objection that even a limited prefectoral role could not be assumed by a civil servant: the function of arbiter between the

services of different ministries, though not so obviously political
as some of the other roles of the prefect, itself had an important
political facet and would in the circumstances of this country
have to be assumed by a political figure. One can see the reasons
for this in the light of British administrative traditions, but the
fact remains that if no political devolution takes place, sooner or
later some formal machinery will have to be taken to ensure the
co-ordination of field services. The more effective this is, the more
possible that something resembling a prefectoral-type institution
may yet emerge.

The final word to this chapter may fittingly be a quotation from
Sir Ernest Barker's *Development of the Public Services in Western
Europe.*

'When we consider the history of the modern state, we cannot but
recognise the debt which all states owe to one another. Each
country has developed according to its own genius; and each has
produced its own fruit. But each has produced some institution
which has served as an example to others; and each, in turn, has
borrowed from each. There has been a rivalry of methods, but it
has not been unfriendly, one country has studied, adopted or
tried to improve the methods of another, and all have combined,
however unconsciously, to promote the growth of a common
European standard of administration and public service.'

PUBLIC ADMINISTRATION

Cause for Discontent

In the establishment of Public Administration as an academic subject, Britain is still an underdeveloped country.[1] Although the title of the Gladstone chair at Oxford was changed from Political Theory and Institutions to Government and Public Administration in 1941, its last three incumbents could not be described as administrative theorists despite Sir Kenneth Wheare's classic *Government by Committee*, Max Beloff's interest in the administration of foreign affairs and S. E. Finer's early *Primer of Public Administration*. At the time of writing, we have only one other chair of Public Administration and that is even more recent: it was specially created for William Robson at the London School of Economics in 1947. There were negotiations for a further chair at the University of Edinburgh, a joint appointment with the Civil Service College in Scotland, but that cannot be attributed solely to academic initiative. At Strathclyde, finally, there is a chair of Administration that happens to be occupied by a Public Administrationist rather than some other. We have no university schools nor even, less grandly, departments of Public Administration. And our Civil Service College itself has only just been established.

Compare Germany. A first chair of Cameralism was founded in 1727 by Frederick William I of Prussia at the University of Halle. The King wanted to balance the legalist training of his servants with some more practical knowledge. Cameralism was the science of managing the royal domain, the farms and forests,

---

[1] A revised version of my 'Public Administration: Cause for Discontent', *Public Administration* (Spring 1972). Note that capitals are used to distinguish Public Administration as an academic subject from public administration, the administrative reality.

mines and manufactories on which the state depended for much of its revenue. Early Public Administration, therefore, was concerned with the substantive fields of government action (the *what* of administration) as well as the general principles of administrative procedures (the *how* of administration). It drew on what then counted as the political sciences, though this called itself, and we might now call it, policy science. When the subject was reborn in America much later, it was deliberately defined to exclude the *what* and emphasise a generalised *how*. But it is worth noting that in recent years there has been a swing back to the earlier tradition of policy science—a concern with public policy and the establishment of schools of public affairs.

Such a school of cameralism was first set up in the Rhine-Palatinate in 1774. In a several years' course it acquainted the student with the available knowledge in practical fields such as agriculture and commerce, as well as more 'political' subjects, economic and fiscal policy for example. At the same time it taught him the techniques of government administration, accountancy, law and management. The addition of a course on moral philosophy strikes another modern chord if one thinks of current discussions about the training of civil servants. However rudimentary the sciences of the time, it thus encompassed everything required for a modern school for officials: economic theories on which to base public policy, technical knowledge of the fields to be administered, general techniques of administration and values for administrators. A later school, in Würtemberg, was even more modern in the emphasis it placed on mathematics. This was the predecessor of the first university faculty of state sciences at Tübingen. Although vocationally orientated, as German university faculties have always tended to be, it meant that Germany already had forerunners of the two types of institutions we now know—the professional school run by the state and the university school—more than a century ago.

Unfortunately they were forerunners in a broken tradition. Public Administration more or less disappeared in Germany thereafter, its place taken by the study of administrative law. This led to the 'monopoly of the jurists' in the public service and a system of training now often decried as formalistic. But it is worth remembering that the emphasis on legal training for administrators reflected a new emphasis on law in administration itself. It came with the emergence of the *Rechtsstaat*, a system of administration which protected the individual citizen against arbitrary decisions by subjecting officials to detailed rules, procedural as well as substantive and enforceable through special courts. British democracy concentrated on responsible, then representative, government: a political system for the control of bureaucrats through ministerial responsibility to Parliament was developed. In Germany the ruler retained control over policy but the bureaucrat came under a rule of law far more comprehensive and far more accessible than our Rule of Law. This explains why administrative law remains a necessary part of Public Administration training in continental Europe even today. One may ask in passing whether the citizen would not be better served if the same were true here.

Tübingen served as the inspiration for a short-lived School of Administration established in Paris in 1848. That, by a hundred years, was the forerunner of the *Ecole Nationale d'Administration*, set up after the last war as an immediate post-entry school for all recruits to the non-specialist higher civil service. And *ENA*, in its turn, was the inspiration of the *Hochschule für Verwaltungswissenschaft* established at Speyer, in the French occupation zone of Germany, with French help. Thus the wheel turned a full circle. It does not have the same embracing intake as *ENA*, nor is attendance at its courses obligatory for young officials. On the other hand, although also a post-entry school, with neither undergraduates nor first degrees, it does enjoy something like university status: it is an institution for teaching and research with the right to award higher degrees and with university-rank professors on its own full-time staff.

Now Britain also has its Civil Service College. Although its programme is based on relatively short courses for established civil servants at various stages in their careers, courses which cannot be considered postgraduate education in the same way as *ENA*'s longer course, taken as an immediate continuation of the first degree, it aspires, like the German model, to academic status. Its Principal and its Director of Studies in Public Administration were drawn from the universities and its intention is to promote research as well as training.

But the inspiration, indirect no doubt, was the French institution. We have already noted the role played by study of foreign experience in the last decade's wave of interest in administrative reform. The Parliamentary Commissioner for Administration was borrowed directly from the Scandinavian ombudsman. The idea of City Manager-Town Clerks was drawn from America, with a side look at Ireland. France, despite patronising scorn for the governmental instability of the Fourth Republic and almost hysterical reactions to the foreign policy of the Fifth, has retained some of its traditional role as mentor of the world. Its codified law and its administrative arrangements, the prefectoral system for example, have in the past been copied at least as widely as have for example, British parliamentary institutions. Recently it has been Britain's own turn to study France. First it was French economic planning, though the National Economic Development Council emerged but a poor shadow of the *Commissariat Général au Plan*. The Fulton committee made more references to France than to America or Sweden, the other countries visited by its members, and its comments were generally favourable. Among its working papers was an account of *ENA*. And in an appendix to the report the school is described as one of the most famous features on the French civil service—'in our view justly so'.

ENA, however, though its syllabus is being reformed, has in the past taught very little Public Administration as administrative science. Whether there is *a* discipline of Public Administration or, more broadly, whether there is *an* interdisciplinary subject, is the theme of subsequent discussion and this is not the place to enter the debate. Nor is it the place to consider the relationship between Public Administration as an academic and an applied subject. But one point is worth making here. While the university department is primarily concerned with understanding (researching the *how* and, more sophisticatedly, theorising about the *why*), the main concern of professional schools is with techniques (the *how to*). The academic may seek knowledge for its own sake (though a theme of this book is that such purity of interest is not desirable); the professional instructor, a utilitarian, wants improved performance. But the two are obviously linked. The administrator will gain something from an academic approach to the subject, not directly practice-orientated. In general terms, a knowledge of the wider system in which he operates will help him understand his own role in life. More specifically, techniques studies outside the context of the disciplines from which they are derived can easily be misunderstood. The medical practitioner, though primarily concerned with diagnosis and cure (techniques), is helped in the same way by an understanding of the scientific causes of ill health. More important, perhaps, is the fact that what can be taught in professional schools depends largely on the research of academics. Public Administration, like medicine, if left entirely to practitioners and the teachers of practice, would simply transmit existing procedures and received wisdom. It is the function of academics to push the frontiers of knowledge forward and thus feed practical training.

It is significant that large textbooks on Public Administration have recently been produced in France and Germany. Their importance lies less in their intrinsic merit (indeed, by comparison to American administrative science they can be described as rather old fashioned) than in the simple fact of their publication. Do they meet a demand or are they hoping to create it? Which came first, the chicken or the egg? Certainly, establishment of chairs (and France established its first chair of Administrative Science in the University of Paris not so long ago), or university departments, or degrees, means not only more research but also more teaching. New courses produce students who in the European, if not the British, context are likely to enter the public service. The civil service schools of France and Germany are largely staffed by practitioners and as new generations of practitioners take over, who as students have themselves passed through theoretically-orientated administrative science courses, the link between the academic and the practical, between theory and techniques, is likely to be strengthened. It will be interesting to see whether a similar pattern is followed in Britain.

In any case, one may well ask whether progress in the field of Public Administration is more likely to come in response to a demand from administrators or whether demand itself depends on the existence of a recognised subject. A subject is not necessarily the same thing as a worthwhile body of knowledge. If administrators are to ask for more than instruction in a miscellaneous bag of techniques, if they are to ask for something actually called Public Administration, they must surely first see the existence of an integrated discipline clearly different from other disciplines which offer the miscellaneous techniques they currently study.

Yet it is British academics themselves who have serious doubts about the existence of such a science—even using that term in its broadest sense—and perhaps with some justification. As we shall see, there are many problems of definition. Even when that preliminary stage is passed, there are questions about the scientific validity, not to mention practical value, of the theories encompassed. Scepticism is a healthy attribute, but the danger in Britain is that we may carry it so far as to prevent the emergence of a subject at all. All new disciplines are tentative in their early days and turn out later to have been full of errors. How many of the early classics of economics are still regarded as valid today? But would economics ever have developed if it had not early gained acceptance as a legitimate discipline? And would it have gained that acceptance if its pioneers had restricted themselves to empirical *ad hoc* studies of limited topics? Even the earliest textbooks of economic theory tried to present an integrated and comprehensive body of principles. The development of every new subject requires the same act of courage. That early theories are likely to be disproved later is less important than the fact that they assure the new subject a place in the academic universe, create a wider demand and thus encourage growth.

Public Administration as a non-professional subject is actually taught at many British universities, either in its institutional form as part of the study of British government or, more sophisticatedly but often somewhat out on a limb in the syllabus of a political science degree, as administrative theory. It is also taught in a variety of semi-professional courses, for example to local government officers. It is astonishing, therefore, that until very recently we have had virtually no textbooks with Public Administration in their title. The works of E. N. Gladden were a notable exception, but they were directed to a rather lower level of student. Compare the American scene. White's *Public Administration* and Willoughby's *Principles of Public Administration* were published in 1926 and 1927 respectively. To pick only some well-known general texts in recent use and to pick them only on the basis of their titles: Pfiffner and Presthus's *Public Administration,* Dimock and Dimock's *Public Administration*, Nigro and Nigro's *Modern Public Administration*, with first editions in 1931, 1953, and 1965 respectively, or alternatively, Simon, Smithburg and Thomson's *Public Administration*, going back to 1950.

It could be answered that we are only just getting over the belief that administration is an art and that there has been no call from administrators themselves for utilitarian textbooks of the 'how to administer' sort. The fact that public servants, central and local, are not recruited from students of the subject has of course been important. Such books are not required for undergraduate courses in political science where political science is treated as a humanities subject, pursued for its own sake (or, by a minority of students, as an apprenticeship to political action), but not as training for a career. With the publication of three books, the year 1970 may have been something of a watershed. Two, entitled *Public Administration* and *British Public Administration*, still remain close to the 'Introduction to British Government' tradition and are pitched below university level, but they obviously reflect a growing demand for a relevant, if not strictly professional, education for middle-rank officials. The third, R. G. S. Brown's *Administrative Process in Britain*, was aimed at more advanced students. After a discussion of the changing role of the civil service, it offers 'an introduction to organisation theory and then applies theoretical concepts to the machinery of government, executive management, policy and planning, the recruitment and training of administrators'. I wrote in my original article that I hoped it was a more significant swallow. Sure enough, it was followed almost immediately by R. J. S. Baker's *Administrative Theory and Public Administration*, M. S. Hill's *Sociology of Public Administration* and Peter Self's *Administrative Theories and Politics*. It is a sad commentary on the state of Public Administration studies that two of the authors are lecturers in Social Administration and only the last a member of a political science department.

The shortage of professionally orientated academic works may be understood in the British context. This, however, does not explain the even more astonishing shortage of academically orientated studies of the administrative system. We have Mackenzie and Grove's *Central Administration in Britain*, a major work in its time but largely institutional. We have F. M. G. Willson's *Organisation of British Central Government*, a detailed but quite straightforward account of changes in structure from 1914 to 1964. We have, especially since the Fulton years, an increasing number of books about the civil service, mainly historical but with some rather old-fashioned sociological analysis. We have the New Whitehall Series, ministry by ministry. We have two volumes of case studies, *Administrators in Action*, reportage uninformed by a theoretical framework, much less by theoretical conclusions. Polemical but far too brief, we have Brian Chapman's *British Government Observed* and, though smoother in style as personal a view, Sisson's *Spirit of British Administration*. There are more books, of course, but taken together they add up to less than one might legitimately expect. They embody little research into what actually goes on inside the administration and contribute even less to the advancement of theory. What theoretical discussion there is tends to be by sociologists writing about bureaucracy: two recent books that spring to mind are Mouzelis's *Organisation and Bureaucracy* and Albrow's *Bureaucracy*.

Compare again the American situation. A fairly random selection of recent books on American administration, chosen from the shelf partly because their titles indicate a range: Simon's *Administrative Behaviour*, Gawthrop's *Bureaucratic Behaviour in the Executive Branch*, Downs' *Inside Bureaucracy*, Kaufman's *Forest Rangers—A Study in Administrative Behaviour*, Price's *The Scientific Estate*, Mosher's *Democracy and the Public Service*, Redford's *Democracy in the Administrative State*. One could easily go on. It is not only the quantity that differs but the range of subject matters and, in many cases, the originality of the approach. Americans may place too high a premium on originality, theorise too easily, and produce too many dead-end original theories; and that in turn makes wholesale dismissal too easy. That we have no Herbert Simon, no Fred Riggs in Britain may be a factor of size: compare the number of political scientists in the two countries, or, indeed, the size of university departments. We cannot hope to rival American research nor, indeed, are we likely on the simple law of averages to have as many original thinkers. But it is chastening to think that we have nothing yet to compare with that theoretically based and empirically supported study of the French administrative system, *The Bureaucratic Phenomenon*. Where, one asks despondently, is the Crozier of Britain? France, after all, has even fewer political scientists and sociologists than we.

The situation is doubly strange when one considers the current fashion in political science to study politics as a system with inputs and outputs. The administration, after all, is the box in which inputs are actually translated into outputs. And that box is inhabited by civil servants. It is not just that they influence the policy-making process by their advice or the pressures they can exercise, though that is obviously true. They translate policy into action in a more technical sense of the term: drafting the laws, making the rules and drawing up the guidelines which alone make it operational and, responsible for its execution, by their everyday actions they give it further shape. The way the box is organised, its patterns of work and communication systems, for example, is bound to affect this process. And it is not only a question of structures, but of men also and their behaviour patterns. The study of administration as a formally organised system of bureaucracy and as a sociological phenomenon, of the decision-making process in its managerial as well as its political aspects, is thus vital to any understanding of British government. It would probably pay greater dividends than, for example, the fashionable analysis of voting behaviour.

One of the facts holding back researchers, of course, is that our administration is nowhere near as open as the American. It has been notoriously difficult to obtain material, though there are welcome signs of change. Our academics also lack the insights offered American scholars who move between government service and the universities with much greater ease. It is true that a few British scholars have served periods of secondment in government departments (and a few, going rather far back now, served as temporary civil servants during the war), but these are exceptions. The structure of our civil service allows no comparison with the much wider career patterns of Public Administrationists in America, nor do university structures in Britain really favour such careers. Periods of public service apart, many Americans combine consultancy work with university teaching. It is said, indeed, that the status of a university department can be measured by the proportion of its professors in the air at any one time—on the way to or from such extra-mural activities. How many political scientists specialising in Public Administration have been used by the government to advise on administrative problems in the way that economists, sociologists and other specialists are? Open invitations to submit evidence to commissions of inquiry, or even occasional invitations to sit on such a commission, are a very different thing from paid, internal consultancy work.

The situation is likely to change, but progress is bound to be slow unless there is a considerable expansion in the number of Public Administrationists in political science departments as well as a change of attitude on the part of the civil service. What needs to be recognised is the dual function of academic research. It can be pursued for its own sake, as part of the disinterested attempt to understand the political system; at the same time it is bound to contribute to a sharpening of administrative techniques. Knowledge *how to* follows from knowledge *how and why*, whether intended by the scholar or not. One might as well embrace this fact and with it a dual motivation. It may indeed be necessary for the advancement of the subject, as usefulness is likely to bring increased research opportunities. It is arguable, in any case, that as universities expand, traditional art for art's sake should be tempered by a commitment to public service: as their cost to society becomes ever heavier, universities should lay an increasing emphasis on those fields which justify the finance of scholarship by utility. The Public Administrationist, in other words, should be one who earns his keep twice over. Certainly, it has been this combination of academic respectability and utilitarian pay-off which has given strength to American Public Administration.

Psephology has developed by comparison with Public Administration not only because its data was more accessible but also because it was readily quantifiable. To that extent it could be organised, and generalisations could be drawn from it, in a way that is difficult with the raw material of Public Administration. The demand is commonly made for more case studies of the administrative process for use as teaching material. Case studies, however, are in the nature of things narrative accounts of unique events. They may give one a better feel for what goes on, they can even be used as vicarious experience, serving as decision-making exercises for trainee administrators, but they contribute relatively little to the development of general theory because little of a general nature can be deduced from them. Broader descriptive studies of entire systems, ecologies even, more anthropological in approach, have in fact been more fertile in stimulating theory. This is shown by the work of Fred Riggs and other American students of development administration (shorthand: the comparative administration movement).

British scholars have perhaps leant towards description on too narrow a front and an approach altogether too empirical. Such sobriety has its strength. But the tendency to scoff at American grand theory is overdone. Often, no doubt, such theory has methodological weaknesses. As often, no doubt, it remains pure theory: its variables cannot be given concrete values or few practical lessons can be drawn from it. A willingness to theorise is nevertheless a prerequisite for the advance from miscellaneous description to an integrated body of knowledge, in other words to the development of a real subject.

It is thus to America that we must largely look if we are to consider the study of Public Administration. This chapter began with a reference to a long defunct German tradition. American universities, in this as in other fields, have been its heirs. Woodrow Wilson, then a Professor of Political Science at Princeton, recommended the study of administration in an article in the *American Political Science Quarterly* as far back as 1887. This hackneyed reference brings out the contrast between the British and the American experience.

Public administration Wilson defined as the machinery for implementing government policy. It could thus be divorced from politics, or, as one would now say, policy-making. The study of Public Administration was the study of the most efficient ways of organising the executive branch of government, its institutions and its procedures. This concept of efficiency tied in well with the scientific management movement started at the turn of the century in America by F. W. Taylor, though with a second, French, parent in Henri Fayol. The approach, later somewhat unjustly decried, was formalist: the concern, that is to say, was with formal structures and rules of procedure. So, of course, was the scientific management movement of the time and, given the state of contemporary sociology, it could be little else. As important, however, and again to some extent a Germanic heritage, was the early and quite un-English concern with administrative law (William Robson a later and untypical exception), an interest which straddled law and political science. It is significant, for example, that the first president of the American Political Science Association, Frank Goodnow, was a Professor of Administrative Law at Columbia. American political scientists concerned themselves with practical aspects of administrative reform. Woodrow Wilson typified this link between academic and utilitarian studies, this overlap of professor and practitioner.

Much has changed since the White and Willoughby textbooks of the 1920s. American universities, showing another aspect of their receptivity to German scholarship, took more easily to the ideas of Max Weber than Britain or, indeed, than Germany itself. The study of Public Administration, having moved from the legal-institutional to scientific management (O & M, personnel, budgeting and all that), turned to the study of bureaucracy and, with Simon as a landmark, to administrative behaviour. Simon, though senior author of the pathbreaking new-approach textbook in Public Administration, is a Professor of Administration and head of the Department of Industrial Management at the Carnegie-Mellon University (previously Carnegie Institute of Technology). This itself typifies two developments. On the one hand, there has been a tendency to submerge Public Administration in Administration *tout court* and, for the behaviouralists at least, to make it part of the general sociology of organisation. On the other, the subject became increasingly under the influence of new branches of economics, developed partly in Schools of Business Administration and centring round the calculus of decisions.

Despite some efforts at unification, in general systems theory for example, this leaves Public Administration with two quite different academic disciplines to draw upon: the quantitative-rational approach towards policy-making favoured by the economist and the human-relations approach towards administrative behaviour favoured by the sociologist. Public Administration now has so wide and diverse a field of contributors, using not only very different approaches to a recognised bundle of problems but actually focusing on a range of rather different problems, that its contemporary history is almost impossible to characterise.

Wilson wrote in 1887 that the science of administration was the latest form of the study of politics. In the light of the developments just mentioned, it is no longer clear that the subject, as practised, is part of the study of politics at all. But a third, more recent, trend also requires mention: the study of policy-making as a political process. Policy studies is now a fashionable term but one that hides an ambiguity of meaning which sometimes leads to practical confusion when those involved in entirely different activities, as likely as not with different interests, meet on the assumption that they are pursuing a common aim. One may conveniently distinguish between normative theories about policy-making, essentially formulae to improve decision-making as a technical process (procedural techniques such as planning, programming and budgeting), and empirical studies of how decisions are actually made, often in terms of the political forces that are inputs into the system and that shape its policy outputs. Examples of the latter approach in recent American textbooks are Sharkansky's *Public Administration: Policy Making in Government Agencies* and Rehfuss's *Public Administration as Political Process*. This has meant a reintroduction of political science into Public Administration and a reintroduction of Public Administration into political science.

Arguably, and it is certainly my argument, such studies are often better seen as part of the study of politics than of Public Administration. They are generally concerned with a traditional question of politics: who gets what? Political scientists have simply realised that administrative institutions are as important an area of input-output transformation as political institutions (Congress for example) and must thus be given a major place in any comprehensive account of the process. That does not mean that this approach is not also relevant to the study of the administrative system as such, to Public Administration that is to say. Clearly it throws a new light on how the administrative system operates just as the sociological approach does.

The point about these remarks is that if all these approaches, and others not mentioned, form part of Public Administration, then Public Administration has become a true crossroads science, so interdisciplinary that its links with political science are outweighed by the range of the links with other disciplines. This can be used as the basis for a declaration of independence for the subject. But whether it then remains a subject in its own right at all is open to debate. It depends to some extent on its purpose. Whatever the purpose, however, there is cause for concern in this confusion of approaches as serious as the underdeveloped state of administrative studies in Britain.

In so far as the academic study of administration is concerned, the situation is perhaps not far different from that now found in political science itself where a number of disciplines (i.e. methods of investigations) are focused on a single object of study—in the one case the administrative system, in the other the wider political system, and what goes on within them. But there is a tendency for sociology to annex large areas of politics and a similar tendency, in the study of bureaucracy for example, for sociology to annex Public Administration, treating it merely as another case of organisational behaviour. This trend is not without danger. It can too easily overlook the very aspect of Public Administration of which earlier political scientists were so aware: the importance of formal institutions and formal procedures. Though business organisations are also subject to law, the role played by law clearly differentiates public authorities from private undertakings, both as regards internal organisation and as regards relations with the public. As crucial is the role of politics. None would deny that giant corporations are subject to political forces, but again politics clearly differentiates public service from other forms of activity, both as regards the pressures to which it is subject and as regards the goals it pursues. If the result of becoming a cross-roads science is to underplay the legal and political aspects of Public Administration, as is likely where theories are drawn from research in wider fields, then it may be that Public Administration should narrow its concern, leave research in management and behaviour to others, and look again to its own traditions.

The situation is rather different if one considers Public Administration as a vocational subject to be taught in professional schools. Administrators are taught a variety of useful disciplines, personnel management by social psychologists for example, or quantitative techniques for decision-making by economists. These specialists often seem to have little in common except their employment in the same institution. It is argued that these techniques are much the same wherever employed. The case is therefore often made for all-purpose schools of Administration to serve both public and private sectors and to include in the former such quite varied activities as health, welfare and educational administration, the administration of public works, scientific projects and development aid programmes, as well as the more traditional central civil service activities. It is a case not without attraction. Division of labour among teachers permits greater specialisation. Common training encourages career mobility and creates professional links between sectors of activity which can only be advantageous.

But there are also dangers. Specialist teachers brought together in this way may have little in common except their employment in the same institution. They may lose the academic strength that comes from membership of an institution focusing on a narrower front. The public service student may find that what the non-Public Administration orientated specialist has to teach is not sufficiently geared to his own needs. It can be forcibly argued that Public Administration requires an emphasis on politics far greater than other branches of administrative study, an empirical emphasis on the political context and a normative emphasis on political goals. And it requires the teaching of politics (and, to some extent, of public law), not merely as a separate course but integrated in all courses.

Meanwhile, to return to the American example, America has not merely civil service schools which predate our own Civil Service College, for example the fairly recent Federal Executive Institute at Charlottesville, but also has long-established graduate schools in the universities. Notable examples are the Kennedy (formerly Littauer) School at Harvard, the Maxwell School at Syracuse, the Wilson School at Princeton and the Pittsburgh Graduate School of Public Affairs. These and others have established a world-wide reputation. Though there are now some graduate courses at British universities—an M.Sc. is offered at the London School of Economics, for example, and a B.Phil. at Liverpool—we have no university-linked schools of Public Administration (the Institute of Local Government Studies at Birmingham is an exception, but its name defines its limitations). We do not even have separate university departments. True, even business schools are a recent phenomenon on the British scene: where business pioneers, may not public service follow?

It remains to be seen, of course, whether the demand will ever be large enough in Britain to stimulate such a development. One would hope so. We may be a small country compared to the United States, but surely not so small that we cannot afford—or fill—at least one such institution. It may be a mistake, however, to wait for consumer demand. Consumer demand is perhaps more likely to follow than to stimulate the development of a subject. And experience shows that subjects are likely to develop faster once they have achieved recognition. To do this, in the academic world at least, they have to establish themselves institutionally by the creation of chairs and then of independent university departments. Until the subject is established it is hard to sell. The relative lack of interest in Public Administration as a necessary part of public service training may well be due to a suspicion that it has little concrete to offer. Old-fashioned businessmen had similar suspicions. As likely, it is due to the fact that there is little concrete on offer in this country. In business schools we imitated America. Economists and businessmen were open-minded enough not to mind. It would be a pity if current disdain for American work in the field of Public Administration were to prevent British scholars —and British officials—from at least exploring this path.

But perhaps the time for independent university departments of Public Administration is already past. Perhaps something wider is now required. If interdisciplinary schools of general administration are suspect because they underplay the political, a different sort of interdisciplinary approach is possible that would emphasise politics in the older sense of the word, i.e. public policy. It may be more sensible to concentrate on Public Affairs. By combining the study of administrative science with the study of substantive policy fields, an otherwise often rather arid subject can be made more concrete and thus more interesting. It may help to combat the generalist's approach that emphasises smooth running at the cost of direction, that designs the noiseless Rolls without much concern for where it is to be driven. Conversely, it allows for a greater injection of political and administrative considerations into the policy studies. This, of course, seems to be the way we are going: thus, one example only, the Centre for Environmental Studies in London.

University departments, however, traditionally concentrate on undergraduate teaching and research by young graduates. Though many courses are vocational in practice, the departments are committed by tradition—and rightly so—to degrees with a full academic content. They do not take easily, therefore, to mid-career training. Nor is full academic content, the study of a subject in depth, easily reconciled with an interdisciplinary education. Graduate research is pursued largely as academic apprenticeship and while it may incidentally have a utilitarian pay-off, this is not a prime consideration. Similar problems arise on staffing. Appointment is rightly on the basis of scholarship but promotion generally depends on publications, making the recruitment of practitioners difficult at senior levels. Other administrative and financial restrictions are too numerous to mention. For these reasons it may be more sensible to establish a more broadly based school of Public Affairs than the policy orientated institutions recently established, university linked to ensure academic respectability but with a fair degree of independence. Such a school would be more flexible in the interchange between scholarship and practice, for example, and in the provision of a non-degree course. It could more easily bring together specialists from different disciplines. It could employ town planners, traffic engineers, social administrators and management experts, as well as economists, sociologists and political scientists. Their common focus would be public affairs, public policy and Public Administration, their common commitment public service.

But such a departure might well require action from outside the universities, where radical innovation is often blocked by natural conservatism as well as the existing balance of sectional interests. And that brings one back to the problem of the chicken and the egg. It is true that consumer demand is more likely to be created by the existence of a recognised subject with a healthy academic record, but it is equally true that change is more likely to come from pressures outside an organisation than from within. In the last resort, therefore, some intervention may be necessary. This is the third cause for concern: who will play the *deus ex machina*?

In this chapter I have noted a number of causes for concern about the state of Public Administration studies in Britain. I shall return to these in the following chapters where I suggest a focus for Public Administration considered as an academic subject, as distinct from the title attached to a mix of courses useful for administrators. That the approach advocated is institutional will not surprise the reader, though I should repeat my earlier disclaimer here: other approaches are legitimate, indeed more widely accepted, and my purpose is largely to attempt a rescue operation for a now unfashionable view of the subject. That the approach should be utilitarian also follows from what has been said earlier, and I look particularly at the role of universities in this respect, at the contribution the academic subject can make to the training of administrators, the reform of government and the education of citizens.

No attempt is made to discuss practical training courses in Public Administration, however, much less the content of multi-subject qualifications for administrators. To pursue this line would take us into a wider range of disciplines, well outside the political science-Public Administration field of this book, just as it would take us outside the walls of university teaching with which this book is primarily concerned. The training of administrators is an important matter and curriculum planning raises many interesting questions. My self-denial is, to be honest, influenced only partly by the focus I have given the present volume. The academic is usually reluctant to accept the practical man's principle, 'whereof one cannot speak from experience, therein one should not meddle'. The academic is usually right: the practitioner's vision is likely to be limited; the scholar, even the ivory-tower intellectual, has new perspectives to contribute. Even so, scholarship in this case requires some expertise, a close knowledge of administrative practice as well as knowledge of the specialised techniques administrators should employ. I cannot claim to possess either in sufficient degree to speak with confidence and I *do* subscribe to the principle, 'whereof one cannot speak with confidence, thereon one should remain silent'.

Focus of the Subject

What is the subject of Public Administration? It all depends for whom, is a legitimate reply. As a subject of study Public Administration means rather different things to different groups of students. Basically, there are three clienteles. They may overlap, sometimes one client may wear two or even all three hats, but they are notionally distinguishable by their purpose. Public Administration is a subject for academics, administrators and citizens; it can be disinterested pursuit of knowledge (liberal education and scholarly research, traditional concerns of the university), professional training (sometimes a university function, more often organised elsewhere), and political debate (originating in the universities, perhaps, but directed at a wider public).

As an academic subject, Public Administration studies how the country's administration is organised and how it functions; more sophisticatedly, it tries to explain why it works as it does; ranging further, it seeks to understand administrative systems in general. In this, it may form part of political science, taking the administration as part, indeed the largest part, of the machinery of government or, more modernly, as an important subsystem in the wider system of politics. There is no monopoly, of course: aspects of bureaucratic organisation may also form party of sociology, while institutional aspects may enter legal studies under the guise of administrative law.

Political science itself is often called a cross-roads science, moreover, and this is only another way of saying that the academic study of Public Administration can take a number of lines, depending to some extent on the disciplines employed in analysis. Examples only: the legalistic approach with its formal anatomy of governmental institutions and analysis of procedural rules; the straightforward description of administrative activities, case studies for example; the behaviouralist emphasis on social interaction within administrative organisations; the policy orientated observer's concern with the decision-making process and its contents. The danger of some of these approaches, however, is that they too easily dissolve study of the administration in wider fields of study (law, contemporary history, sociology of organisations, policy as such, the political process). There is nothing to be said against this. Indeed, one should be glad if the practitioners of other disciplines recognise the importance of administration and give it a place in their studies, but if we ourselves embrace all these disciplines we become the clients of other subjects and may— as Public Administrationists—be left without a subject of our own. That, to some extent, is the point I made in my first chapter about the methodological temptations that face the jack of all trades.

But here it is another another point I want to make. The student (a term which embraces the researcher) may wish to study the administration as such rather than other fields which happen to include certain aspects of it. His interest may be concrete, just as another enjoys reading about exotic tribes or medieval history, or more scientific, moving from description to explanation and from explanations of the specific to generalised theories. In either case the purpose of study can be the study itself, a form of art for art's sake. That this can be combined with the utilitarian purpose of training and reform I shall argue, but it is notionally distinct and may not be combined in practice, any more than students of political science need always have a practical purpose.

Public Administration is also vocational, a label pinned to useful subjects for professional administrators or those who intend to become professional administrators. The emphasis then is not on the *how* or the *why* but on the *how to*: how to organise the administration, operate its procedures, manage its staff, calculate its policies and much else besides. If professional training is to involve more than the transmission of experience by the experienced, if practical instruction is to be underpinned by theoretical understanding, then what is offered the practitioner is likely to resemble that which is offered the academic clientele. Moreover, if techniques of administration are to be taught which are better than current practice, instructors will have to rely on academic research: frontiers of knowledge are rarely pushed forward in other ways.

More important is the fact that such use of the Public Administration label is somewhat misleading. I referred above to useful subjects in the plural and it is obvious that much of the knowledge required by administrators goes well beyond any study of the administrative system, however approached. It embraces a wide and ever-widening range of management techniques. In addition, they may require some knowledge of the substantive fields they are to administer, and each of these, again, may involve a variety of approaches, some focusing on the technical aspects, others on the wider implications of alternative policies. Public Administration used in this context is no longer the title of a subject but the title of a curriculum or a qualification. There is nothing wrong with this usage: what is argued is simply that the subject of Public Administration is something rather more specific—a part rather than the whole of the curriculum. Much confusion can be avoided if the distinction is kept in mind. Without it, certainly, it becomes impossible to begin defining Public Administration as a subject in its own right.

Finally, there is Public Administration as what, for want of a better word, I shall call civics, training for citizenship or, more generally still, education for democracy. There is the view that ordinary citizens (or schoolchildren and students, the citizens-to-be) should be taught something about how the administrative system of their country operates. This is desirable for utilitarian reasons—so that, increasingly administered, they can better make their interests known, pursue their claims, protect their rights. More fundamentally, it is desirable for the sake of democracy—so that they can participate more effectively at least at the grass-roots levels of government, not necessarily to pursue their own interests but as part of the civic culture (a useful phrase if one separates it from the technical content given it by recent American political science) on which democracy of consent depends.

Another aspect of Public Administration as civics is the writing which is directed at the informed and influential public, including administrators and politicians, and seeks to improve the governmental system. This again may have utilitarian or democratic motives, greater efficiency or more responsible government for example, though we must beg the ambiguity of such shorthand terms. The link between the three spheres of Public Administration is obvious. True, the idea that science should concern itself with the relief of man's estate as well as the advancement of learning is sometimes more honoured in the breach than in the observance, more often in political science these days, perhaps, than in most other social disciplines, but the original purpose of the study of government was not to cultivate knowledge for its own sake: it was squarely reformist. Public Administration must, I am sure, focus not only on theories about how the administration works or about how to administer, but also—and arguably more important— on ways of making government better.

The purpose of the remainder of this chapter is to consider what the subject of Public Administration can be if it is to be a subject in its own right. Practical illustrations of the approach I advocate have already been given in earlier chapters where I have considered some contemporary problems of administrative reform. In the next chapter we shall look instead at the fathers of the subject, not as potted history of now discredited theories, but to illustrate the abiding relevance of their approach.

Public Administration is the study of public administration. The ambiguity is obvious enough. We slip easily from one use to the other, from public administration as the subject of study to Public Administration as the name of the study itself. Public Administration is often used as the title of a university course. We do the same when we label courses about the governmental system Government or, indeed, when we describe the study of political systems as Politics. Our usage becomes more confused, however, when we go one step further and employ the same term for descriptive accounts of the system and for theories about it. Whatever convenient label we attach to courses about the British system of government, we are pretty clear that theories about the governmental system are part of political science. But we have no convenient name for the body of theoretical knowledge we have acquired about the administrative system. This is a rare example of linguistic poverty in the Anglo-Saxon, connected partly, no doubt, with inhibitions about the use of the word 'science'. The Germans have the long-established term *Verwaltungswissenschaft* and the French have more recently accepted *science administrative*. Both are understood to refer to *public* administration. The English translation, administrative science, does not have the same specific connotation and will, therefore, not serve as a parallel to political science.

The implication of an administrative science is that it focuses on administration in general. Now it may be that administration is sufficiently similar, whether public or private, for it to be treated as a single subject. Even allowing for the fact that administration circumscribed by law and subject to politics is bound to have a character of its own, administrative procedures and the behaviour of administrators will have much in common wherever found. But definition of a subject by focus on an activity—the activity of administering—is misleading in the context of Public Administration, however legitimate it may be for the purpose of defining other subjects of study. The subject of study in political science is not political activity or even, current fashion notwithstanding, political behaviour: it is the political system. The fact that very similar forms of behaviour can be observed in trade unions, companies, clubs and, indeed, almost any organised group, merely indicates that the sociologist can study aspects of the political system as part of the general study of social behaviour. The same is true of Public Administration. If it is to differentiate itself at all, the focus of Public Administration must be the public administrative system as a whole, its formal institutions and its rules of procedure as well as the way it really works. And it is the formal institutions, it will be argued, which, though by no means all important, actually define the subject of study.

It is sometimes said that the social sciences all take the same reality as their province—man in society—and examine different aspects of the relationship between them. Each science examines different aspects of this complex of relationships between men, organisations and events. The social sciences, and on this view it is easy to slip into saying the behavioural sciences, differentiate themselves not by selecting different men, organisations or events as their field of study: they do so by concentrating on different types of relationship. Sociology concerns itself with the structure and interlocking of social roles; social psychology looks at the problems of the individual within the organised group.

But political science is a little different. Unlike sociology, social psychology or, indeed, anthropology, it does not look at the entire social complex from a special point of view. It defines itself by the entity it studies. It is concerned not purely with a type of relationship, with the political, though there is an element of this in most definitions of political science, but with the political *system* as a whole. Arguably, this is even truer in the case of Public Administration because the subject matter there is rather more obviously circumscribed. It may be hard to define society except in terms of relationships, it may even be hard to define the political system in concrete terms (though something is gained if one uses instead the term governmental system), but *the* public administration had a clear institutional framework. The basis of Public Administration studies, therefore, is an entity, not an approach. If administrative science is the *how and why* of administrative behaviour, Public Administration is both less than this because administrative behaviour is a wider subject, and more than this because the administrative system consists of more than behaviour. This fact has led some Frenchmen to borrow *Administration Publique* from the English, as in the title of a recent university textbook, the emphasis, admittedly, being on description of the structure and 'real working' of administrative institutions rather than on theory. If administrative science will not do as a label, therefore, and if Public Administration sounds too descriptive, one should presumably talk of public administration science. But this is too clumsy and usage is against it.

There is another problem about the term Public Administration, and here I return to what I said above with reference to one clientele. What administrators want to learn is not only the *how and why* of the administrative system, perhaps not even the *how and why*, but the *how to*. In so far as they are concerned with the efficient organisation of work, they will draw on such new disciplines as systems analysis and communications theory. In so far as they are concerned with the organisation of men, they will need the help of social psychologists. And their concern is not merely with management but also with policy-making. For this they will turn to the economists whose specialisation is rational choice in the use of scarce resources. In other words, if one thinks of Public Administration as something for the professional administrator, it can easily become a label for the entire range of knowledge he may find useful. It becomes interdisciplinary in quite a different sense: not a combination of methods of investigation focused on a single subject matter, more or less integrated, but a set of basically unrelated disciplines, even if more or less geared to his needs. For this reason, perhaps, the French preferred until recently to talk of *sciences administratives* rather than *science administrative*, meaning sciences for administrators rather than the scientific study of the administrative system. Public Administration is used in this sense in such names as School of Public Administration or Diploma in Public Administration. It is not the name of a course but of a curriculum. It is almost impossible to avoid this, as indeed other, ambiguities. Terminology does not really matter very much so long as one is clear what one is talking about. It matters only when the complexities of meaning are ignored and argument slides, as it too often does, from one sense to another without clarification *en route*.

Certainly, to return to our apparent truism that Public Administration is the study of the administration, we are not really in much danger of mistaking the theoretical discipline for the concrete reality. Much argument about the scope of public administration theory nevertheless rests on terminological confusion. One reason for this is that there is not a straight one-to-one relationship between them. The study of Public Administration does not concern itself with all that goes on within the administrative system. Unfortunately, the adherents of different schools of Public Administration often start with different definitions of their subject matter, different definitions of what, within the system, they consider their special concern. Much of the argument about how the science of Public Administration should develop depends on such definitions, though this is often forgotten in the subsequent debate. Definitional arguments easily acquire a scholastic character all of their own and become as sterile as they are divisive. In the last resort every scholar can appeal to Humpty Dumpty and make his words mean exactly what he wants them to. It is possible, against this, to appeal to consensus, at least where consensus exists, but it is equally true that many breakthroughs in the social sciences have been the result of a redefining of accepted terms by the pioneers of a new approach. Some definitions, moreover, turn out to be more useful than others, though this itself raises the question: useful for what?

The point here is simply that any study of Public Administration is selective. It generally limits itself to what it considers the truly administrative in the administrative system. Technical questions relating to the substance of policy, as distinct from the actual policy-making process or techniques to be applied in the rational making of policy, are thus generally excluded.

Many textbooks certainly start on these lines. That they often give their opening pages to stating the obvious is another matter. Perhaps it is just a convention, a proper way of doing things; perhaps even the obvious appears an insight to the uninitiated—the number of pages spent in this way could perhaps be used to measure the degree of sophistication expected of new students. Politics, we are told, is an unavoidable fact of human existence. So is economics. And so it would seem, is administration. Wherever two or three are gathered together, political, economic and administrative relationships are bound to arise. And it all goes back to the ancient civilisations of which we have record, the Egyptians by preference. Thus Simon and his collaborators: 'When two men co-operate to roll a stone that neither could move alone, the rudiments of administration have appeared.' Almost as broad, two decades and a more old-fashioned approach earlier, is Luther Gulick's 'Administration has to do with getting things done, with the accomplishment of defined objectives.' Beyond proving the universality of administration, and thus the importance of the subject, all this contributes little to further analysis. Some looseness of language is already apparent, however. There are those who emphasise the activities of men working together to accomplish common goals and those who emphasise the organisation of such activities. I shall return to this problem. It is worth noting that a separation between ends and means is often assumed in such definitions. This creates other problems to which we shall also return.

More important in its consequences, perhaps, is the next stage of definition: what is *public* administration? How do we isolate a sector of this apparently universal activity for special study. We may note another verbal ambiguity here. So far I have referred to study of the administrative system. On the face of this usage, system is defined by its functions—the public administrative system is identified by the performance of the functions of public administration. But how do we identify public functions? It is a problem that does not arise, of course, if one starts with a different sort of introduction to the subject altogether, not with man in society but with the structure of government and a distinction between executive and political institutions. We can then say, and that is the approach I wish to advocate, that Public Administration is not primarily about an activity, it is about a set of institutions: *the* Administration. In earlier days Americans, inspired by the separation of powers, had the convenient phrase *executive branch of government*. But in American textbooks of Public Administration, as indeed of political science itself, such an opening is now rare.

There are those, of course, who say we should not isolate a *sector* of reality at all. For the sociologist organisational behaviour in the public sector is only one aspect of behaviour in organisations. In the same way, of course, he may see politics as simply another aspect of social behaviour and regard with distrust the erection of a separate discipline of political science. And given the currently fashionable belief that we are all sociologists now, the political scientist, and even the Public Administrationist, may feel bound to agree. Two questions certainly arise. First, as all human activity forms part of a seamless web, are not all divisions within the social sciences bound to be arbitrary? Second, may such divisions, if made, not distract from the existence of general laws; may the student of public administration, for example, not easily miss the significance of what the sociologist has learned in his wider field?

For the Public Administrationist, nevertheless, the answer may be different. To him, the question whether public administration differs significantly from other forms of administration may be irrelevant: he may well admit that all forms of administration share common characteristics, that there are general laws of administrative behaviour, general principles of administrational organisation, but he can borrow these from the research of other scholars. He is interested primarily in analysing the working of the governmental system. His definition, then, may be a simple institutional one: public administration is administration in the public sector. Alternatively, and more sophisticatedly, he may claim that public administration differs significantly from other forms of administration and can thus be defined by its character as well as by the institutional framework in which it occurs. Character, however, is an altogether less concrete starting point than institutions and, as the definition of a subject matter, shades into far too many uncertainties.

The simplest definition of public administration is that it is administration by the state. Though not so simple in fact, because it depends in turn on a definition of the state itself. That is no problem for the European but perhaps something of a problem for the British student. I have already discussed in an earlier chapter whether such a thing as *the* state is to be found in Britain at all, but the theme must be raised again. At one level that is a question for the political philosopher and as such does not concern us. But what of the state as a formally recognised entity capable of administration? Nearly every European textbook on constitutional or administrative law will start with a definition of the state. Our own textbooks are astonishingly silent by comparison. In E. C. S. Wade and Phillips' *Constitutional Law*, for example, it is used only three or four times and that with reference to international relations: we recognise the existence of foreign states which have certain rights in Britain (e.g. the immunity of state property) and we recognise that our own government has certain prerogative powers, arising out of its relationship with foreign states, in the performance of acts of state—the actor, however, being the Crown and not the state. For domestic purposes it does not appear to exist as a legal institution at all. The situation is not different as we look at H. W. R. Wade's *Administrative Law*. He does say at the start that 'if the powers of the state are classified as legislative, administrative and judicial, then administrative law might be said to be the law which concerns administrative authorities as opposed to others'—but it is clear that the word state has no formal connotation in that sentence: it is dropped thereafter, and he continues that 'the administrative authorities can be easily recognised: the Crown, ministers, local authorities, police and so forth'. The absence of any real concept of the state, used though we are to it, does make the definition of public administration more difficult.

Like all political systems, we do of course have government and we can say that public administration is governmental administration. Government, however, is a term of political science rather than law and no easier to pin down. More practically, therefore,

one might say that public administration is administration by
public authorities. But what are public authorities? We cannot
define them, as Europeans would, as organs of the state. And we
have no obvious definition of our own. H. W. R. Wade merely
says that they are easily recognised, but it says something for the
astonishingly pragmatic approach of British jurists that he simply
leaves it at that. But all difficulties are not met so easily. What
about public corporations, for example? Public they are, but are
they part of public administration? The most important corporations are industrial concerns run on commercial lines. Their
administrative structures and their administrative procedures are
not significantly different from undertakings in the private sector.

This may tempt one to take evasive action, defining public
administration, after all, not in terms of the institutions in which
it occurs but by its characteristics, by its difference from other
forms of administration. Something of the sort occurs in European
countries in relation to the definition of administrative law. In
France, for example, public law applies to those actions of the
state—the great majority—which are public functions, private law
where it is acting like any other individual. It is thus possible to
distinguish the rules governing the public and private property of
a local authority, the latter not having a public interest element,
or, in the case of nationalised industries, to distinguish rules applicable to the operation of a public utility and those relating to
ordinary industrial or commercial activities. All this, however,
depends on the elaboration of a doctrine of public services by the
administrative courts, and this we do not have either.

It seems, therefore, that while one could probably define public
administration formally in terms of the special rules to which
public authorities are subject, or the special powers they enjoy,
such a definition is likely to be circular in the absence of a clear
legal framework. Public administration is administration by public
authorities and public authorities are authorities which administer
according to the rules of public administration (or, more restric-
tedly, public administration is administration by public authorities
in so far as it is bound by such rules). Broadly, however, we all
recognise governmental institutions when we see them and we
recognise the difference between administration by governmental
and other bodies when we meet it. Perhaps it is best left at that.

All this may sound very academic and without practical consequence. Definitions do, however, have a considerable effect on
the way a subject is presented. We may start with what is essentially political, stressing such aspects of administration as ministerial
direction, answerability to Parliament, consultation with interests,

responsiveness to outside pressures, awareness of public opinion. We may emphasise the legal aspects, the extent to which it is subject to control by the courts, and other forms of control such as audit by the Comptroller and Auditor General or investigation by the Parliamentary Commissioner for Administration. We may stress formalisation by internal rules relating to public expenditure or civil service staffing, for example. Or we may pick out the power of public authorities to take legally enforceable decisions. Against this, there are those who will argue that such a focus may distract from the similarities between public and private administration. It can be argued that there is only one phenomenon called administration, that administration is administration is administration, that its subdivision means overrating secondary characteristics. This is quite likely to be the view of the student who starts from organisation theory or decision theory, the sociologist or the economist or, indeed, where such creatures are found, the administrative scientist.

The case for the unity of administrative studies has been argued often and forcibly. Against this, it is argued here that the special factors to which public administration is subject, the political and the legal environment in which it operates, are so inextricably intertwined with the administrative process as to make it quite different in character from other forms of administration. Even if this were not true, even if the similarities were really as important as the differences, this would still be no reason to submerge Public Administration in the study of administration.

This is particularly true if we are primarily interested in the political science focus, the working of the institutions of government, rather than generalisations about administrative behaviour. That we may have to draw on other disciplines for useful knowledge is no reason to demolish the frontiers and thus allow the subject to disintegrate. The study of human physiology, to take an example from another field, depends extensively on research into animal physiology, but it has not been found necessary to amalgamate the two. There are, indeed, obvious practical arguments for separation in both cases: medical studies are geared to the understanding and treatment of Man; Public Administration is geared to the understanding and 'treatment' of governmental systems ('treatment' to be understood here as the improvement of administration, whether by the advocacy of reforms or the training of administrators).

The whole argument has arisen very largely because it is now common to describe administration, and thus public administration, as an activity. This is part of that fashionable trend in political science as a whole which approaches the subject in behavioural rather than institutional terms. That is the behaviouralists' right. But the subject can be defined in institutional terms. We do recognise *the* administration when we see it. As a recognisable institution, it is a legitimate subject for study. Public Administration centred originally on the organisation of the executive branch of government and there is much to be said for a return to this. Indeed, if it is to be a subject in its own right at all, therein lies its best hope. All other approaches will submerge it, sooner or later, in other disciplines.

And that would be a loss. Public Administration as an independent subject is worth promoting not simply as a matter of academic interest but because of the contribution it can make to the welfare of society. Its American origins lay not so much in the study of existing governmental organisation as in the study of how government should best be organised. Modern political science has tended to abdicate this responsibility, and it has done so in part because it has preferred the study of real behaviour to the study of formal rules and institutions. The arguments for a return to the institutional approach I stressed in my opening chapter and they do not require rehearsing here. Let me make just one point. Rules and institutions, unlike behaviour, though sometimes 'unreal', are more likely to be the deliberate expression of values. A reformist science must therefore be 'formalistic' at least to the extent that major improvements in the governmental system generally require the alteration of rules or the restructuring of institutions. Public Administration should be the study of *the* administration, descriptive, theoretical and normative. But in the last resort it is efficiency and democracy, a practical and a political concern, that should be its justification.

The Founding Fathers
and After

This chapter looks at the origins of the 'intellectual history of Public Administration as a scholarly subject'—to borrow a rather grand phrase from another writer. Although the genealogy of Public Administration can be traced back to the cameralism of the eighteenth-century Germany, this was a line that ended without issue. Precursors can also be found in earlier French and English writing. It is to America, however, that we must turn in the main because that is where most of the intellectual development took place.

From matter to method, from an attempt to define the subject matter of Public Administration to the different ways in which the subject has been approached—that would give a neat progression of chapters. The problem, as we have already seen, is that the two are not independent. This, as much as anything, accounts for the 'crisis of identity' label so often pinned to debates about the state of the discipline. It would seem logical that matter should determine method, that once *the* administration has been identified, appropriate techniques of investigation can be discussed. Sometimes, however, the reverse seems to have occurred, a favoured method determining what is to be studied, its focus either limiting the subject to certain aspects of public administration or enlarging the subject in a way that submerges public administration in wider fields. It is difficult, nevertheless, to avoid jumping between the two. The perceptive reader, indeed, will have noticed that I have not really avoided this myself. I argued in the last chapter for a definition of Public Administration as the study of *the* administration in its formal attire because this gave us a clearly defined subject matter of our own in a way that administrative behaviour or the policy-making process do not. But I also argued that the merits of an institutional approach lay in its reformist usefulness, and to that extent my definition followed from the purpose I advocated.

The history of Public Administration thought shows the same unavoidable relationship. Much can only be understood against the background of its time, not only contemporary states of knowledge, though these are also important, but contemporary ideas about the ends such knowledge should serve. Changing content and changing purpose are thus two strands continuously intertwined. The reader may feel that the return to the origins undertaken here place an undue weight on the past, on writers now discredited and scholarship absorbed in later works. He may be irritated by reference to the same old classics yet again. Understandably, he might prefer a straight account of the state of the discipline today. My own feeling is that Public Administration has now advanced in so many directions that it is almost impossible to pattern the current literature. Much now involves the applications of sophisticated theories from new and complex disciplines, sometimes to the extent that it can only be understood as a special aspect of some other science, so that the old-fashioned student of government, even the generalist in political science, may simply cry enough. If one tries to include all the advanced techniques for administrators as well, coherence disappears entirely.

Traditional theory is easier to discuss, not just because knowledge was less advanced in those days, but because the literature was for a generalist audience. But my return to the origins is not entirely a coward's way out: just because the approach then was relatively simpler, the work of earlier days offers an altogether more convenient set of pegs for reflection on issues that still lie at the heart of the subject. The historical ground has, of course, been well covered elsewhere and readers are likely to be familiar with K. M. Henderson's *Emerging Synthesis in American Public Administration*. Andrew Dunsire's recent *Administration: The Word and the Science* is invaluable. No claim to originality of research is made here. The purpose of this historical survey is simply to illustrate some of the points I wish to make in the context of this book.

One writer puts the origins neatly, combining all its aspects on a single sentence: 'The study of American Public Administration developed in the late nineteenth century as a branch of political science, then preoccupied with legal relationships, strongly orientated towards reform rather than research, and conceived simply by most of its tiny band of practitioners as the study of government.'

British political science had its origins in history and philosophy, though much could be described as institutional-descriptive if one also includes the quality journalism of Bagehot and Dicey. In continental Europe, on the other hand, the subject developed in the law faculties, rather than in the Arts, partly because civil servants and, indeed, many politicians, took law degrees, partly because law was regarded as a general education and legal studies thus given a broader content than in Britain. In America jurisprudence was also a godfather of political science. The Germanic influence on American scholarship played a role. Another reason was the existence of a written constitution which tended to reduce many political questions to questions of law. The new multinational state had problems of political socialisation and one of the ways in which the government tried to deal with this was through the educational system. This was a third factor and it has been put thus: 'there was a mushrooming of civics courses providing indoctrination into citizenship, and of courses preparing for participation, in one role or another, in the political structure—above all courses in public administration, constitutional development and public law.' Civics meant knowing the constitution, understanding the formal machinery of government and absorbing democratic values; in pre-behavioural days it could mean little else.

This brings me to the second point concerning the origins of American Public Administration. Political scientists were committed to teaching the American system of government (a form of indoctrination, if you will) and to making the American system of democracy more perfect. In that commitment they differed from many of their successors. Modern political science came to concern itself with 'real' processes rather than with formal institutions and the values they are intended to embody. It engaged in disinterested fact-finding surveys and in theory for its own sake. We may beg the question of hidden values in this proclaimedly value free approach: it certainly involved a shift of emphasis from problem-centred research and advocacy of reform in scholars' publications. In the last few years there has been something of a shift back among seniors of the profession as well as the protagonists of a 'new' political science on the left. For a time, however, realism led paradoxically to the ivory tower and even now the modernised civics approach fits uneasily with the rest of the discipline.

A legalistic approach unsupported by a political philosophy does not necessarily lead anywhere different. The majority of lawyers, indeed, have never been reformist. But—and this is the third point here and has been my argument all along—a complete rejection of legal-institutional studies is even more likely to lead to a neutralist position in political science. Societies, after all, are governed by laws and through institutions. Whether one regards these as surface phenomena or not, if one wishes to reform society one must amend laws and alter institutions. This is no less true for the subject of Public Administration. Most improvements of the governmental system, even quite limited changes in the administrative process, usually require some formal implementation.

It is customary to trace the history of modern Public Administration back to 1887 when Woodrow Wilson, then Professor of Political Science at Yale, published an article in the *Political Science Quarterly* entitled 'The Study of Public Administration'. He recommended his readers to study the administrative institutions of government as well as the political. Previous neglect can be explained in several ways. Government departments must have appeared duller than Congress, the civil service duller than the presidency—and most political scientists in Britain today react in much the same way to suggestions that they should study the machinery of administration. Less in the lime-light, it was also less amenable to instant analysis—and in Britain today access is still a problem that deters the potential student.

More important, perhaps, was the assumption that administration was a mere conveyor belt, mechanically executing the instructions it received: so long as the laws were good, their implementation could be taken as a matter of course. In early days, when the tasks of government were few and the administrative machine simple, this view was plausible, even if never true. But critics were becoming aware that the machine was not perfect: administration was not an automatic process, inputs did not become outputs unchanged. Inefficiency, even corruption, was noticed. Hence the need for studies to improve the system. Though corruption is not a problem in contemporary England, a recent scandal notwithstanding, inefficiency is still sometimes thought to be, *vide* Fulton. It later became apparent, of course, that even an honest and efficient bureaucracy was an influence to be reckoned with in the process of transforming ideas into policies, policies into legislation and legislation into executive action—but that is not the point here.

This is something of a digression from Wilson's own argument, however. He declared—and this is his claim to rank in the pantheon of Public Administration—that one could distinguish the political and the executive functions of government and that consequently one could be studied separately from the other. This would permit a group of scholars to concentrate undisturbed on the problems of the administrative machine. If Public Administration was to establish itself as a field of study in its own right, its practitioners would naturally seek to define it in a way that allowed it to isolate itself from the wider field of political science.

The distinction between executive and legislative institutions, enshrined in the constitution, lay ready to hand—so ready that Wilson could say it was 'happily too obvious to need further discussion'. Many have argued since, with some force, though also with some misunderstanding, that it was altogether too easy, so obvious, indeed, that it was bound to be superficial. Leave this aside for the moment. It may nevertheless have been tactically necessary. Universities have tended to the view, pedantic perhaps, that before a new academic discipline can establish itself it must prove its credentials by showing either a subject matter distinct from those of existing disciplines or methods of investigation of its own if it wished to share a subject matter with others. A prerequisite of autonomy, in other words, was the definition of frontiers. The first criterion must have seemed more appropriate at the time as relevant methodologies had hardly been invented. It was not until later that different branches of managerial science could establish themselves on the basis of different techniques (sociological and mathematical for example). What the field of Public Administration is was later to become a perennial agenda item: Wilson's was an attempt to avoid some of these demarcation disputes.

There was another reason why he wished to draw a frontier around the subject, more often stressed by later critics. The task he set Public Administration was 'to straighten the paths of government, to make its business less unbusinesslike, to strengthen and purify its organisation, and to crown its duties with dutifulness'. The purpose, in other words, was to make government a more efficient machine. The establishment of a new discipline allowed a useful distinction to be made. Wilson was a reformer, but he wanted Public Administration to become a reformist science with self-imposed limitations. The political reformism of political science involved values, thus disputes about values: administrative science accepted the values—the policies—determined by the political system and concerned itself with their rational implementation. Over-simplified though this was later shown to be, it did allow the subject to get under way. Public Administrationists could devote themselves to the scientific analysis of facts and the formulation of scientific principles. They had first to be motivated by a sense of public duty, a point I made earlier in the chapter; that given, they could devote themselves to the scientific analysis of facts and the formulation of scientific principles. Value free, because they dealt with means rather than ends, they could reach agreement, first about the facts and then, as knowledge progressed, about principles also.

Wilson was no doubt aware of the contradiction that lay at the heart of his approach, even if he chose for tactical reasons to ignore it. The goal he set Public Administration involved both management science (businesslike administration) and political theory (purity and dutifulness). The latter, despite the moral overtones of language, could, of course, be interpreted as just another way of saying managerial efficiency (the faithful execution of duties), but the roots of reformism in Wilson's time and in subsequent decades were indeed political. Attacks on the spoils system played a major role, for example, and these had a distinctly moral flavour. An end to patronage in the appointment of officials, as distinct from the appointment of better-qualified officials (i.e. purity without expertise), would not necessarily have made the system more efficient. Nor, indeed, would the subjection of officials to more effective public controls necessarily have had this effect— not, at least, if efficiency is defined in straight management-science terms as obtaining a desired output at minimum cost.

Public Administration, in other words, started with its own set of democratic values, not so much hidden as taken for granted. The Public Administration movement was in fact part of the 'clean government' movement. This alliance could be criticised in retrospect because it encouraged a restricted view of the subject, a concern with the immediately practical, which might have prevented the development of broader theories had not other scholars, with other interests, later entered the field. It remains to be said, however, that it was reformism that provided the necessary motivation for the subject, just as much later the major theoretical breakthrough of the Comparative Administration movement was motivated in part by a sympathetic interest in the needs of developing countries and of development administrators.

Reformism could not be separated from politics for another reason. Its programme could only be achieved by political means: by persuading Congress to legislate, the President to make rules, state and local authorities to act, or the public to bring pressure to bear on them. This fact, together with a view of 'dutifulness' which meant, among other things, that the administrator should be responsive to public opinion, postulated a politically informed society. The task of Public Administration was thus to educate the citizen as well as the administrator. This fitted well with American notions of participant democracy, later called civic culture. The state universities, moreover, had been deliberately established for the welfare of society rather than as bastions of pure learning. Their function was to train professionals, agronomists and engineers for example, and, more generally, to give as many students as possible an education in citizenship. The widespread teaching of political science, including at least some aspects of Public Administration, must be seen in this light.

Following Wilson's call with some time lag, there appeared a number of detailed works describing the internal structure of American government and advocating improvements, often based on principles drawn from comparative studies, largely untheoretical, or on more or less common-sense assumptions about human behaviour, with some borrowing from the new works on management science. The first real textbooks were Leonard White's *Public Administration* and F. W. Willoughby's *Principles of Public Administration*, the first published in 1926, the second in 1927. Both claimed to be writing for students of political science, citizens interested in public affairs and public officials. Their books remained standard texts for a time; White, indeed, was republished as late as 1955. It is only fair to add that although both works looked superficially like practical textbooks, this was not their primary purpose. White, a Professor of Political Science at Chicago, said in his preface that his approach was analytic and critical, but it was in the critical aspects that his real intention lay. Willoughby headed the Institute for Government Research in Washington, an organisation to promote the scientific study of government in order to discover principles which could lead to its improvement. The two books could be read as detailed evidence to a commission of inquiry on administrative reform.

Both authors started from the separation of politics and administration. Willoughby drew an analogy from business: the legislature was the board of directors, the chief executive was the managing director and the administration was responsible for management—with management defined, rather differently from today, as the simple application of board policy. More strangely, in hindsight at least, they believed that the organisational problems of executing policy were more important than those of the policy-making institutions, nor were they terribly concerned with problems relating to the substantive content of policies: the contemporary American political system seemed reasonably well organised to them; it was the administration that needed reorganising. According to White 'administration has become, and will continue to be, the heart of the problem of modern government'.

He wanted to make American government more effective as executor of the democratic will and to this end emphasised Wilson's purity (the elimination of patronage for example) and his dutifulness (better control of the administration by legislature, courts and public). Willoughby, director of a professionally orientated research institute rather than member of a university department, set somewhat different goals: 'It can hardly be questioned that the great political problem now confronting us is that of securing economy and efficiency in the actual administration of government affairs.'

Despite the authors' introductory remarks, it was never quite clear for whom they intended the knowledge they had to offer. By spreading their appeal to three quite different audiences, however, they produced books that were not really tailored to the needs of any: too specialist for the student, too long for the layman, not practical enough for the practitioner. This confusion of clientele reflected some of the ambiguities that I noted earlier and that are still with us. They dealt in some detail with topics that were to become the staple diet of vocational courses, though not practically enough to serve as manuals for practitioners. Some of what they wrote, about personnel matters for example, could be read as good advice to administrators. This was largely concerned with structures and rules, formal ways of organising staff. But it neither explained the existing regulations in detail nor did it cover human relations techniques. To that extent, again, it did not really deal with the actual daily problems that arise in the management of staff. The academic material, historical and comparative, on the other hand, was of little use to the serving official. The analysis of alternative methods of organising the public service may seem wasted on those who work in a service whose rules they cannot alter as readily as their counterpart in industry. Young officials, still learning about the administrative system, are unlikely to be in a position to implement reformist proposals for many years to come. In so far as these books were intended for the influentials, that part of the content is understandable—though, given the detail, one must allow for a more serious public readership than in our time. The question I am asking here, however, is what they expected of the student readers, whether those intending to join the public service or those already in it. The answer presumably— and it may be thought relevant to the content of courses for administrators today—is that one should give such students a reasonably academic background and that one should treat them as the influentials of the future.

Both authors were strongly influenced by management studies.

While accepting that the business of government was different from the business of private enterprise, White thought it more likely that government could learn from industry than *vice versa* because only the latter was driven to continual improvement by competition. In an important sense, moreover, they wished to emphasise the similarities rather than the difference. White started from certain assumptions: that administration was a common process, showing similar characteristics wherever found; that it should be studied from a managerial, rather than a legal, point of view; and that general principles could be discovered which would turn the subject from an art into a science.

It was easy enough to distinguish administration as such from its 'technical phases'—the subject matter of which could be found in specialist books for students of public health, highway engineering and other useful branches of government activity. The limitations of his approach become obvious, however, when one looks at what his common process of administration actually consisted of. He defined his subject as 'the management of men and material'. This meant concentrating on certain functions, common to the work of most government agencies, it is true, but far from the whole field of management nevertheless. The main sections in his book dealt with organisation, staff and control; Willoughby added material and replaced control by finance. Both actually included topics that related to the governmental rather than the administrative system in a strict sense: control by legislature, courts and public in one case, control of public expenditure in the other. Despite this, the emphasis was on matters that were to become the diet of textbooks for some time, broadly speaking Organisation and Methods, personnel management and the rules of public expenditure. The point I want to make is simply that this tended to reduce Public Administration to the universally required but rather narrow specialism of office management. The view of administration as office management can still be found in some places: it is not uncommon, for example, among the middle-range 'generalists' of British local government who recognise the professional's expertise in substantive policy decisions and in the operation of largely technical services, but who hope to raise the status of their own supporting office activities. The fact remains, however, that senior civil servants are only involved in this sort of work for part of their time and much of it can in fact be done by specialists, by staff rather than line (specially trained personnel officers, qualified O. & M. units).

It was convenient, of course, for Public Administration to define management as the most efficient use of resources available and to take resources as office staff and office supplies. That insulated the subject from politics, but it depended on an interpretation of efficiency that reflected an inward-looking approach: it overlooked the fact that the purpose of government offices is not to run smoothly and efficiently but to prepare and execute policies relating the distribution of national resources to the needs of the population. An efficiency that ignores this is dangerous because it is likely to encourage wrong priorities in administrative organisation. It leads to a vice that has been attributed to senior civil servants and that I have found in local government officers taking the Diploma in Public Administration—that of the Rolls Royce enthusiast so pleased with the silence of his motor that he has little time for the scenery *en route*; a greater concern, in other words, with the smoothness of the machine than with its policy outputs. But governments are only efficient if they take the right decisions. If we want to allow for a politics-administration dichotomy, separating the political and the administrative branches of government on the one hand, eliminating values from administration on the other, then it must still be said that an administrative system is efficient only if its procedures ensure that rational (i.e. properly calculated) policy options are submitted to the actual decision makers.

Both authors assumed that the existence of natural laws of administration could be discovered with relative ease once scholars put their minds to it. Willoughby could write that if governments were to be efficient 'there are certain fundamental principles that must be observed' and could virtually leave it at that. It was easy enough, later, to describe this belief as naïve and to label their principles 'proverbs of administration', as did Herbert Simon in a much-reprinted article of 1946. But what they were doing was to follow respectable traditions of political science. Willoughby generalised from what seemed basic elements common to the best-administered systems, American and foreign, public and private, past and present. The method of study, in other words, was historical and comparative. The great students of comparative politics, from Aristotle to Bryce, had derived their principles of good government from the same procedure.

That this method missed much is obvious: behaviour patterns that made a nonsense of formal structures, for example, and complex ecologies that undermined comparisons. The political science of their time was not all that scientific. How much more scientific ours is, is another matter: I do get the feeling that every empirically based, theoretically deduced generalisation of our own time is immediately shot down by those with other data or other methodologies, leaving scientific political science with little agreed content. That is a digression. The point I want to make here is that the later scholars have tended to lose in clarity of theories what they have gained in sophistication of methods.

The relative ineffectiveness of contemporary social scientists has been attributed by Yehezkel Dror to their reluctance to make less than scientifically reliable recommendations. Unfortunately, knowledge develops so rapidly nowadays, and is so conscious of its own imperfections, that certainty seems quite unattainable. A by-product is the bewilderment of practitioners who become reluctant to seek the advice of reluctant academics. The optimistic over-simplification of its founders was necessary to get a scholarly subject under way and to arouse interest outside the narrow bounds of scholarship. Proverbs of administration served a purpose. Tongue only half in cheek, it may even be that they still serve us better than a science which looks as if it may remain in its birthpangs during the lifetime of present decision makers.

The principles of good administration dealt with such standard questions as the allocation of functions, chains of command, span of control, line and staff—all that was involved in the construction of formal organisation charts. There were similar precepts to cover staffing, centring round the notion of a professionally qualified, depersonalised, hierarchically organised career service. It is easy in hindsight to criticise White, Willoughby and their contemporaries for their emphasis on formal arrangements rather than, say, human relations techniques, but their reformist intent must be born in mind: staffing in the public service, to stay with that example, is closely regulated. It is an easy in hindsight to criticise them for their rather superficial investigations of organisational behaviour, but there one must remember that social psychology had not yet established itself as a branch of management science, nor had political science turned behavioural. The early Public Administrationists claimed to draw many of their maxims from the comparative study of administrative systems. More often, they used comparisons to illustrate intuitive knowledge, possibly the reflection of direct experience. A rather simple concept of democratic government always lay in the background. Max Weber's theory of the ideal-type bureaucracy was not without influence. Even more, they depended on the scientific management movement in industry.

The adherents of this movement maintained that management was management regardless of the activity managed, a proposition by no means as self-evident as they or, indeed, later schools, assumed. The fact remains, however, that its theoretical foundations were laid by students of the private sector. Much of the evidence came from industry and much of the literature dealt with industrial organisation. It is nevertheless worth tracking back to its leading exponents, for when the attack on the proverbs of formal organisation came, it came as part of a wider attack on this school.

Frederick Taylor is usually accorded the title of father of scientific management, the date fixed at 1911 when his *Principles and Methods of Scientific Management* was published. An efficiency expert, his main interest lay in devising ways of getting maximum results out of routine industrial work. That need not concern us here. More relevant is the fact that Taylor's science dealt with an abstract man, as abstract as the economist's: it observed him from outside, studying the routines he performed, and not, for example, his motives. In so far as this approach was followed over the next decades, management science became as formalistic as the Public Administration of institutional reformers, even if formalistic in a different sense. A second founding father was Henri Fayol with *Administration industrielle et générale* in 1916. He focused on the other end of the scale, on management functions, the top rather than the bottom. While Taylor obtained his evidence from actual work studies, Fayol drew mainly on personal eperience. He was nevertheless a schematist in the French intellectual tradition and ended with categorisations which were logical rather than empirical, notably of management functions. A third approach can be seen in James Mooney's *Principles of Organisation* a 1947 revision of Mooney and Reiley's *Onward Industry* of 1931. Although they were General Motors executives, they drew on the lessons of history. In that, they resembled Weber, White and Willoughby, but the emphasis on administration-in-general led to even wider comparisons: state, army, church and industry were all raided for evidence. The main theme was hierarchy—the organisation chart again.

The work that influenced Public Administration more directly, perhaps, was that of Luther Gulick and Lyndall Urwick, in particular the *Papers on the Science of Management* they edited in 1937. They tried to get away from the democratically biased reformism of earlier Public Administrationists and to lay the foundations for a more rigorous value free science. In his introductory essay Gulick defined administration as 'the accomplishment of defined objectives'. The objectives could then be taken as given and attention concentrated on methods of accomplishment. On the face of it, this involves some odd notions about what administration is about in the public sector—or at least what the

Administrative Class of the civil service (however named) actually do. Apart from the fact that senior officials play an active role in the formulation of policy, the truth is that objectives are rarely spelt out so precisely by the policy-makers that civil servants have merely to think about techniques of execution: however detailed the brief, it still has to be translated into rules of application—and even within these rules much discretion is likely to remain. Different sets of rules, different attitudes in the exercise of discretion, will colour the policy and modify the end product as it affects the individual citizen.

A possible answer is that the Gulick–Urwick School was not so naïve as this simple criticism would seem to suggest. Their position need not depend on defining administrative institutions but on defining an administrative function which includes only part of the work of those who are called administrators. It depends then on a distinction within public administration between the tasks of organising the system on the one hand and, on the other, those of policy-making (or policy-advising, if we are to remain within the democratic myth) and of discretionary decisions.

Gulick, however, defined the functions of top executives in a way that cut the ground from under such an attempt to make sense of the ends-means dichotomy. According to him, executives were responsible for planning, organising, staffing, directing, co-ordinating, reporting and budgeting (the mnemonic POSDCORB). His definition of the three somewhat ambiguous terms in this heptad does not help us much: planning is 'the working out in broad outlines of the things that need to be done and the methods for doing them to accomplish the purpose set for the enterprise'; organising is 'the establishment of the formal structure of authority through which the work is arranged . . . for the defined objective'; directing is 'the continuous task of making decisions and embodying them in specific and general orders, and serving as the leader of the enterprise'. These are the tasks of a chief executive in a business enterprise geared to the maximisation of profits—where the purpose is sufficiently clear for him to choose the policies needed to accomplish it, and where these policies, in turn, provide a sufficiently clear framework for him to take the general decisions of implementation.

POSDCORB fits less well with a definition of administration as the accomplishment of defined objectives in government, for there the objectives are multiple: business policies are in theory means to a single end; public policies are more likely to be ends in themselves. One can get round this by a narrow interpretation of the planning function, excluding substantive policies and concentrating on planning the machinery of government. Even then, an administrative science must surely include the organisation of that part of the policy-making process that lies within the executive branch of government. Administration, then, is not merely concerned with the accomplishment of defined ends but with their definition also. Any attempt to exclude the latter from Public Administration is likely to encourage the office management view of the subject and thus turn it into a rather narrow specialism. Having said that, let me nevertheless make a distinction. The quantitative techniques of policy-making form part of other disciplines, and it is as such that they form part of a syllabus for administrators. On the institutional view of Public Administration I have been advocating in this book, it is with the organisation of the machinery to apply these techniques that the subject is primarily concerned.

Let us accept, then, that the administrative sciences include several specialisms and that Public Administration is the science of organising the administration. Gulick defined the objectives of scientific management as the efficient accomplishment of the work in hand with the least expenditure of manpower and material. Values could be ignored or, more sophisticatedly, the values of the policy-makers and of the environment in which administrators work could be treated as constants. This immediately raises a problem. Businessmen may be open to the appeal of value free prescriptions because, in theory at least, the managerial problems to be solved are never in doubt: the least expenditure of work and material compatible with the output to be achieved (the output can be taken as a constant, its determination a question of economic, not administrative, science). But this cannot be said of the politicians responsible, in the last resort, for the organisation of public services.

In a democracy politicians are bound to judge administrative procedures by several criteria. One may certainly be efficiency calculated by cost, but conformity with unquantifiable values is just as important. The reformism of earlier Public Administrationists could be rationalised as a belief that honest and accountable officials were more likely to implement policies efficiently than corrupt and irresponsible ones—but in fact clean government was seen as a desirable end in itself. Fairness is not the automatic servant of efficiency, whether in internal matters such as staffing or in dealing with the public, but it is certainly a test of good administration and often means administrative procedures that have little to do with the sort of efficiency defined above. Security of tenure and regulated promotion procedures are internal examples. An obvious example in external relations is the emphasis on legalism in continental Europe. Systems dominated by administrative law start from the assumption that the citizens must have a right of appeal to special courts against any decision which affects him: if courts are to investigate appealed decisions, then decision-making procedures must be formalised, even at the cost of efficiency. Another example: the desire to minimise friction within the administration (e.g. good staff relations) and in relation to the public (e.g. to avoid political embarrassment for the minister) may influence administrative procedures; indeed, it may become another test of efficiency. This, of course, brings one to the point that efficiency can be defined in many ways or by a combination of tests. The trouble with this is that some are not quantifiable in the way costs are, nor can they be reduced to compatible terms—a fact which undermines the scientific intentions of scientific management.

One can go further. Administrative reform is rarely intended simply to cheapen (or expedite, or even make more effective) the implementation of existing policies. More often, it is related to the implementation of new policies or, more vaguely, to changing notions about the functions of government. This emerged very clearly from the Fulton Report which advocated changes that would enable the administration to play a more positive role in the policy-making process of government. In public administration the management scientist cannot concentrate on institutional engineering within an otherwise static stystem: the Public Administrationist is as concerned with the definition of efficiency as with achieving it.

There are really two things I am trying to say here. The first is simply that public administration is different from other forms of administration, hence Public Administration cannot be a science of administration in general. The second is that efficiency really involves very complex notions about what a good system of public administration achieves. One can think of several 'ideal' models: the neutrally efficient (cheap and effective implementation of given policies); the legally formalised (protection of citizens through administrative law); the publicly responsive (minimising friction with its clientele by interest group brokerage or good public relations); the technocratic (taking responsibility for policy initiation and valuing public welfare above public opinion). There are doubtless more and they can all be permuted. This makes comparison between systems along a bad–poor–good–better–best scale difficult, though not impossible, as I have suggested in an earlier chapter on comparison as a practical activity. Such practical comparisons, however, as I have also suggested, do not allow for generalisations of a truly scientific sort.

The reference to science brings me to another problem. The intentions of the scientific management school were also practical: 'The science of administration is the system of knowledge whereby one may understand relationships, predict results and influence outcomes.' This means the ability to make statements of the sort: 'Under conditions x, y and z, conduct A will produce B and conduct A' will produce C' (x, y and z may be taken as norms of the system and constant). Now, clearly if one can make statements in this form, one has the beginnings of a science in the technical sense of the term (not to be confused with the older sense of science as an organised body of knowledge). The trouble, of course, lies in the fact that the social sciences are rarely experimental. Only rarely can one maintain environmental factors constant, as in a laboratory, and simply alter conduct A in order to determine what the product of A' will be. It is possible to experiment within organisations on a modest scale, but even then one would have to assume that such changes have no affect on the supposedly constant environment if one is to make the statement that a change in conduct from A to A' will produce changes in output from B to C and not also changes in the environment to x', y' or z'; indeed, the successful move from B to C may depend on such environmental modifications.

But let us leave this problem aside. The point here is that although reform (i.e. experimentation) is almost continuous in public administration, it is rarely geared to the requirements of the administrative scientist. To obtain the comparisons he needs, he has either to compare the same system over time or, more often, to compare different systems. The ecological complexities are such, however, that it then becomes very difficult to define the relevant environmental factors and even harder to find situations which are identical. I have already suggested that such difficulties are not insurmountable for rough and ready judgements, but that is not what is under consideration here. What it may mean is that statements about relationships are more easily based on understanding how individual systems work than on comparisons. It may be easier to move towards general explanations from what at least appear to be causal relations within a system than from apparent correlations between systems. Too much of the early work, however, failed to explore causal links in detail and preferred to generalise from comparative descriptions. An additional weakness, one stressed by later critics, may be noted: as all organisations involve human beings, and it is only human beings who act, explanation—the causal chain—in the last resort needs an analysis of human behaviour. This involves other methods of study which, unfortunately, create problems in their turn if one tries to integrate them in a science of administrative institutions.

In fact, the principles of scientific management were not really based on scientific research. We get sweeping historical surveys, broad accounts of industrial practice, impressions of participant observers, generalisations from direct experience, assumptions about human behaviour, with a good deal of intuition thrown in, the whole put together in a formally logical pattern. What was missing was hard data based on empirical studies on a manageable scale. To be fair, this approach has a respectable tradition. It was that of Machiavelli, for example: reason imposed on history and experience, using history and experience as a store of illustrations. Scientific management was a form of rationalism, based not only on assumptions about the rational behaviour of administrators but also on the assumption that principles of administration could be deduced by common sense. Put more unkindly, of course, it started with what appeared logical preconceptions rather than the data itself.

This was partly because those concerned were practical men rather than scholars, prepared to do some reading, to think, particularly about their own experience, and to write—but not to do much fieldwork (the exception was Taylor, but he is hardly relevant here). Their background had another—paradoxically contrary—result. They were not really theoretically minded enough, despite their rationalism, to produce any properly integrated theory to explain the working of administrative institutions. In the end, their propositions consisted of a series of only loosely connected principles.

All these criticisms are easy to make. Too easy. It is not clear that a more rigorous approach leads to more useful advice. In devising institutions, as well as in policy-making, governments have generally to act on the basis of imperfect knowledge supported by a feeling for what is possible and how things work. The latter, conveniently labelled intuition, can have solid roots in experience. For the rest, it must often rely on *a priori*, apparently logical assumptions about human behaviour and causal relations. That all these sometimes prove erroneous goes without saying—too often, perhaps, if one considers the record of the governments we know. Does empirical data score much higher on accuracy? Are the methodologies applied in its interpretation more foolproof? Where governments think they are making decisions on the basis of hard facts and scientific calculations, they seem to go wrong no less often. As for political scientists and the modern exponents of a scientific approach to Public Administration, one has only to read the literature to see how contradictory their conclusions are, how much of their time, indeed, is spent in challenging each other's data or showing the errors in each other's methodologies. In the light of this sad history, we may have something to learn after all from the approach of earlier practitioners of the subject.

To return to the earlier history of the subject, a very different approach to the study of industrial orgnisations developed concurrently with the one I have just discussed. This, broadly, was the human relations approach, with the Hawthorne research of the late twenties as a convenient starting point and the name of Elton Mayo, though only one of several pioneers, as a convenient peg. The Hawthorne study showed that factory workers' output was less influenced by physiological factors such as lighting (as the Taylor school approach to the design of work procedures might have supposed) than by the emotional satisfaction derived from membership of a work group. From this socio-psychological approach, concerned with the influence of personal relations on individual attitudes, thus on morale, output and efficiency, the focus broadened to sociological studies of organised groups. Observers found that members of organisations followed patterns of behaviour that did not necessarily correspond to the procedures officially prescribed, and that underlying such patterns there were attitudes (norms of behaviour) that did not correspond to the goals the organisation had set. Simplified, this meant that the study of formal structures—organisation charts and rules of procedure—was replaced by the study of how people really behaved.

This, then, simplifying again, was the behaviouralism that was later to dominate the study of organisations, giving, the reader will expect me to add, a very one-sided view of administration. Organisations, whether industrial or administrative, were described as social systems. Social systems are composed of relationships: the interaction of individuals with one another and with the system itself. The relationships the schools examined in its early days, however, were only a small part of the complex elements that actually make up a system. They concentrated on the behavioural variables, taking the institutional framework and externally determined values as given—to be taken into account, of course, but only in so far as they were translated into the perceptions and behaviour patterns of group members. In terms of these early researchers' limited interests in increased efficiency through improved morale, this was reasonable enough.

It meant, however, that they felt little need to explain why a system was formally organised in the way it was, nor were they much interested in how the formal side worked. The advice they could give to management on the basis of their research, however useful in its field, was thus limited in scope. This was the more true because their research focused on small groups relatively low in the hierarchy. Even when attention shifted from production workers to bureaux administrators, the small group emphasis was bound to remain because of the emphasis on personal relationships: individuals only interact in ways that can be conveniently observed in relatively closed groups. Though social systems can be extended to include an entire organisation, even the entire administration, in direct human relations terms these are rather amorphous entities and one is likely to end up with models that have little hard data content. The approach, moreover, is more suitable for workshop and office studies than for analysing the higher levels of administrative activities. Though it is undoubtedly important to study the behaviour of policy-making officials and the values they hold, these require a much wider range of explanations.

The real contribution of this school was to emphasise the extent to which the shared values of a group influence its members, to indicate how these values develop and how they can be influenced at lower levels. While the scientific management school hoped to improve efficiency by elaborating principles of organisation, the Hawthorne school sought to achieve this by improved morale through informal leadership and better human relations. Useful personnel management techniques emerged as a result of the broadening of this approach. But this again leads to a specialised skill, a subject for public administrators but not the subject matter of Public Administration. Even from this point of view, too enthusiastic an espousal of the human relations approach is not without dangers. I have stressed that the public service is generally organised in a more formal manner than other occupations. By seeking the informal, by seeking the elements common to behaviour in all organisations, public or private, one may tend to underplay the large blocs of activity that are nevertheless channelled along prescribed procedures.

As a way of understanding how the administrative system operates, it has serious limitations. Undoubtedly higher civil servants have their values just as clerical officers, a point well made earlier by Max Weber. But these are less likely to be the result of social relationships within the system. It must be remembered that a very much wider range of values is at issue when one considers the attitude of those engaged in the policy-making process than if one is concerned with the work attitudes of those engaged in more or less routine activities. Some of these values are likely to be determined by the environment in which the administration operates, others by the social class or profession to which the administrators belong. There may be administrative traditions into which officials are socialised through education and early experience. The formal principles regulating the careers and activities of higher civil servants will not be without influence. Obviously enough, patterns may emerge that run contrary to the formal goals of the system, contrary even to the ideologies the bureaucracy claims to accept: the desire to increase one's own sphere of influence; a reluctance to innovate where this upsets career interests; group loyalties that clash with service loyalties. Many influences together determine the way in which senior officials see their role in the governmental system: historical, constitutional, legal, social, political, ideological, professional, organisational and educational. One may attempt to map these, in rough outline at least, leaving many territories marked 'here unknown quantities dwell' or even 'unquantifiable forces here'.[1] But even then the interrelation of forces is so complex that one is likely to be faced in the end with a broken mirror. Certainly, behavioural surveys will illuminate a corner, but the only result may be to raise additional questions that cannot be answered in this way.

The main impression one has of the mood of the post-war period is its eagerness to reject traditional approaches, notably the belief that Public Administration was concerned with the elaboration of principles of good administration. Three lines of attack on the received wisdom can be distinguished. The first point regularly made was that means inevitably contain ends. Principles were normative rather than scientific, quite explicitly embodying the goals of the American way of democracy as well as numerous hidden values. This vitiated the objectivity of the approach and deprived the principles of the universal application they were supposed to have. As the values themselves came to be questioned, the principles were doubly undermined. The second criticism was directed at the supposedly factual and analytic parts of the research exercise. It was not hard to show that principles were based on assumptions about what actually happened rather than on empirical data, on often questionable assumptions, errors then compounded by generalising on the basis of false analogies.

---

[1] I tried to do this in a paper entitled 'Framework for Comparative Research on the Political Role of Higher Civil Servants', *Res Publica* (1974 No. 2).

Finally, it was said that principles could no more be geographically universal than ideologically so, because the working of administrative systems were as culture bound as the values they served.

Dwight Waldo's *Administrative State* of 1948 can be taken as keynoter of this attack on traditional American Public Administration. He criticised the pseudo-factualism that ignored values, the formalism that by-passed the real, the unwarranted assumption of rational behaviour and the narrow definition of efficiency. The same attack was to be found in Herbert Simon's 'Proverbs of Administration' article of 1946. Simon showed that every principle of good administration advocated by the scientific management school had an equally plausible counter-principle, just as every proverb has its counter-proverb. This was not just an attack on the rational administrator, a man as fictitious as the economic man of theory, but on rationalism itself: on the belief that knowledge can be expanded by rational argument, by the logical deduction of principles from self-evident assumptions. Assumptions apart, it is fairly obvious that one can often construct different—internally logical—arguments leading to different conclusions.

There is a danger, however, in throwing out old-fashioned rationalism. It has the merit of giving the subject matter it treats a framework. Its abandonment led to a Public Administration rich in empirical studies, almost richer in theories, but no longer able to present itself as an integrated body of knowledge. Some form of integration is essential to establish a coherent discipline. The search for unifying theory is a natural instinct of scientific man and therefore continues: its latest, most ambitious, most difficult and most abstract form is general systems theory. Because of the explosion of empirical data and the multiplication of divergent theories, however, it becomes ever more difficult to present the subject in a coherent manner. One recent writer put it thus: 'No single person or group has been able to assimilate everything that has happened, let alone code, classify and arrange it in a coherent framework.' The virtual impossibility of integrating a multiplicity of approaches in a single theoretical framework may be accepted; more serious in its consequences, perhaps, is the fact that it is not even possible to organise them convincingly in an expository framework that has some sort of didactic logic.

This may be the price of scientific progress but the cost should be borne in mind: as the subject becomes more confused, so it become less attractive to the practitioner. What is at stake here is not the simplicity of ideas; economic theory does not necessarily lose its attraction as it becomes more sophisticated so long as it retains clarity of profile and apparent logic. Not surprisingly, practitioners now demand quantitative techniques of policy-making, a branch of economic theory, rather than principles on which to organise the machinery of government; Public Administration has tended to undermine itself as a subject.

The different approaches now employed involve far more than methodological disputes within a discipline. They stem from different disciplines and use different languages. They tend to focus on different aspects of the administrative system, often treating their part as a strip of a wider field: organisations, behaviour, decisions, policy. If one is not careful, the material is dissolved in a series of patches that do not make even a patchwork quilt. In the process, Public Administration all but disappears. Behind this development lie differences of view, or little view at all, about the purpose of studying public administration. This again has serious practical consequences for the subject. A reformist aim is more likely to hold students together, even if they differ on methodological grounds, than a disinterested pursuit of science; it is more likely, it hardly needs saying, to attract outside interest.

One can nevertheless discern a number of trends in post-war years. To carry the subject along these lines is to move from the founding fathers to the great names of modern times and that is not the purpose of this chapter. What follows, therefore, is some reflection on the problems of the discipline as I see them rather than a fair discussion of schools and their masters.

Broadly, the trends I want to discuss here fall along a spectrum of theoretical generality. At one end there is what has been described as the new realism, the detailed account of specific events that is associated in America with the Case Program Series under the editorship of Ed Bock. Basically, this is the historical approach—'instant history', perhaps, but, more important, history of the 'factualist' school that claims to describe things straight—'as they really were'. The attempt to portray a 'case' in its totality, all the factors, for example, that influenced a decision, depends like good history on literary skills of presentation almost more than on the clarity of its analytic framework to read convincingly. Indeed, the assumption is not merely that so many variables are involved that each case is the result of a unique combination of forces and thus itself unique; the variables themselves are so complex that they are bound to present a disorderly picture. As the *types* of variable forces also vary between cases, this means that case studies present, as one writer puts it, 'an incorrigible resistance to systematic categorisation'.

If well done, cases may usefully give the non-practitioner student a feel for reality and an insight into the actual work of administration—vicarious experience, so to speak. The danger, however, lies on the other side of the coin: emphasis on the totality of a case, on the necessarily unique combination of many different factors, self-avowedly makes it impossible to generalise on the basis of a series of case studies. In that sense, the approach is really a counsel of despair. Hyper-factualism is anti-scientific, if science means theory building. This is taking the approach to its extreme, of course, but this extreme is its logical implication. It is not even clear that one really gets a better description of events. Superficially more accurate, it may at the same time explain less than an account which starts with a theoretical framework. A preconceived framework may certainly lead one to overlook important data, but this is just as likely to occur without: influences below the surface may be missed, as may be wider environmental factors; the story itself may become so complex and so lacking in connections that in the end it is literally meaningless. Straight history is history that signifies nothing.

At the other end of the scale of generality, that of grand theory, there was what might be called the cultural breakthrough. Earlier studies tried to derive general principles of administrative organisation from comparisons that made a simple assumption. Although they drew on administrative, industrial, military and even ecclesiastical experience, they assumed that administrative structures had common features because they were essentially concerned with the rational execution of set tasks, whatever the political context or the wider socioeconomic and cultural environment. With the growth of development aid programmes, however, administrators were given the opportunity of testing this assumption in the field. The difficulties they had in transferring their administrative experience to more exotic places led to the realisation that even executive structures were culture bound, operating differently in different environments rather than according to some universal internal logic.

For the Public Administration theorist, the realisation followed that one must compare administrative systems in their environment, and from this it was but a short step to comparing whole systems. This approach, of course, is associated particularly with the work of Fred Riggs, starting with *Agraria and Industria* in 1957 and becoming even more sophisticated in a host of subsequent publications. As the horizon of students widened, the end result became barely distinguishable from work in the field of comparative politics. Though, arguably, this was for a time the best

developed field of whole-system comparative politics, it became less
and less part of Public Administration as a recognisable subject.
There were lessons for the practitioner in all this, but they were
largely of the negative sort, warning him that things were likely
to be different elsewhere and that the baggage he took from
America could not simply be unpacked in the third world. Nevertheless, the impression one gets is that the broader the comparisons, the more general the theory and, to that extent, the less
useful in applicable detail to the practitioner.

In between came the theoretical approaches to specific administrative system. True, these also tended to place *the* administration
in a wider context—organisations in general for example—but the
attempt was made to explain, however, one-sidedly sometimes, how
it really functioned and how it might be improved. Herbert
Simon's *Administrative Behaviour* of 1947 is an obvious landmark.
It is easy to link much of this with the behavioural approach in the
social sciences, but it is well to remember that behaviouralism
is a much overworked term that tends to mean whatever its
users wish it to mean. Really it means no more than a primary
focus on behaviour rather than rules and institutions. We have
already seen its use by the industrial psychologists. Drawing
on sociology and psychology, social scientists could study the
administrative system as a pattern of behaviour that depended
on a network of human relations. As Public Administrationists
became involved, however, the focus shifted to decision-making
behaviour: the administration was studied as a decision-
making process. The sub-title of Simon's book was in fact
'A Study of the Decision-Making Process in Administrative
Organisations'.

There is an important implication in this approach. The
administrative function is no longer seen as the organisation of
offices or the management of men, as earlier Public Administrations defined it, but as the taking of decisions. At the
highest levels, certainly, decisions are the main output of the
administrative system. This is a somewhat ambiguous notion,
however, because two rather different sorts of decision are
involved. The contemporary interest in public policy leads to a
consideration of the contribution of administrators to the policy-
making process. This can be seen as a subject for empirical studies
(how policy is actually made, who influences whom) or as a field
for techniques (how policies should be made, what procedures
should be followed). The first is broadly the concern of politics,
the second of management science. The Public Administrationist
is concerned with both, because both are relevant to any reform

of the administrative machine, though, as I have argued, neither is his own subject.

But there is another sense in which virtually all administration is about decisions. There is sometimes a tendency to separate decisions from actions, the decision to do something from the act of implementation. But looked at more closely, every action an official performs is also a decision. Simon was concerned with the process of choice which leads to action. A decision may be simply to execute an order from above or to apply a rule that allows no choice: there are clerks and manual workers who do no more and with that we need not be concerned. But one does not have to go far up the hierarchy before an element of discretion enters, or at least some judgement in finding the applicable rule. This is another way of saying that while administration was often discussed in the past as if it were the art of organising how to get things done, or even the art of actually doing things, less attention was paid to what should be done. This may itself have been the result of the democratic politics-administration dichotomy which inhibited Public Administrationists from thinking along decision-making lines. It is well to remember, however, that what may appear to the legislator setting the ends as means best left to the administration will appear to senior administrators as ends; the means a senior official sets his subordinates to implement will appear as ends lower down the scale and these officials will in turn set means to their own subordinates; and so on down the line. In that sense, certainly, one can study not just the policy-making process at the top but all administration as a decision-making machine.

Whether one wants to study that behaviourally is another matter. It depends to some extent on the relative importance one thinks formal and informal procedures have in determining the outcome in each case. I would argue that behaviouralists tend to underrate the former and thus miss many of the differences between behaviour in the public and private sectors. In internal matters (staffing, expenditure and contracting, for example) and in their relations with individual citizens, public administrators are bound by a far denser network of regulations than their private counterparts, even in Britain and *a fortiori* in the administrative law countries of continental Europe. It depends also on one's purpose. It is not just that public administration is different, it should be different: administration according to rules is the real meaning of the Rule of Law. If the democratic Public Administrationist is concerned with the protection of the citizen against discretionary decisions apparently taken by administrators in accordance with informal behaviour patterns that develop within administrative organisations, then he will wish to study institutional and procedural arrangements to counteract such tendencies.

All this was perhaps something of a digression. Let us accept that decisions lie at the heart of all administration—the truism that all administration, like all life, involves an element of choice. Simon was in fact concerned to bring together the two aspects of Public Administration I mentioned at the start: academic understanding and practitioner techniques. When he said that the vocabulary of administrative theory should be drawn from logic and the psychology of human choice, we have exactly this. Psychology gives us the how and why of actual administration, logic the techniques for better decision-making. There is an attempt here to free the subject from some of the normative assumptions of earlier Public Administrationists by concentrating on organisation for rational decisions (or as near rational as possible) rather than on economy, or even effectiveness, in implementing set policies. The decision-making approach can thus be given a practical purpose. It can, indeed, be worked into an institutional and procedural approach, and Simon did so. So can policy studies if their real concern is less with explaining the politics of a country than with devising policy-making machinery: the best example of this is the 'meta-policy'— or how to make policy—of Yehezkel Dror in his *Public Policy-making Re-examined* of 1968. Much of Simon and Dror (and they are cited here to signify approaches) is relevant to improving the institutional and procedural framework of administration. If one moves beyond this, one soon enters the field of techniques for administrators, thus moving from Public Administration as a subject in its own right to Public Administration as the label attached to a mix of specialist courses for administrators.

At this point we must back-track for a moment. With the attacks on traditional Public Administration from the camps of sociology and social psychology came other attacks from political science. These showed the difficulty of making an analytic distinction between the administrative and policy-making functions of government and challenged the desirability of any attempt to separate them in practice. This change of heart in America was associated with the New Deal and growing government intervention in social and economic affairs. If one wants a post-war peg, Paul Appleby's *Policy and Administration* of 1949 will serve as an apologia for the politically involved administrator. I have myself argued in an earlier chapter for the development-committed civil servant. Clearly, however, this line challenged the definition of Public Administration as established by the founding fathers.

Demand for active government led to appreciation of the fact that much administration is actually a political activity. What would earlier have been regarded as a vice now became a virtue. Interest shifted from the efficient execution of set policies to the executive's ability to play a useful role in their setting. The call was for executive leadership. The trend was reflected in the first postwar textbook, *Elements of Public Administration*, edited by Fritz Morstein Marx: this, he declared, is a broadly political rather than merely technical book.

Public Administration changed as the subject it studied—the administration—came to be seen in a different light. Administration was seen to contain political elements. To be properly understood, moreover, the administrative system had itself to be placed in a political context. There was a new emphasis on environmental factors. In his *Reflections on Public Administration* of 1947, John Gaus launched the notion of the ecology of public administration, bringing into the subject of Public Administration a consideration of external determinants: political, sociological, cultural, geographic, technical and ideological. This led on the one hand to the Comparative Administration movement referred to earlier. On a narrower front, concentrating on the explanation of a single system, one can look at Ira Sharkansky's *Public Administration* textbook of 1970, to take a recent example.

Sharkansky's declared purpose was to bring together the information that is most relevant to an understanding of the larger political process. This involves facts and theories about the administration itself, its organisation and methods, its attitudes and behaviour patterns— but also external attitudes and behaviour, interactions with public, parties, interest groups and other branches of government. Focus is the conversion process which turns inputs (attitudinal dispositions as well as specific demands) into outputs (decisions allocating resources). To some extent, to be fair, the book differs from other Public Administration texts in format rather than content: many of the same topics are considered. Although the conversion process takes place in a subsystem composed of structures and procedures as well as attitudes, however, these are seen as 'withinputs', inputs that operate within the system, rather than as problems of administrative organisation. A political scientist might study other subsystems, parties or legislatures for example, in much the same way. I am not arguing, therefore, that the approach is wrong, simply that it is the approach of a political scientist and to that extent cannot provide the core of an independent subject called Public Administration. This links with another danger of focusing on policy that I have already mentioned. Such concern is likely to swamp interest in the host of decisions smaller than policy, and often more formal, all the way down the scale. These are more obviously administrative decisions and, taken together, of great importance to the citizens they affect. The machinery involved is politically less interesting but as worthy a subject of study.

There is another general point that may be made about the input-output approach, which also relates to what I have just said. It has meant the introduction of systems framework into Public Administration. Systems theory can be as vague a term as behaviouralism. In general, it means that *the* administration is seen as a system (or subsystem) of forces that interrelate. True, formal structures as well as behavioural patterns are the channels along which these forces move, but in the last resort one is left with an abstract picture. This, of course, is why we get the concept of the black box in which a rather mysterious transformation of inputs into outputs takes place. Originally the black box tended to be *the* administration. Political scientists observed inputs and outputs from outside. As they studied it from within, one got more inputs (withinputs in Sharkansky's phrase)—but the black boxes never quite vanish, if only because behaviour in the last resort involves the unopenable human mind.

It is quite possible, on the other hand, to think of more concrete systems if one wants to use a systems analysis. There is, for example, the railway system. This is an interrelated network of lines and stations with an operating schedule set by headquarters. The public administration system, I would suggest, can be seen in much the same way. The stations are the bureaux, the lines the procedures along which business is channelled according to laws and regulations. If one does not ask how the men at headquarters, legislators or senior officials, came to make these rules, one can concentrate on the administrative process. This way of seeing things does give us something more tangible to work on—the equivalent of bricks and mortar and printed timetables. Moreover, if the administrative system is defined in formal, rather than behavioural, terms, we do have a subject of our own.

The fear, as I have already said, is that Public Administration is growing in so many directions and has got involved with so many other disciplines at its periphery that it is in danger of disappearing as a recognisable focus of study. To establish the centre of a discipline is a problem of definition. This is too often regarded as pedantry, diverting us from the business of real research. To allow freer pursuit of that business, we may prefer frontiers only roughly sketched and frontier posts left open. A centre is needed, nevertheless. As another writer put it recently 'a field without a centre has no circumference'—and without a circumference, I might add, we face infinity. It may be, he comments, that our focus will shift, our subject matter change, hopefully leading us to concepts that explain more than we were originally able to. But one is bound to counter: what is it we want to explain? The social sciences as a whole want to explain almost everything apart from the physical laws of nature, but we are not omnicompetent social scientists. I have already suggested earlier in the book that we should start with the concrete administrative institutions that we know because we can see them. Within that framework, we may consider organisational behaviour, everyday decision-making, the policy process—but only in so far as this helps to explain how the institutions really work. And this we want to know primarily as a test to set against existing arrangements and as a guide to future arrangements. We want to know whether our institutions need reform because they do not function as intended, and we want to know what sort of changes are likely to achieve these intentions. Rather than prospect in alien territories too often, however, we would do better to import their goods as required. If we concentrate in this way, we may be able to show those concerned that we do have a subject to offer.

Science, as they say, marches on—inevitably more complex. It is foolish to yearn for a return to earlier, simpler days. The academic is committed to the advancement of knowledge, even if the result is a world ever harder to comprehend. The simplicity of the founding fathers is not to be recaptured. But let us remember the coherence of their subject and the clarity of their purpose.

The Universities' Role

In this chapter I want to turn from the discussion of Public Administration as a subject in its own right to Public Administration as a programme of courses. The proper training of administrators is not the focus of this book. This is because the contents of a training programme are necessarily technical and cover a much wider ground than the study of government. That the subject of Public Administration as I have defined it should form part of any programme goes without saying, but I have already discussed it at length and there is little I can say about the other subjects that need be taught. The only view I will venture here is that administrators should receive an education as well as training: as the French would say, and as a former director of the *Ecole Nationale d'Administration* actually said, 'the solid elements of general culture'.

To my mind this involves two things. First, it seems to me that training in the use of techniques (or, as senior officials like to think that the manipulation of techniques is a matter for specialist subordinates, training in familiarity with their use) should be underpinned by a proper understanding of the theories on which such techniques are based. That a little knowledge is a dangerous thing may be a platitude. It may also be one of those proverbs to which there is an anti-proverb: too much knowledge inhibits action. Nevertheless, fools do rush in where angels fear to tread: a technique, the theory of which is not understood, can be more dangerous than no technique at all. One is told that administrators on short training courses switch off when the lecturer turns to theory. This lack of intellectual curiosity is odd, given that our elite civil service is chosen largely on the basis of intellectual superiority, but let that pass: perhaps it lies in the nature of short courses that they cannot shake off the busy practitioner's impatience with anything that cannot be applied tomorrow morning. All I am saying here is that there is a range of sciences, human and quantitative, that they should understand in the proper sense of the word—and this means academic instruction.

My second point is that senior officials deal not only with techniques of organisation and techniques of decision-making—they deal with concrete problems of society. The *ENA* director also said: 'The science of public administration is essentially a human science . . . it should not be forgotton that administration is not an end in itself but a means towards the increasing well-being of man.' I have already stressed the dangers of the administrator who is more concerned with the smooth operation of the machine than with the direction in which it moves. Good administration is a matter of content as well as of form. To be a good administrator means to understand the content. This implies an understanding of policy fields; not just of the political and administrative issues involved in education or health, for example, but of the 'technical' facts and theories that underline alternative policies. Only then can they fulfil their responsibilities as active participants in the policy-making process, can they match their assessment of what is politically and administratively feasible by a notion of what is in the best interests of society. To this end, again, some academic study is required.

The word academic was pinned deliberately to the two fields of study mentioned above—deliberately because thought turns naturally from it to the universities. My concern in the present chapter is not with the content of administrative or technical courses. The focus of this book is on the study of government in universities. But, because I am concerned with universities as well as the study of government, I want to discuss the wider role universities should play in teaching and research of public administration.

This is not the place, however, for yet another discussion of the true nature of universities or the role they should play in the modern world.[1] That, over the years, has been a favourite topic for specialists in all academic disciplines and none. The flow of books has now reached flood proportions, though with Britain mercifully lagging behind America. And if we appear to live in a period marked by uncertainty of purpose, our academic predecessors

[1] What follows is a revised version of my 'Public Administration as a University Subject', *PAC Bulletin* (now *Public Administration Bulletin*) (December 1971).

seemed to have lived through similar crises before us, less dramatic, of course, because they were spared the concurrent crisis of authority. Nevertheless, public investment in higher education has now reached levels which make uncertainty more serious, the consequence of wrong decisions, or even non-decision, increasingly expensive. A misplaced emphasis in higher education or in research now wastes more resources more quickly—and that at a time when resources are desperately needed elsewhere. Wrong policies may deprive the community of the universities' full contribution to its welfare—and that at a time when such contributions are important.

The traditional function of the university is often thought to be the pursuit of learning for its own sake. Scholarship is a valuable experience for the individual. More than that: universities are the guardians of universal scholarship—and thus civilisation—passing on the knowledge acquired by earlier generations and adding to its stock. The image is that of a community of scholars, undisturbed by practical, professional or contemporary considerations. There are still many academics with this self-image. Yet it was never really true. Traditionally, the general education of the Bachelor, doubtless well below present-day standards, was followed by professional training in theology, law or medicine. We all accept, nevertheless, that no culture can survive without a measure of art for art's sake.

But what could be an important function of a few universities, as we had in the past, can hardly be the major function of the multitude we have today. There are, for a start, not that many scholars around, either junior or senior. The 'more means worse' argument may not apply to university intake if one is considering the general educability of youngsters: how many can—or wish—to pursue learning purely for reasons of personal interest is another matter. In the recruitment of university teachers the number likely to be lifetime researchers, capable of making significant contributions to knowledge, must somewhere reach its limits. Corners of the universities must remain sheltered from the immediate pressures of life, as were the medieval houses of religion—but even then, the number of monks and nuns in closed houses, praying for the salvation of mankind, were generally outnumbered by those involved in society and dedicated to good works. The problem of modern universities is to find the right balance between the two. The high financial and social investment they now demand makes it even harder to maintain the supposed traditional stance. The pressure is strong—and rightly—to shift the balance and widen the role. Strong also is the resistance. Partly this may be explained by laudable attachments to high scholarship; less charitably by the scholar's isolation from the world and its needs, some ignorance, some indifference, fostered by security of tenure; more politically by university self-government with its inevitable premium on the vested interests of existing members and by the difficulty of obtaining a change of direction by an institution run by a congress of interests.

The expansion of polytechnics has not been entirely due to the fact that they offer the Government a cheaper method of further education, though there is some truth in this and it is by no means unreasonable. It is also because they have often been more willing to develop new courses, perhaps because their own government is simpler, perhaps because their staff is less tradition-bound, perhaps because they have their own imperialist urge to carve out new territories, but above all because they see their clientele very differently. In so far as the university teaching of Public Adminis-tration is concerned, I have already remarked that Britain remains an underdeveloped country. We have no university schools, nor even departments, of Public Administration (if one excludes the more specialised fields of Local Government and Development Administration). We have a few postgraduate degree courses, attached to Politics departments and taught by Politics lecturers whose main duty is generally the teaching of British Government as a humanities subject to undergraduates. Though still at a relatively low level (and the emphasis is on the word 'relatively' rather than on the word 'low'), there is more activity in the polytechnics than in the universities.

The self-image of universities is nevertheless changing under current pressures. Not fast enough, however. Society, faced with ever-rising bills, may reasonably expect the gearing of higher education to social needs rather than to the self-culture of a privi-leged group. When applied to students this is only a half-truth, for even a general education may bring indirect benefits to the larger community (this recently fashionable argument, however, now seems to be under some challenge in so far as the benefits are seen in terms of economic development). It applies with more force, perhaps, to the employment of academics who can too easily spend not three but forty years cultivating their own gardens. Academics are too easily convinced of the importance of their own subject. As they still control British universities, despite all protes-tations about government interference, they tend to perpetuate the emphasis of more leisurely days. Outside control is marginal at best, partly, of course, because universities, like other institutions, are limited to incremental planning while the bulk of their activities remain fixed by earlier generations of scholars. Yet the situation is little different in the new universities with greater planning opportunities, notwithstanding their claims to modernity.

Universities have gone some way in adapting their courses to meet the existing career demands of their students, but only some way. They have shown little initiative in reshaping degree structures in a way that would help to change career patterns to meet the real needs of modern society. Science faculties, for example, train excellent scientists. Economics departments produce good economists, even some businessmen. Between them, however, they do little to produce the managerially orientated technologists or technologically orientated managers (technocrats for short) that we require. Our social science faculties are little better. Welfare workers are trained in some places, of course, and there are other examples. But Politics departments produce neither politicians nor public officials—nor, indeed, anything else recognisable. Of all the social sciences, in fact, Politics seems the most resolutely to cultivate a humanities outlook, offering knowledge about modern society, it is true, but largely for its intrinsic interest rather than for any use value. The minority of students who enrol believing in their youthfully unsophisticated way that the purpose of understanding the world is to change it are soon disabused, as much by the attitude of their teachers as by the realities of life. Very few choose the subject with lower keyed but more practical hopes—as a preparation for public service. In this, of course, Politics departments respond to, and in turn reinforce, the British cult of the amateur: higher education is not relevant to careers and careers are not to be chosen until after it is completed. And yet the notion of Politics as another art for art's sake subject is astonishing when one remembers the high hopes of the founders of the London School of Economics and Political Science.

Perhaps it is as well that Politics departments do not turn out a stream of intending politicians: if they hoped to enter the established system, they would be largely unemployable (a matter of numbers, quite apart from the question of what qualities make a successful politician); if too many remained footloose in the counter-establishment we might have grave social problems. The fact that most British students leave university at 21, earlier than their German or many of their American counterparts, and are thus more easily socialised into established careers, is a blessing in one respect even if it has marked disadvantages with regard to their career preparation. To what extent departments should turn out administrators is another matter, depending on what one thinks the preparation of administrators should be and where it should be done. To that question I will return.

The situation is more serious when one looks at the research carried out in such departments, at how academics spend the non-teaching time at their disposal, ranging from behavioural surveys at the worm's-eye level to systems theory at the cosmic, from textual analysis of past thinkers to studies that are essentially political history. All academically respectable—but remarkably little that is directly useful, even indirectly influential, except on very optimistic notions about the extent to which the writings of political theorists, whether behavioural or philosophical, can be absorbed in the mainstream of social thought. Again there are reasons for this. Scholars, left to themselves, are likely to research in fields that interest them most and the chances are that these are not fields of practical concern: men with practical interests, after all, are less likely to become academics in the first place. But even if the research is practical in a broad sense, the choice of subjects will still reflect the academics' personal interests and there is no guarantee that these will coincide with the socially important issues of the time.

For research to focus on such issues, researchers need to feel wanted, to feel, as few in Public Administration can at present, that their contribution is valued by the administrators. This involves more than access to material (the current academic demand). It means direct collaboration in the world of general administrative reform at all levels, not only at the Fulton–Maud–Kilbrandon heights of generalisation, but also at the level of everyday problems of internal organisation. As the focus shifts from general administrative principles to concern with substantive fields of policy, it involves collaboration in planning over many fields of governmental activity. This, in turn, means membership of internal committees, internal consultancies and participation in the administrative process.

But it is not just a question of personal satisfaction through personal involvement. Research depends on finance. The number of academics specialising in Public Administration is small and their time is often largely committed to university work. For research to be carried out effectively on any worthwhile scale, departments or schools of Public Administration need to be established with sufficient staff to permit flexibility in teaching and reserach arrangements and to allow for cross-fertilisation between different specialists: large enough, also, for team work and research assistance. An alternative, less satisfactory because involving short-term *ad hoc* arrangements, with a consequent loss in build-up of expertise, is the direct commissioning of work. It may well be the case, nevertheless, that the direction of research is most likely to change if there is a paying client. Abhorrent though it may be to traditionalists and radicals alike, there would be no harm if an element of market demand were introduced into Politics departments, as it already has been in many others. Complaints by radical students that academics were being further absorbed into the establishment, were involved in maintenance of the *status quo*, would doubtless increase—and students' unease would doubtless have a measure of justification. One would certainly want political theorists to remain independent and one might even wish that a larger proportion than at present were prepared to jeopardise establishment respectability by subjecting the existing order to radical critique. But it is just as arguable that some of the rest should contribute practically to reform within the existing order. If there were a 'Warwick University Ltd' of the sort caricatured a while ago, so long as there are other universities also, it is hard to see what should be wrong with a university geared to industrial needs and thus helping to improve living standards (as well as company profits) by its work. One would rightly suspect university departments closely linked to political parties (though it is surprising how little use has been made by British parties of academic psephologists compared to some of their foreign counterparts), but one would need to be very far to the left indeed to have the same suspicion of the administration as a client of Public Administrationists.

One can thus see two needs: for more professionally orientated education and for more practically orientated research. Returning to the former, I do not suggest that undergraduate courses should necessarily be professionalised. Now that the polytechnics are well established, it may be right that social science faculties should, in the main, regard their undergraduate courses as general education in the tradition of the Arts faculties from which they sprang. Even then, a greater concern with socially useful careers could well be combined with a liberal education. And one can, in any case, overstate the principles of liberal education. University students of law and medicine, after all, take strictly professional degrees and it has not yet been suggested that we should follow the American pattern of making these studies postgraduate. We cannot yet afford a general education for all up to the age of 21 and there is not much evidence that all would want it. Too many students already wonder what they are doing and why; disenchanted by what seems a lack of purpose in their studies, they all too easily lose heart and end up with neither a useful degree nor real depth of culture. The fault lies partly with their lecturers, though it is not the lecturers' fault—there is no reason why scholars should automatically be good teachers, after all. But the fault lies equally with the students, and again it is not their fault—there is no reason to assume a universal inclination to pursue learning for its own sake. The point is simply that career-orientated courses may provide clearer motivation for many and thus produce better work and better results. Whether such people should be taught in non-university institutions, in polytechnics and other colleges, is open to debate—certainly, these are often much better at teaching.

The division of functions at the moment is less a matter of principle—general education here, practical education there— than a matter of historical accident. Preparation for the older professions, though often originally through apprenticeship and their own guilds, has now largely found a place within the universities. In the case of some of the newer professions sometimes it has, sometimes not. A good case can often be made for the non-university sector, relative costs and flexibility apart. There is the desire to limit the size of universities (though British universities are laughably small compared to most others). Extension of subjects, and thus the growth of departments, brings organisational difficulties. The more sections a university has, the more conflicting demands there are for resources, the harder it is under the existing system to make university policy: the alternative, strong central government within the university, seems entirely unacceptable to vested sectional interests at present. But these are general points.

A more specific point is that courses specialising in Public Administration may have to be pitched at a level below that acceptable to universities. Some Public Administration courses necessarily train for posts below those normally occupied by graduates—lower management, in other words. The lack of training here, not only in Public Administration but in most sectors of activity, is perhaps even more serious than at higher levels. In the university one thinks naturally of the old Administrative Class of the civil service and its equivalents elsewhere—middle management, with expectations (in the civil service) or hopes (in business) of promotion to the top, where organisational engineering and policy-making become central functions. The improvement of services, however, depends as much on the supporting staff. Training for such clearly involves simpler courses, courses with a different content and, equally important, a different sort of teaching from that which universities can give. It may also be better organised on a day-release or sandwich basis, more effectively linked to a job and perhaps more in line with the students' own desires—and the universities are not really geared to such arrangements.

The provision of Public Administration courses for prospective senior administrators is another matter. But should these be taught at undergraduate or postgraduate level? Administrative theory in all its ramifications and the wider ramifications of policy science are too advanced for 18 to 20 year olds. It is hard to believe that one would get very far in an undergraduate course or that, if one did, the students would really master the subject. If the experience of Economics is anything to go by, it seems increasingly to be necessary for students to undergo postgraduate training, or some form of in-job training, to work usefully at any real level. The fact that a full Public Administration course must involve a wider range of disciplines, not to be understood superficially, makes it even more difficult. To that extent such a course at undergraduate level may be a waste of time for students, leaving them insufficiently skilled if they enter the administration immediately on graduating and merely duplicating in simpler terms what they will learn if they go on to graduate schools.

Another point may be made here in passing. Unless there were a dramatic increase in the recruitment of trained administrators, taking the public service as a whole and in its widest sense, with a clear policy of preference for relevance known to school leavers when they make their university applications, it is unlikely that the intake into professionally orientated undergraduate courses in Public Administration would be sufficient to make this a viable enterprise. Probably, indeed, one would not wish sixth formers to have to make such decisions anyway. If one did, moreover, there would be some obligation on the authorities to employ those who successfully completed the course. And this would mean that someone else, presumably admission tutors, would have to judge at 18 whether candidates have the making of future administrators. An absurd situation. The present system, whereby future senior civil servants are recruited at the relatively immature age of 21, even allowing for recent attempts to make the system more flexible, is bad enough: neither in Germany, for example, nor in America is the attempt made to judge a man's lifetime potential so early.

The teaching of some Public Administration as an element in a wider undergraduate course, in a Politics degree for example, is another matter. Here one thinks of the subject more narrowly, not as training in a range of professional skills, involving a variety of disciplines, but simply as the study of the administrative system (the *how and why*, not the *how to*, of administration). Any study of the British system of government, even, more fashionably, of the British political system, demands some examination of the administrative machine which both implements policy outputs and constitutes a major factor of the policy-making process itself. The subject is, on the whole, more adequately dealt with from the institutional than from the systems point of view. Perhaps this is because in Britain we have hardly begun to develop a sociology of the administrative system (neither studies of the background of senior civil servants nor case studies of particular decisions contribute much to this). In the field of comparative politics, theoretical and empirical work is much further advanced, though almost entirely American in origin and concentrated until recently on developing nations. This aspect of Public Administration provides important material for the Politics student: indeed, more country studies are now available as a fill-in for broader theoretical models in this field than in any other field of comparative politics.

Some aspects of Public Administration may be taught at undergraduate level for yet another reason, not as a professional subject, not as political science, but as part of civics. A general education in civics, at school or university, has never been part of the British tradition. British Government, a growing but relatively small A-level subject in schools, is taught as a subject like others, just as Politics at the university is studied as a subject like others. Compare America, where the study of Government is long established at both levels, or Germany where, since the war, efforts have been made to establish it in schools as part of an education for democracy campaign. Again, one foresees cries of horror from the right that thinks all teachers socialists and from the left that sees the face of the establishment in headmasters and education officers. Such courses may certainly be used to extol the existing democratic order (often in terms of its principles rather than its practice), to socialise the young into ruling values and thus maintain the *status quo*. One has only to read the A-level scripts of 17- and 18-year-olds to see how many believe that the British system of government is the envy of the world (unless they are dissembling in the mistaken hope of pleasing their examiners, but for that such candidates seem too unsophisticated). Radical teachers, on the other hand, may use such courses to undermine the established order—as part of the 'long march through institutions' that some of the revolutionary left in Germany, for example, have come to believe a more effective technique than direct action.

Politics students, of course, are more critical—the danger, indeed, may be that lecturers will adapt themselves to the anti-establishmentarianism of the vocal minority, for the sake of peace in the classroom if for no other, rather than that they will brainwash the silent majority. If courses in British Government were more generally taken at university level, by less critical students—that is, those reading subjects based on the accumulation of unchallenged facts, engineering for example—one might be more worried about the transmission of an accepted ideology, conservative in implication and often quite unrealistic. The problem of implicit values and the relation between theory and practice would then doubtless arise.

Nevertheless, we all live in an increasingly administered society and it is increasingly important that we should understand the system if we are to use it rather than let it use us. In this sense, at least, there is good reason for giving some factual instruction in Public Administration to all—the emphasis being on those levels of administration with which the citizen is likely to come into contact, on immediately useful knowledge rather than principles of administrative reorganisation. Where students are preparing for careers which will bring them into contact with the administration in a professional as well as a private capacity, as is often the case with doctors, architects and engineers, for example, such courses would be even more relevant. To these points I will return.

This has been something of a digression in so far as the concern of this chapter is with Public Administration as a comprehensive syllabus, reasonably advanced and with professional orientation, and we may return to the questions: training from whom, at what level and in what institution?

Universities could not gear their undergraduate degrees directly to the teaching of Public Administration even if this were desirable. For one thing, central government does not have a large enough intake of non-specialist graduates to account for a significant proportion of student throughput spread over a host of university departments. Even if local authorities were added, bearing in mind the emphasis on specialisation there, it would not make much difference. And given the reasonable desire to get some of the nation's best graduates (even if it were with some preference for relevance), recruitment is bound to remain nationwide, making it difficult to conceive of pre-entry training concentrated in one or two universities. In France, on the other hand, students who wish to enter the higher levels of the civil service as non-technical administrators pass through the *Ecole Nationale d'Administration* for post-entry training. The youngster who seeks a career as a technical administrator gets his entire university-level education, undergraduate as well as graduate, in a limited number of special-ised civil service schools. This brings one to another point. In Britain there is a dispersal of talent (entrance qualifications are, overall, probably not significantly higher at Oxbridge or the LSE than at provincial universities); in France there is a concentration. The technological *Grandes Ecoles* are more prestigious than the university science faculties and are likely to attract the best school leavers; the Paris law faculty and the Paris *Institut National d'Etudes Politiques*, paths to *ENA* are more prestigious than their provincial counterparts or even than the equivalent of our Arts faculties in Paris. This naturally involves the schoolboy (and girl) in an undesirably early career decision (though it is worth remem-bering that those who wish to become doctors or engineers have to make their choice even earlier in Britain, given the relatively narrow specialisation in our sixth forms). The other side of the coin, however, is that such concentration of students would allow a more rational organisation of degree courses than the present dispersal of intake.

Even if it were desirable to force youngsters to make an early career choice, this would in fact be a harder choice to make in the case of public administration than in many others. Public adminis-tration is not a career comprehensible to the young in the same way as medicine, law or engineering: they meet doctors and see them at work as heroes in films; the only civil servants those who do not come from privileged families are likely to see, or whose work they are likely to be able to understand, are clerical staff. Public Administration is taught at present in the context of Politics degrees and Politics students must contain a higher pro-portion without defined career aspirations than almost any other group of social science students, while most Arts students at least know they have a let-out in school teaching. Indeed, students reading Politics are often not even clear what the subject is about, quite apart from where it will lead. Those opting for under-graduate courses in Public Administration will neither know what to expect from their studies nor what their studies will fit them for. Some will hope to learn how to administer, others simply to find out how the administration works. This ambiguity may easily undermine a course, leading the teacher to an uneasy see-saw between two approaches and a disjointed series of topics, ranging from theoretical Weber to even more abstract Riggs on the one hand, and from cook-book Urwick to the more sophisti-cated practical recommendations of Simon on the other. This is not likely to satisfy either sort of clientele. Those interested in political science are likely to avoid it if other choices are open, if only because it sounds rather dully utilitarian, while those who want something useful are likely to be disappointed by much that appears abstract.

But the situation is rather different if a Public Administration course is considered at postgraduate level. A career orientation is then reasonable. It should be possible to concentrate students in a limited number of centres. The question remains, of course, whether professional graduate schools of this sort should be within the university or attached to the administration. In the long run, it would be unreasonable to expect candidates to apply unless there was a reasonable guarantee of employment at the end. One of the strengths of the *Ecole Nationale d'Administration* is that it is both a postgraduate and post-entry school. Another strength, of course, is that it can use practising administrators for its teaching staff. (Comparisons between Britain and France would be difficult in this respect as French administrators, for a variety of reasons, tend to have a more academic outlook than their British counterparts and thus take more easily to the teaching of theory). A third advantage is that students can use internal, perhaps confidential, documents in their classwork (case studies) and can also do periods of work in the field, attached to sympathetic officials who have gone through the same school. It is clearly easier to construct and reconstruct courses according to the needs of the service in an internal school than by negotiation with universities and university teachers, both jealous of their independence. Assessment of candidates, too, remains internal, perhaps thought more reliable, certainly easier handled, than assessment by academic outsiders. A school closely linked with the administration thus has obvious educational advantages. If training is to be post-entry, moreover (and this is the only safe way of guaranteeing a career to the trainee), it also has advantages from the point of personnel management: it is more complicated to send civil servants out to the universities, presumably on paid leave of absence, than to organise their studies within the service.

For these reasons there is much to be said in favour of civil service schools. A possible proviso is that measures need to be taken to ensure that their standards are equivalent to those of a university. This is clearly the case with *ENA*, but the point to remember is that *ENA* restricts itself to a full-length postgraduate programme of studies. The Civil Service College, by comparison, offers a wide range of short courses at many levels, many mid-career, and may suffer as a consequence, perhaps in standards (pressure of work and the stultifying effects of too much repetitive low-level teaching), more likely in prestige. If there is a case for fuller professional training in Public Administration for entrants into the higher civil service—and the case, of course, is not accepted at present—there would also be a case for splitting the college into two, one an academic institution, the other a centre for the provision (or co-ordination) of shorter training programmes.

The foregoing conclusions, however, only apply if considerations of training are paramount. A university is concerned with research as well as education, and in the case of Public Administration research is as important as education. It is important so that we can understand the administrative system better as political scientists. But it is equally important because training and research are necessarily linked: what can be taught depends on what is known—a truism, no doubt, but relevant nevertheless. If training is not to degenerate into a repetition of received ideas, then the frontiers of knowledge (another relevant stock phrase) must be continually pushed forward. And whatever efforts individual lecturers may make, if they are scattered through a host of Politics departments, often small and with a majority of members whose interests are really quite different, the results are bound to be meagre. Research thrives best, new ideas develop more easily, projects are best organised, when a considerable number of scholars work together with a common focus of interest. Research in Public Administration is still extraordinarily limited, especially in the field of theory, where there are strong suspicions of Americanism, but even in the traditional British field of empirical work.

It is hard to see how there can be a significant expansion of research under existing university arrangements. Extra staff could, of course, be taken on if studies were commissioned by the administration or if the Social Science Research Council showed a greater preference for the socially useful. University-financed appointments, on the other hand, are linked directly to teaching needs; they depend on student numbers, now, moreover, largely on undergraduate numbers. The number of Public Administrationists any one Politics department can employ must thus remain very small so long as Public Administration courses form only a small part of its syllabus. This, perhaps, is the real case for one or two university-based Public Administration centres. It does not mean the transfer of existing staff or the elimination of existing undergraduate courses: Public Administration should, indeed, be included in all Politics degrees. What it does mean is a concentration of postgraduate taught courses and independent postgraduate research in a number of centres where staff research is also recognised as a special function.

Such a development would facilitate staff secondment to ministries and work on government-sponsored research: people can be spared in a large organisation in a way that they cannot in a small. There could also be a rapid expansion of research in a larger organisation. And that means not only research concerned with practical issues of immediate importance but also the development of theory. It is only the latter, in fact, that can ensure the real establishment of Public Administration as a subject. Once a worthwhile body of theoretical knowledge is available in published form, focused on the British administrative system, attitudes towards recruitment in the civil service are more likely to change and the emphasis placed on professional training may increase—but that is a longer term possibility and does not alter the immediate concern.

Let one revert, however, to the teaching of Public Administration degrees or diplomas in the universities as a broadly based, reasonably advanced, hopefully professional qualification. A number of these have been developed, though it is a nice point whether they are intended to meet or create a demand. (The clientele, in any case, is less likely to include prospective civil servants than local government officers and 'undecideds' with general interest in some sort of administrative career.) Such developments notwithstanding, there is still a considerable reluctance to expand professional degrees, particularly where these involve an interdisciplinary syllabus, cutting across departments, even faculties. Competing demands and a certain reluctance among some members of university planning committees to finance such developments out of limited university funds at the cost of general undergraduate education and academic research are a partial explanation. The snobbery of certain faculties when vocational training is mentioned is matched by their conservatism when it comes to proposals that do not fit well into existing departmental patterns.

University structures certainly place difficulty in the way of interdisciplinary degrees. One sees this even at the undergraduate level where joint degrees are common enough. They are often weakly organised: students left wandering between departments without co-ordinated supervision; courses stuck together without much regard for their interrelation because teachers do not collaborate easily across departmental boundaries. A postgraduate syllabus in Public Administration that consisted merely of juxtaposed courses in a wide range of disciplines, very different from each other in their methods, would merely strengthen the scholar's suspicion that overall the subject will not be studied in sufficient depth to ensure academic respectability. And, indeed, it would be foolish to deny that a genuinely interdisciplinary syllabus poses serious problems. Each teacher must teach his own discipline according to its own methods if the student is to obtain a sound grasp of the skills involved. To do this well, to remain up to date in his subject, some would argue that the teacher is best rooted in the department of his discipline, working with colleagues in his own field. This, of course, is a possible argument against schools of Public Administration which bring together experts in different fields: they might lose contact with their own science. The fact remains that while different disciplines must be taught, the focus—the illustrations chosen in applying techniques, for example—must be geared to the common interest, in this case the administrative system and the policy-making process. This means that lectures given within different departments for their own students will not do, that parallel lecture courses covering the same techniques but with a different focus must be arranged. Shortage of staff is the immediate cry. More staff, financed from earmarked funds, seems the only answer unless inroads are to be made into the traditional eight to ten hours student contact that academics regard as their established right.

What does all this mean for Politics departments? It is not likely that they will develop a professional orientation. Quite apart from the fact that the interests of the overwhelming majority of their members do not lie in this direction, the professional market for their students is not large enough to influence them. But the departments are, in any case, probably not the right place for postgraduate courses of this sort. Proud though we may be of the title 'master science', the majority of disciplines needing to be taught fall outside the province of political science even at its widest definition. That the focus in each case should be the administrative system or political issues, that administrative and political considerations need to be taken into account, does not outweigh the fact that the basic techniques involved are to a large extent those of other disciplines.

And yet politics remains crucial. This is more than a matter of focus (illustrations used, problems discussed). It is also a question of method. The problems of management are very different in the public service from those in the private sector, not just because different things are dealt with, but also because the environment is different: important factors have to be taken into account which courses in business management, for example, are likely to ignore. Organisation in the public service is circumscribed by a host of special formalities and broader constitutional limitations such as ministerial responsibility. Its activities are subject to the scrutiny of the press and the reactions of the public. In its individual decisions, discretion is generally limited by the principle of equality of treatment and often by rights of appeal to the courts. Policy-making, too, involves a very different range of factors: non-quantifiable goals, party policies, parliamentary and interest group pressures and public opinion. It is not only that the ends of policy often remain economically intangible; the framework in which policy is made also involves economically irrational considerations. If all this is to be built into management theory for the public service, it is bound to be a rather different sort of theory from that applied to other sectors of activity. For this reason it may, after all, be necessary to take the various specialists concerned out of their traditional departmental environment, for there they seem rather unlikely to come into contact with such considerations.

The case, then, for schools of Public Administration, can be argued along several further lines. First, existing departmental structures inhibit the development of genuine interdisciplinary courses. New structures, uninhibited by tradition, are in any case more likely to innovate. Second, students are better looked after in a separate school than if left to fall between numerous departmental stools. Third, teachers are more likely to focus on common problems, and to develop theories which will take account of special considerations, if brought together in this way.

Having said all this, it may well be that the need is actually less for schools of Public Administration than for schools of Public Policy. This is not the place to go into the distinction between administration and policy again. Let me simply note that more than a terminological difference is at stake here. There is clearly a level at which training for administration in the public service does not involve policy in any real sense. This applies on the whole to lower management, to those concerned with office organisation, personnel work, accounting procedures and the like (the staple diet of earlier American textbooks on Public Administration, in fact). True, there is not always a clear distinction of personnel. At the highest levels the two functions are united (senior civil servants advise ministers on policy and direct the executive services in their ministries)—and lower-ranking officials may rise eventually. Their number, even taking the public services as a whole, is nevertheless relatively small compared with that of lower and career middle management (the latter term taken to mean those with no real expectations of rising to policy levels). These require general and specialist administrative skills of a sort that do permit a distinction (even if not absolute) between administration and policy. The point has already been made, however, that at this level training involves courses better given in non-university institutions.

The trouble with policy-based courses is that they are even more interdisciplinary in nature than administration-based ones. This is particularly true if one is concerned with problem areas, the contents of policy, as well as the general question how policy-making should be organised (meta-policy science). In so far as policy is concerned directly with the reform of governmental institutions (ombudsman and all that, for example), it fits well enough into Politics departments. But institutional reform as such is only a very small part of government programmes. These are generally related to particular fields of governmental activity: health, education and welfare, housing and urban development, economic and regional planning—the list is long. Here, broadly, there are four elements, four sorts of consideration and four sorts of knowledge required, three more or less common to each field, the fourth different in each case. First, the analytic (quantitative techniques of policy-making); second, the administrative (how to organise); third, the political (what is politically desirable and what is feasible under existing political conditions); fourth, the substantive (what are the problems of health, education, welfare or whatever it may be, what is 'technically' desirable, and what, technically, can be done about it). The last of these considerations involves a different sort of expertise in each case and therefore increases considerably the number of different sorts of specialists required. A Public Policy school, therefore, particularly if it is concerned as much with research as with training, really needs to be something of a miniature university in itself, bringing together representatives not only for all the social science departments but all other faculties as well.

A version of the old specialist versus generalist debate may be introduced here. The Public Administrationist should undoubtedly familiarise himself with a substantive field of activity if he is to understand either the policy issues or the administrative problems involved; the doctor, educationist or town planner should, for his part, understand the political and managerial implications of any proposed reform. It is important that each should learn something from the others' expertise. For this purpose, there is much to be said for placing them in an environment that forces them to collaborate, that will create links strong enough to balance those of their own discipline. Institutional arrangements will help to do this (authority structures) and so will physical arrangements (a shared building). These will reinforce an otherwise often weakly integrative common focus in teaching (shared students) and in research (joint projects). The advantage of such schools would be two-fold: because of the involvement of specialists, they would contribute more effectively to policy formulation (research) and they would at the same time turn out much needed hybrid specialist/generalist administrators (training). In so far as one can generalise about a country with so many diverse academic institutions, this is the way in which America is going, and it seems to be the way we are going also, with the Centre for Environmental Studies as the first swallow. An example of the opposite direction —a Public Administration rather than a Policy school—would be the Institute of Local Government Studies at Birmingham. There is room for both.

Any major change, however, of whatever sort, seems unlikely to come about as the result of the initiative of the universities themselves. This brings me back to the issue of government interference. The danger to universities lies not in any suspected extension of state control but in their own autonomy and their stubborn refusal to accept some form of social control. It is time for the state to assert its legitimate rights. It has a right as paymaster: one that should not be so easily shrugged off by those who allow themselves to be paid from public funds and enjoy security of tenure—that they should claim the right to exclusive management of the vast public capital invested in universites into the bargain might seem almost shameless to less fortunate employees elsewhere. It also has a right as guardian of the public good: whatever criticism one may make of the system, elected governments subject to parliamentary and public pressures are undoubtedly more democratic than co-opted university senates. Academic standards must be preserved, and so must scholarship for its own sake—but within limits; the state, for its part, should ensure that a reasonable proportion of university expenditure (and that means a growing proportion) is directed into useful channels.

While individual teachers must remain free to speak their own minds in their lectures, weighing the evidence as they see it, just as judges adjudicate freely in the cases to which they are assigned, there is no more reason for individual professors (or the small groups of lecturers that form departments) to devise their degree programmes as they see fit than there is for judges to write the law. In many areas, of course, this is generally accepted—if not formally, then at least informally: while universities differ slightly in what they teach medical students, there is a broad consensus about what the qualified medical practitioner should know. This, however, is not the case with Politics degrees—understandably, perhaps, as there is nothing Politics graduates are expected to be able to do.

Less understandably, it seems to be the case with Public Administration courses also.

There is a good case for some form of state intervention—state control in this context meaning control by bodies representative of, and responsible to, the society that supports the students and pays the academics, that will employ the students and may expect to benefit from the research of the academics. Whether such bodies are Parliament and parliamentary committees, Government and government departments, research councils, grant committee or something else again, is another matter. In the field of Public Administration, at least, it might reasonably be seen as the responsibility of public authorities. The point has been made that they may prefer to organise their own in-training institutions, negotiating *ad hoc* arrangements with the universities on occasion and commissioning the occasional *ad hoc* research from them—and that this may be an efficient way of doing things. But one reason for this is also that public authorities have fallen over backwards to respect the autonomy of universities. Both sides have lost as a result. In the case of Public Administration, certainly, development as a university subject on a worthwhile scale, in terms of research as well as teaching, will be best promoted as things stand by some form of outside intervention. Physician heal thyself is not a reliable precept.

The Civic
Contribution

In my preface I made it clear that this was an advocate's book. The threads that hold it together are arguments for a certain way of studying government and a certain stance the academic should take with regard to government itself. For the inevitable repetition that follows I apologise. In a concluding chapter I hope that it is not unreasonable. I apologise at the same time, in retrospect also in this case, for a book that will have struck the initiated reader as decidedly old fashioned. Of that, too, I warned in my preface. This is partly a matter of style. I hope, after all, to say something convincing to the layman as well as the professional academic. It is also, however, a matter of content. The academic reader will not have overlooked the way I have avoided any real discussion of sophisticated modern theories. He may have felt that this was largely because I did not understand them sufficiently well— and some, to be honest, I do not. But let me make a virtue of this vice: if the discussion has centred on approaches to the subject that are now old fashioned, it is because I believe an old-fashioned approach worthy of a voice amidst the scientifically sophisticated works now reaching us in ever larger number from across the Atlantic.

In this chapter I am less concerned with the proper academic approach to the subject than with the subject's proper usefulness to society. I am largely concerned, in other words, with the study of government as a subject for the public. It is natural—and fitting also—that the academic should conclude any account of his subject as he sees it by turning outwards, showing its wider relevance to the world in which he lives and thus its claim to wider attention.

Students who choose to read political science in Britain are not choosing a useful subject.[1] A few may hope to find a key that will unlock the door to a better society but most, even of that small group, are soon disillusioned. Even fewer select it for vocational reasons: political scientists rarely graduate into real-life politics. Where the choice is a positive one, not merely boredom with traditional school subjects or hope for a soft option, the reason usually given, nevertheless, is an interest in politics. The admissions tutor's answer is likely to be that political science is not about politics as the layman understands it: the issues that are the stuff of politics are the province of other departments. Political science is theory—about institutions, behaviour, ideologies, it is true, but theory nevertheless, which the student, if he is not to get bored again, must appreciate as science for science's sake. Like any other liberal arts subject, it is taught as an intellectual exercise, part of the liberal university's function of expanding the mind.

The situation is rather different in America where Politics courses are taken by students reading a wider range of subjects, generally in the form of an Introduction to American Government. A recent and widely used textbook starts with a section entitled 'The Value of the Study of Political Science' and this, in turn, has two subsections: 'Political Science as Training for Citizenship' and 'Political Science as Career Preparation'. Public Administration studies can be seen under the same three aspects—as liberal education, as preparation for professional employment, or as background to better citizenship. Public Administration as part of a political science course for undergraduates is likely to emphasise the disinterested search for knowledge—analysis of the administrative subsystem as an important element in understanding the larger political system. Public Administration as a vocational course will teach the student a range of useful skills based on other sciences as well as the science of politics. Let us consider Public Administration as civics.

To quote the textbook again: 'Citizens of democracy are particularly obligated to inform themselves on public matters; if they are to make any real contribution to the governmental process, they need a considerable understanding of the nature and objectives of the government. Persons who receive the advantage of higher education have a greater-than-average responsibility for the assumption of civic obligations.' This view is commonly held in America, home of grass-roots democracy and the 'civic culture', and explains the roots political science has taken in liberal arts colleges and universities. 'We are the only people who think him

---

[1] What follows is a version of my 'Public Administration as Civics', *Teaching Politics* (May 1972).

that does not meddle in state affairs—not indolent, but good for nothing.' Pericles of Athens might have been an American citizen. Compare Britain, where understanding of the governmental process is still regarded as a specialised subject rather than part of the intellectual baggage of the educated citizen.

Public administration is part of the governmental process. The administration is not merely the means by which policies are implemented—it plays a considerable part in their formulation. It is important, therefore, that the citizen should have some knowledge of how that part of the system works, doubly important if he wishes not merely to understand but also to participate—to meddle effectively—in the policy-making process.

Public Administration is even more relevant to the ordinary citizen at the ordinary level of everyday life. It is a truism to say that we are all being increasingly administered, that we are subject to an ever-increasing number of governmental regulations, and that we depend upon public authorities for an ever-increasing number of services. It is no less a truism to say that we must know the 'who, how and why' of the decisions that affect us if we are not to get lost in Kafka's castle. And it is not just a question of understanding the castle's lay-out but of making its keepers work for us, of claiming our rights or challenging decisions that seem wrong. The man in the street has only the haziest notion of how the system operates. It is not simply that he does not always know his rights (i.e. understand the policies): he often does not know where to find the mysterious and undifferentiated 'they' who take the decisions that affect him in a host of offices that he can barely identify. Local councillors and Citizens Advice Bureaux, useful though they are, are no real answer to this problem. Even the better educated and more vocal middle class is often frustrated by its ignorance. Aspects of Public Administration can thus be usefully taught as part of elementary civics to schoolchildren, even if mainly at the level of who is responsible for emptying the dustbins and where do you complain if they are not emptied. At sixth-form level some quite sophisticated instruction is possible and, if geared to apparent needs, might not be unpopular. Even the Arts student would benefit from such a course.

A knowledge of the administrative system may be even more important for the citizen in his professional than in his private capacity. Many professions, industrial managers, architects, social workers, doctors, to name only four, come into regular contact with the administration during their work. They need to understand the regulations that affect them and the organisations that apply them—the formal procedures and the formal structures—

but also, more important perhaps and perhaps harder to look up in a reference work, the reality of administration: the way the bureaucracy works, the influences likely to impinge on it, the attitudes it is likely to develop, the way its decisions are likely to be made. This is the case for Public Administration courses as part of almost all professional training, each, no doubt, with a rather special angle as regards the legal and institutional aspects of the syllabus, but all with a common element, the common characteristics of the administrative process.

A well-informed society is more likely to develop a civic culture. For the less highly motivated individual, understanding the system is likely to pay dividends—and the dividends will increase as the citizen comes to depend more and more on the system for licences, permits, allocations, allowances, benefits, subsidies and the other good things it can grant or withhold. But civics means more than using the system, more even than participation. The whole notion of civic education is closely linked to the notion of reform. To quote another American textbook chosen for its elementary character (intended, in other words, for the non-specialist): 'The function of political science is to discover the principles that should be adhered to in public affairs and to study the operations of government in order to demonstrate what is good, criticise what is bad or inefficient, and suggest improvements.'

As political science has become more 'scientific', it has tended to forget what used to be commonly accepted, that the function of learning was the service of man. Public Administration has largely avoided this withdrawal from life, partly because of the professional orientation of the subject: its large student clientele in America generally has a practical interest, its American teachers often practical experience. Even in Public Administration, however, signs of withdrawal can be found. The number of disinterested academics is increasing, theorists, that is, who, either by scholarly inclination or through attachment to the ideal of a value free science, are more concerned with exploration than prescription. The pure theorists nevertheless remain in a minority. They are most likely to be found in those parts of the subject where it most closely approaches straight political science (cross-cultural comparisons of entire administrative systems) or straight sociology (general models of bureaucratic development). Much of the subject, however, is still too mundane to attract the dedicatedly ivory-tower scholar.

There are, of course, two entirely different ways in which Public Administration research can contribute to the improvement of government. The first aims to improve administrative techniques such as O & M, personnel management, Planning–Programming–Budgeting systems and operational research, and should be absorbed in the professional training of administrators. This is not under discussion here. It is the second type of research that is relevant: study of the administrative system in order to suggest ways in which the machine itself might be reorganised. It is true, of course, that techniques and institutions must be related—structures and functions are interdependent—but again it is not this level of improvement that is under discussion. The reform of administration, however, shades at a certain level—the level at which its colour turns political—into the reforms of government.

More or less professionally orientated courses in Public Administration, as well as courses for liberal-arts Politics students, often include material of this kind. For the humanist student, there is some point in this. Political science at its best has always had a normative concern with how the state should be ordered to be at its best. For the professional student, on the other hand, such discussion tends to be a little meaningless. It may be interesting, even intellectually stimulating, to consider major reorganisations of central or local government, but the students concerned are not likely to be in a position to implement (or even influence) such schemes until many years after graduation, if then, and by then the situation is bound to have changed anyway. There is a danger in lecturing students as if they were going to be in really influential positions immediately on entering the public service: it may give an 'academic' air to the course, often unwarranted by its total content, but is also likely to alienate the more down-to-earth of its participants.

Public Administration research in its reformist aspects is really directed at the educated citizen, the opinion-formers and the influentials, rather than the professionally orientated student (though, in his wider capacity, it certainly includes him). In that sense, the task of Public Administration is to educate the public as well as administrators—not, here, in how government *is* but in how it should be. This notion fits well with American belief in a participant democracy underpinned by state universities as mass educators for citizenship. Traditional British philosophies have been different, of course: government in the context of a 'deferential society' with the 'habit of authority' on the one hand, and elitist universities dedicated to scholarship on the other. But society is changing and so are universities—though they, as I have just argued, do need a push along the road.

In any case, for some years now in Britain the governmental system has been under continuous debate. 'What's wrong with?'

and 'let's reform' have been the slogans. We have been going
through a concentrated phase of inquiries into administrative
reform which is still far from completed. There is the roll call of
reports: Whyatt, Willink, Plowden, Maud I and II, Mallaby,
Fulton, Seebohm and Kilbrandon, not to mention the White
Paper opening Mr Heath's administration. A good deal of thinking and some research has gone into these, even if at a rather
superficial level in scientific terms—but that as much for paucity
of funds and shortage of researchers as for lack of interest. There
were, after all, only a few score of Public Administration specialists
in British universities and they were generally occupied with other
work. What has been significant, indeed, has been the limited
contribution of academics to administrative reform. Some gave
brief evidence to commissions and committees, some wrote
articles—but if one looks along one's bookshelves, will more than
a dozen real studies be found that centre on major contemporary
problems of government organisation?

And yet—and this has been a central point of my argument so
far and is central here—the study of Public Administration grew
in America out of a concern for reform: though it changed beyond
all recognition over the years, much of that concern has remained.
Perhaps it is because (until very recently, at least) America
retained rather more of what we now derisively label a Victorian
belief in progress or, more specifically, in modernisation, and
deliberate modernisation at that. This depended on a belief in
reason, the possibility of improving things by the application of
rational, even scientific, thought. The British establishment, if not
actually conservative (in the non-party political sense), viewed the
contribution which academic research could make to administrative reform with a scepticism quite startling by comparison. For the
American view it is worth quoting some sentences from Jefferson,
enshrined in one of the four tablets in his Washington memorial:

'I am not an advocate for frequent changes in laws and institutions.
But laws and institutions must go hand in hand with the progress
of the human mind. As that becomes more enlightened, as new
discoveries are made, new truths discovered and manners and
opinions change, with the change of circumstances, institutions
must advance also to keep pace with the times. We might as well
require a man to wear still the coat which fitted him when a boy as
civilised society to remain even under the regimen of their bar-
barous ancestors.'

What has been called Public Administration as civics is essentially part of this tradition—the belief that students of government have a duty to search for ways of improving the government of their country and to work for its actual improvement, either by direct participation in government or by influencing the influentials.

This prescriptive approach to Public Administration is as old as the subject itself. In America it goes back directly to Woodrow Wilson. For him, as we have seen, the importance of the subject lay in the contribution it could make to straightening the paths of government, to making its business more businesslike, to strengthening and purifying its organisation, to crowning its duties with dutifulness. In present-day terms, the scholar sought ways of making the system more efficient and more responsible—twin goals, one of management science, the other of political science.

Much the same was true of the next major writer in the field, Frank Goodnow, whose *Politics and Administration* discussed reforms that might bring governmental practice closer to the ideals on which the system was founded. It was not only because it was the style of the time, nor even because Goodnow was a Professor of Administrative Law, that the approach was what we now call formalistic, that is to say legal and institutional. I have stressed the point throughout that reform almost inevitably has formal implications: it can only be implemented by changes in administrative structures or by changes in the rules governing administrative procedures. The sort of efficiency techniques that can be adopted within the existing framework (e.g. the application of analytic skills in decision-making or of human relations skills in personnel management) were later discoveries. They are, moreover, changes that can be made internally, requiring neither political nor legal action. The reformist outsider of the time, however, advocating changes in civil service organisation for example, had to campaign for legal and institutional reforms. These could not be put through by the administration itself; they required action by the political branch of government. He necessarily appealed to a different audience from that of the modern expert trying to sell the latest analytic technique to the civil service.

This becomes very noticeable when one considers the first real textbook, Leonard White's *Introduction to Public Administration*, published a quarter of a century later. That is to say, it looks like a textbook—it dealt with topics that were to become the staple diet of Public Administration courses—but it was not really intended as a guide to management techniques for the administrator. White, a Professor of Political Science, wanted to make American government more effective as executor of the public will. His proposals for civil service reform were directed to this end, as were his proposals for better control of the administration by the legislature, the courts and the public—issues clearly not part of a training course for civil servants. And, indeed, he indicated the audience to which his book was directed: the student of political science on the one hand, the citizen interested in public affairs on the other; officials, he added, might also find value in it. The whole could be read, as I have already suggested, as evidence to a commission of inquiry.

Though the other major textbook of the time, W. F. Willoughby's *Principles of Public Administration*, extended the technical field, the purpose was not very different, and this I have also discussed. As director of the Institute of Government Research, he headed an organisation whose aim was the scientific study of government in order to discover the principles which lie at the basis of sound administration and which would, if applied, promote efficiency and economy—these being the great problems he saw confronting America. The point to stress, however, is that he also considered this to be a political problem. His book was written for political scientists and officials—but, as far as the latter were concerned, largely to mobilise them as influentials for reform plans based on generalised principles. This was clearly shown in the way the question of finance was handled, not as techniques to be taught (e.g. accounting procedures), much less a branch of economics, but by reference to the budget as an important mechanism of control.

Both, in other words, saw the function of the scholar not in training but in analysis and prescription. They advocated changes in the formal structures and formal procedures of government—in institutions and in the rules. This formalism was inescapable: civil service organisation was regulated by law, as were those financial procedures which assured the control of public expenditure. And for this reason their proposals were directed at the influential public. Despite the titles of their books, despite their textbook-for-administrators appearance, they really belonged to that part of political science which, at a higher level, is concerned with devising the best constitution for the state.

The approach became less clear in later years. One can argue that the Taylor–Fayol–Urwick school of management efficiency was on the whole concerned with internal, non-political reorganisation, and thus more obviously intended for the administrator. This cannot be said of the behavioural school from Mayo to Simon and beyond which, though also concerned with practical questions of organisational efficiency, developed a sophisticated sociology of organisations more likely to appeal to the scholar than the practitioner. That Simon offers valuable insights into decision-making, prescriptions often quoted, is true enough. But the theoretical weight tilted the scales. This line of Public Administration does not have the same apparent reformist character, the same primary concern with the improvement of administration for political reasons. Against this, of course, one can see that the behaviourists —using that imprecise but reasonably understood label—laid the foundation of a more seriously based science of the administrative system, a science for the disinterested student as well as the practitioner—something that can hardly be said of the guidelines set out by White and Willoughby.

But the civics approach to Public Administration is not dead in America. The first post-war textbook, *Elements of Public Administration*, edited by Fritz Morstein Marx, stated clearly in its preface: 'The principal aim of this book is to deepen the reader's understanding of the administrative process as an integral part of contemporary civilisation.' The focus was political (the role of the executive in a democratic society) rather than professional–technical or sociological–scientific. Much the same was true of Paul Appleby (then Dean of the Maxwell School of Public Administration) in *Big Democracy* and *Policy and Administration*, the former dedicated to John Citizen and Bill Bureaucrat. Both were arguments for the political involvement of the administrator, a reversal of earlier trends. To that extent such books were teaching civics, not to the ordinary citizen but to Bill Bureaucrat himself.

In the recent past it seemed that the civics approach—whether teaching democracy or advocating reform—was nevertheless out of fashion, certainly among the more distinguished contributors to what was until recently the new science of Public Administration. This has been largely concerned with developing theories of administrative behaviour. Take a post-war textbook like Simon, Smithburg and Thompson's *Public Administration*: its broad scope clearly indicates that it is a course textbook rather than just a contribution to administrative theory—but the concern is nevertheless with analysis and hypothesis rather than with prescription. True, it discusses alternative ways of doing things, and to that extent may tell the reformer what is possible—but it has no message. It could be argued, of course, and for a time it seemed plausible, that the time for messages was past; that administration had become so complex that little could be achieved by political–legislative reform; that what was required was internal adjustment, changes in style and attitudes, use of new techniques—in other words, better-trained administrators.

There is now a 'new Public Administration' in America, as there is a 'new political science', on the left and marked by its concern with underprivileged citizens. It does not enter my discussion here because it no more seems to advocate legislative reforms than the ultra-scientific school—not for reasons of scientific neutrality in this case but for political reasons. Essentially anti-establishment and anti-established structures, it seems to advocate a form of internal change by ideologically committed practitioners (an undermining of the system from within, a critic would say) that it is not my purpose to advocate here, much as I approve the revival of commitment. In any case, the literature of this branch of the new left in political science, unlike some others, does not yet seem to have become part of British courses.

It could be argued, similarly, that what the liberal-arts political science students were interested in in the interval between the post-war generation and the last few years was understanding systems, not principles of reform. But this attitude has changed more clearly in Britain. We have a more critical generation again. Some study the social sciences in order to change society. At present, student revolutionaries condemn the socio-political system as a whole, demanding fundamental changes and often contemptuous of smaller but immediate reforms. If the mood changes and such demands prove ineffective, and unless we follow the German pattern of sabotage from within by the 'long march through institutions', political science, and Public Administration with it, may well return to its earlier concern with middle-range democratisation.

It has been said that political science largely grew out of 'a curative urge and an engineering itch—but it outgrew them too'. The same could be said of Public Administration. True, many Public Administration teachers in America participate in the work of government, directly or as consultants—and in the latter capacity they are clearly involved in works of reform. But these are often at the level of internal questions and to that extent non-political. And their interests sometimes reflects less of a curative itch than a market response—theirs is a new paid professionalism. Many have, as a result, taken care not to risk their effectiveness within the administration (less charitably: their outside earnings) by taking public stands or by campaigning on major issues of reform. The cult of scientism may have contributed to this: if one spends too much of one's time analysing why things are as they are, one becomes sceptical of the possibility of rational change. Such scepticism was a useful antidote to earlier reformist optimism —optimism about what the reformist could persuade public and politicians to accept; optimism about the effectiveness of formal changes, once accepted. Careerism and scepticism—both have brought benefits to Public Administration, both have limited its scope. The time has perhaps come for a move back to older traditions.

And yet, of course, proposals for the reform of democracy, for the improvement of government to make it a more effective servant of the democratic society, are not enough. The bookshelves are full of dusty proposals, barely read when new and soon forgotten. How are the Public Administrationist's proposals to be turned into practice? He can influence the influentials—the traditional approach. But that has limited possibilities as influentials are in the main establishment-minded. The need is to influence a wider public—*the* public, in fact. And here one is back at the starting point: Public Administration as civics—Public Administration taught not merely so that the citizen understands the administrative environment that controls so much of his life, not merely so that he can use it to his benefit, but also—and above all—so that he can contribute more actively to the continuous reshaping of society. That, of course, should be an essential part of education as such, and it may seem exaggerated to place Public Administration high on the list of subjects that should contribute to educating the full citizen. But in the last resort—and increasingly so—it is administration that governs his life: all other activities, even if they are the source of his real satisfactions, take place within the framework of an administered society. Political science was called the master science but now Public Administration holds many of the keys.

Index